What Makes Education Catholic

WHAT MAKES EDUCATION CATHOLIC

Spiritual Foundations

THOMAS H. GROOME

ORBIS BOOKS
Maryknoll, New York 10545

Second Printing, February 2023

Founded in 1970, Orbis Books endeavors to publish works that enlighten the mind, nourish the spirit, and challenge the conscience. The publishing arm of the Maryknoll Fathers and Brothers, Orbis seeks to explore the global dimensions of the Christian faith and mission, to invite dialogue with diverse cultures and religious traditions, and to serve the cause of reconciliation and peace. The books published reflect the views of their authors and do not represent the official position of the Maryknoll Society. To learn more about Orbis Books, please visit our website at www.orbisbooks.com.

Published by Orbis Books, P.O. Box 302, Maryknoll, NY 10545-0302.

Manufactured in the United States of America.

Library of Congress Cataloging-in-Publication Data

Names: Groome, Thomas H., author.
Title: What makes education Catholic : spiritual foundations / Thomas H. Groome.
Description: Maryknoll, New York : Orbis Books, [2021] | Includes bibliographical references and index. | Summary: "Offers the spiritual foundations that should define/suffuse Catholic education, at every level, to ensure that Catholic schools are providing the education that they promise"— Provided by publisher.
Identifiers: LCCN 2021016701 (print) | LCCN 2021016702 (ebook) | ISBN 9781626984479 (print) | ISBN 9781608339105 (ebook)
Subjects: LCSH: Catholic Church—Education—Philosophy. | Catholic Church—Doctrines—Education. | Catholic schools. | Education (Christian theology)
Classification: LCC LC473 .G76 2021 (print) | LCC LC473 (ebook) | DDC 371.071/2—dc23
LC record available at https://lccn.loc.gov/2021016701
LC ebook record available at https://lccn.loc.gov/2021016702

For Colleen and Ted

Contents

Preface

So, what makes education Catholic? What does it mean to place *Catholic* before such terms as *education, teacher,* or *school*? How can the deep spiritual values of Catholic faith shape and, hopefully, be rendered as promised?

The etymology of the word *education* is debatable. Does it originate from the Latin *educere* and signify "educing out of" people the potential and wisdom that is already within them, developing their inner capacities and insights? Or are its roots in the Latin *educare,* signifying "to lead out"—as in leading people out into new horizons and the world of knowledge and meaning that already await them? As this text proposes, we do well to embrace both emphases, drawing out from *within* and mediating in from *without.* For now, it is enough to note that both imply a significant intervention in people's lives, one that is to engage their full human potential and access for them their rich legacy of learning as human beings.

To be a *teacher*—an *educator*—is to shape the very lives of students. Without sounding pretentious, teachers are ontological agents (from the Greek *ontos* meaning "being"); willy-nilly, we shape students' very *being*—as both noun and verb—*who* they become and *how* they live. What an august vocation and sacred trust! Teachers walk on the holy ground of students' lives; as the poet Yeats cautioned, we must ever "tread softly" lest we "tread on their dreams" ("Cloths of Heaven").

From the nature of *education* and the vocation of *teacher,* therefore, conducting a *school* is a most significant and strategic civic enterprise. Schools shape the quality of the public realm through shaping the human agents within it—its citizens. They serve a critical social function toward the personal and common good of all!

Given, then, that *education, teacher,* and *school* are so significant for people and society, we well ask: How might the term *Catholic* qualify or further distinguish those terms and to what end?

Most patently, Catholic Christianity is a *faith* stance toward life in the world. A *Catholic* education, then, suggests educating *from* and *for* faith of some kind, grounding its foundations in a faith posture

ix

toward life and proposing a similar take to students. While it should
be informed by the best of educational philosophy and research, and
committed to academic excellence, its defining characteristic is to be
faith-based education—otherwise, why *Catholic*? At a minimum, this
means encouraging students to live their lives with a sense of Ultimate
Horizon—God, if you will—in order to find meaning and purpose, and
values to live by. Such faith-based education should prepare students
to engage in the immanent of life with a sense of the Transcendent.

Furthermore, Catholic faith is shaped by both reason and revelation,
the latter high-pointed in Jesus, the Christ. The Horizon revealed in
Jesus is of a personal God of love and compassion, who outreaches into
our lives with grace—God's effective love at work—to enable us to live
well together and with hope as human family. Surely, being grounded
in such faith foundations will encourage a distinctive *education*, *school*,
and *teacher*. But what would lend such distinction in practice? And
how do we ensure that Catholic education delivers as promised?

This is not an insignificant question. Might it be no exaggeration
to say that it pertains to the present and future state of our world?
When one considers the vast network of Catholic schools, ranging
from kindergartens to research universities (some fifty-five thousand),
located on every continent, in two hundred countries, and serving over
one hundred and fifty million students, it likely constitutes the largest
single system of education in the world today. Its funding varies greatly,
ranging from church-sponsored schools that depend on student tuition
to those funded by governments and managed by the church, often
with elected boards of governance.

A growing phenomenon in Catholic schools now is that an ever-
increasing number of students, faculty, and staff are from other or no
faith traditions, and indeed, many of their Catholic participants are
more cultural than affiliated in their faith. This expanding horizon
for Catholic education should be welcomed rather than resisted. In
his Apostolic Exhortation *Christus Vivit* (*Christ Lives,* March 2019),
Pope Francis states boldly that Catholic schools must "seek to welcome all young people, regardless of their religious choices, cultural
origins and personal, family or social situation. In this way, the Church
makes a fundamental contribution to the integral education of the
young in various parts of the world" (no. 247). This being said, such
a worldwide system of schools, so influential to the lives of so many
persons and societies, should be clear about the education it promises
and then fulfills.

Maintaining the Catholic identity of this worldwide network of
schools is far from inevitable; now, more than ever, this must be

deliberately chosen and crafted. There was a time, not so long ago, when the identity and curriculum of Catholic schools seemed assured by the overwhelming presence of religious sisters, brothers, and priests as their teachers and administrators. For example, in 1950, vowed religious made up some 90 percent of the faculty of US Catholic grade and high schools, and laypeople were 10 percent; in 2020, this figure was reversed and more, with vowed religious making up less than 3 percent of the faculty. Of course, laypeople are equally capable of conducting a system of Catholic education, but they need to know and be prepared to render what this asks of them.

That the Catholic Church and its schools will meet this challenge is likewise far from inevitable. Simply note that many distinguished American universities were originally sponsored by a faith community: Yale by Episcopalians; Princeton by Presbyterians; Boston University by Methodists; and another, founded by Puritans to educate church ministers, was named after Rev. John Harvard, its first benefactor. Today, such institutions claim, and vehemently, no religious or spiritual identity. They assiduously avoid such association, embracing the *Enlightenment* posture that any semblance of faith would prove inimical to their academic freedom and to the critical rigor of their scholarship. Consider, for example, great American Catholic universities—Notre Dame and Boston College, Georgetown and Fordham, and others— how might they avoid going the same route and rise in our time to the challenges of continuing to offer a faith-based and formative (yet fully enlightened) university education?

The anti-faith legacy of modernity and its assumption that enlightenment would eradicate religion continues into our now postmodern times, well described as a *secular age*. While secularization is most obviously measured by the falling off of religious practice and influence, its more challenging feature is that the social conditions for faith have changed radically—and not in faith's favor. Instead of an "enchanted age" (Max Weber)—not so long ago really—when faith and its practice permeated the whole sociocultural ethos, disposing people to follow suit, now conditions are reversed to propose "exclusive (of God) humanism" as a more *reasonable* alternative to a transcendent take on life (Charles Taylor). The tradition and rationale for faith-based schools cannot be taken for granted!

And yet, there is also growing evidence that our postmodern era is becoming more open to faith than modernity was and that more and more postmodern people are, in fact, "believers without belonging" (Grace Davie). To some amazement, many *enlightened* social commentators and thought leaders are recognizing again the need for a

* Should be conserved w/ small, poorly funded schools

"well-reasoned faith" that can provide a spiritual foundation for the public realm and especially to inspire its social ethic.

So, might it be possible that we are emerging into a new era of opportunity and a need for faith-based education? Of course, this should never mean proselytizing participants—students or teachers—to embrace a particular faith identity. Yet, giving access to a faith-inspired education that engages the souls as well as the minds of participants and leans them into a gracious Transcendent Horizon of meaning, purpose and values, can offer heightened hope for life lived well and for the common good of all. It does so precisely by drawing upon the full potential and capacities of the human person, offering an education that engages what the poet Yeats named well as "the marrow bone" of people rather than simply "the mind alone" ("Poem for Old Age").

SPIRITUAL FOUNDATIONS AND VISION

Much of public education is currently dominated by an empirical and disengaged rationality that favors science, technology, engineering, and math (the STEM curriculum). Such a mode of knowing is needed, of course, and yet alone is highly limited. It is unlikely to be formative of participants in humanizing ways or to encourage their shared responsibility for the common good as well as their own. Indeed, the ennui of spirit that is so evident in postmodern societies, coupled with the lack of moral compass in the public realm, suggests that faith-grounded education that engages the emotive and ethical (the soul) as well as the rational and empirical (the mind) was never more needed. The very challenges of our era, then, may well offer new opportunities and, indeed, an urgent need for truly *Catholic* education.

Such education must ground itself in a spiritual vision and then engage the very souls of its students. Note that much of the current scholarship regarding education, even in Catholic circles, is dominated by the social sciences and their empirical research. The empirical is certainly a valid and vital way of knowing and can make practical and tested recommendations to improve education of any kind. However, all education needs an empowering vision if it is to fulfill its ultimate purpose to promote human well-being. As the author of the Book of Proverbs wisely noted, "Where there is no vision, the people perish" (Prov 29:18, KJV).

Surely, Catholic education can draw a life-giving vision from its rich treasury of spiritual wisdom bequeathed by its Jewish roots, from Jesus of Nazareth, and then from across its two thousand years of engaged faith tradition. This legacy can lend a spiritual vision for Catholic schools, encouraging them to educate for both their immanent and transcendent purposes, encouraging in students both a horizontal and vertical perspective on life in the world. And while I write from a Catholic perspective, my foundations and proposals are broadly Christian. What I propose here can ring true for schools sponsored by other communities of Christian faith—Episcopalian, Lutheran, Methodist, and so on.

By simple logic, Catholic schools are to reflect the deep values, truths, and wisdom of this faith tradition as they pertain to the practice of education. Because so shaped by faith, we can say that the foundations of Catholic education are spiritual more than philosophical, arising more from faith than reason (though the latter is a crucial partner). Spirituality is variously understood now and especially in what is alleged to be a "new age" for it. From a Catholic perspective, however, the generic sense of spirituality is simply *faith put to work*. To ground Catholic education in its spiritual foundations, therefore, means to take the core values and wisdom reflected in Catholic faith and put them to work throughout the whole ethos and curriculum of a school. For example, and at its core, Catholic faith reflects an essentially positive understanding of the human person, is committed to the dignity and rights of all people, and is convinced of their potential to be agents for their own good and the common good of all. Imagine, then, what such faith might mean when put to work as a spiritual foundation of Catholic education.

I hasten to reiterate that this does not require all participants in Catholic education—teachers, staff, and students—to be confessing Catholics. All, however, must embrace the spiritual values that ground and identify *Catholic* education, with non-Christian participants inspired, perhaps, by echoes in other religious or humanist traditions. Here, we raise up the core spiritual values for education that confessing Catholics can embrace and put to work out of faith conviction. Yet they are, in fact, universal values that can be embraced by any person of good will—educator or student. Pragmatically, however, it is imperative that Catholic school principals be spiritual leaders who embrace and can articulate the school's faith-based vision, and that they have a core cadre of faculty and staff who are effective custodians of the spiritual foundations of the school.

Furthermore, such education must reach beyond teaching *about* Catholic values, truths, and wisdom; these must be put to work as formative for students throughout the whole curriculum. Consequently, all participants in Catholic education can at least learn *from* the values it represents to enrich their own lives and spiritual journey, and those from Catholic traditions can be disposed to learn *into* them as their identity in faith. In Chapter 10 we take up the particular challenge this offers for religious education in Catholic schools that have religiously diverse student populations. For now, and at a minimum, education done *from* such faith foundations can encourage students to embrace a transcendent rather than an exclusively immanent stance toward life. In other words, by educating *from* faith, Catholic schools are to educate *for* faith as well—yet ever respecting the particular faith and spiritual values that people may choose as their personal posture toward life in the world.

JESUS AND THE
CATHOLIC INTELLECTUAL TRADITION

But where, pray tell, should we search for the spiritual foundation and vision of such faith-based education? My proposal surely sounds like a tautology: *Jesus Christ is the heart of Christian faith and thus should be at the heart of Catholic education.* At first blush, this seems obvious. But truth be told, focusing on Jesus as portrayed in the Gospels is something of a new consciousness for Catholic Christians (more below). Following on, to bring an *educational* hermeneutic to contemporary Jesus scholarship is still work to be done; I hope to make a small contribution here.

Ask any Christian what is the heart of their faith and Protestants are most likely to say "the Bible" and Catholics "the church." The Bible, the church, and then the creeds and commandments, the sacraments and symbols, the values and virtues, and so on are all constitutive of Christian faith. Yet, as the *Catechism of the Catholic Church* well summarizes: "At the heart . . . we find a Person, the Person of Jesus of Nazareth, the only Son from the Father" (§426; hereafter CCC). By simple logic, the "heart" of Christian faith should be the "heart" of Catholic education.

Note well the CCC's insistence on both—the historical person, Jesus (a carpenter from Nazareth), who also was, in Christian conviction, the Christ of faith (Son from God). In Christian doctrine the two natures—human and Divine—existed in one person and without compromising either. Both should shape the *heart* of Catholic education, with the gospel portrayal of Jesus modeling and inspiring a distinctive kind of life-giving education and the Risen Christ being the source of hope and grace for realizing its learning outcomes.

To pose Jesus, the Christ, as the "cornerstone" (Acts 4:11) of Catholic education means to return to its scriptural foundations in the New Testament and likewise to the Hebrew scriptures (commonly called the Old Testament) that nurtured Jesus's own faith and pedagogy. In Chapter 1 we begin this retrieval of what New Testament scholar Jose Pagola describes as a "historical approximation" of Jesus, given that the Gospels are primarily texts of faith, and especially as relevant for Catholic education. This reclaiming of the centrality of Jesus continues throughout the whole text.

Focusing on the core values of Jesus as reflected in the Gospels enables us to appreciate all the more the hope that God offered to humankind—and thus to those who would educate—by raising him up, as Christians believe, as the Christ of faith (Chapter 2). We propose that God raised up Jesus precisely that we might educate for hope. We will also note how the values of Jesus continued to shape Catholic education across the centuries as we distill pedagogical wisdom from some great historical proponents of the Catholic intellectual tradition (Chapters 3, 4, 5, and 6). We have much to learn for Catholic education from two thousand years of tradition, and yet Jesus must ever remain the "heart" of it all.

In Chapters 7 to 10 we continue to ground the deep spiritual foundations of Catholic education, retrieving further aspects of the gospel curriculum of Jesus, coupled with contemporary Catholic theology as relevant to foundational issues for educators in our postmodern era. In sum, learning from Jesus for Catholic education runs throughout the whole text, with suggestions for every aspect of its curriculum today. Note parenthetically that here *curriculum* means not simply *what* is taught but also *how* (the pedagogy), for *whom* (understanding of person), *where* (the learning environment), and *why* (the intended learning outcomes).

I noted above that focusing on the human person, Jesus, can be a new consciousness for Catholics; we are more accustomed to relating to the Risen Christ of faith, the Son of God, the Second Person of the Blessed Trinity, and so on. This is due to a variety of historical circumstances, but perhaps the most causative is that the doctrinal section of traditional Catholic catechisms, which so shaped the "sense of the faithful" up to the Second Vatican Council (1962–65), was based solely on the Apostles' Creed. So, the catechisms took each article of the creed and catechized it, typically using a question-and-answer format.

The problematic for a comprehensive catechesis, however, was that the Creed's article "born of the virgin Mary" is followed immediately by "suffered under Pontius Pilate"—as if Jesus had no life between his birth and death, and in particular overlooking his three years (according to John's Gospel) of public ministry and teaching. And just as the Creed skipped the public life of Jesus, the catechisms did likewise—lending little awareness of it in Catholic faith and practice.

In addition to this, until the Second Vatican Council Catholics generally were not Bible readers and had only a limited and one-year cycle of scripture readings at mass (unlike the current three-year cycle that is more representative). Gratefully, we have made progress in embracing the scriptures as central to Catholic faith, beginning with Vatican II. However, it takes time to erase old patterns; more traditional Catholics, at least, still tend to "think church" as the core of their faith. Instead, we should first "think Jesus," including for Catholic education. This shift to "the centrality of Jesus Christ and of his Gospel" has well marked the pontificate of Pope Francis (*Directory for Catechesis*, no. 102).

The good news is that critical biblical scholarship, after many "quests for the historical Jesus," can now say reliably what were the core themes and commitments of his public ministry as reflected in the faith of the first Christian communities. Such scholarship draws upon the findings of biblical archaeology and historical anthropology, analyzes the literary forms of the scripture texts, makes comparison between Christian texts and other ancient manuscripts, and employs a host of other scholarly research methods.

This has heightened appreciation of Jesus's public ministry by locating him in his sociocultural context as a first-century Palestinian Jew, in a world ruled with an iron fist by the Roman Empire, and with which his core teachings were often in contrast. This situating of his teaching ministry in its historical context heightens the often radical nature of the gospel and of his call to live for the reign of God.

The upshot is that New Testament scholars can suggest what José Pagola calls "an historical approximation" of who Jesus actually was, the sociocultural characteristics of the time and place in which he carried on his teaching, and the core values and truths he taught and lived—often against the grain. This will greatly aid our imagining of what his teachings and pedagogy mean for us today, and in particular, for the curriculum of Catholic education.

Jesus's values and perspectives, and especially his teaching praxis—what he did, said, and taught—are surely germane to education that claims Christian faith as its spiritual foundation. Indeed, the most frequent description of Jesus and his work in the four Gospels is as teacher and teaching—so described over one hundred times. So our hermeneutical interest will be that of educators, explicitly focusing on what Jesus taught, how he taught it, and toward what "learning outcomes"—our key concern. Allowing for the differences between his and our historical contexts, Catholic educators are to teach in keeping with what and how Jesus is portrayed to have taught, having his curriculum inspire and shape our own.

Even as the pedagogical praxis of Jesus is to inspire Catholic education and lend its spiritual foundations, Christians believe that this same Jesus was the Christ, the long-promised Messiah, "raised up by God" (Acts 2:24) as Savior and Liberator of all humankind. Christian faith is that Easter has changed the course of history, turning it, however slowly, toward realizing God's reign of fullness of life for all people and creation. Christian faith holds that this paschal mystery, that is, Jesus's living, dying, and rising, released into human history what Saint Paul repeatedly describes as "God's abundant grace" (see, for example, Rom 5:17; 1 Tim 1:14; 2 Cor 4:15) and is for all people and creation.

Christians believe that we are assured now of God's love at work in all people's lives and for free—*gratis*. God's grace is to empower people's own best efforts to live well, wisely, and always with hope, even in the most difficult circumstances. Such faith-for-hope conviction can encourage a most life-giving vision to inspire Catholic education, not with historical naivete but with confidence that the great potential of students as human beings and their best efforts toward their own and the common good are empowered and sustained with God's help. That such grace is available to all people, whether they believe so or not, has been a constant Christian conviction since the early centuries of the church; it is a core spiritual foundation of Catholic education.

Certainly, drawing upon Jesus the Christ as model, inspiration, and source of empowerment does not imply and certainly should not require that all students, faculty, and staff in Catholic schools confess him as their liberating Savior. Again, because the values he represented are universal—love, mercy, compassion, peace, justice, honesty, responsibility, and so on—the education they inspire can enrich the lives and lend spiritual wisdom to people of any or no religious background. Indeed, the symbol of Jesus being raised up by God is the *Christian* grounding of hope for all. However, people from other traditions can benefit from such hope mediated through a Catholic education, even as they find their own personal symbols of faith and spiritual foundations for keeping their hope alive.

As hinted earlier, and following on from Jesus, Catholic education has been forged and enhanced by a long conversation with the traditions of Western philosophy and education that began with the early Christian encounter with Plato, Aristotle, and the Greco-Roman culture. From the beginning this encounter encouraged education marked by some crucial partnerships of faith and reason, of revelation and science, of knowledge and wisdom, of academic rigor and formation in values, and so on. Such partnerships constitute the rich legacy of the *Catholic intellectual tradition* and can be a powerful resource for Catholic education today.

Chapters 3, 4, 5 and 6 draw upon the wisdom of some chief exponents of the Catholic intellectual tradition regarding education, such as Augustine and Aquinas, Julian of Norwich and Angela Merici. Shaped by its original faith in Jesus Christ and by its encounter with the philosophical and sociocultural movements across the past two thousand years, especially in the West, the Catholic intellectual tradition offers a rich spiritual legacy for how to craft Catholic education in our time.

Chapters 7, 8, and 9 take up some central themes for Catholic education as informed by contemporary theology, highlighting the spiritual foundations it suggests. With a view to the whole curriculum of Catholic education, Chapter 7 reflects on an essentially positive understanding of the person as a relational being intent on the common good of all (anthropology cum sociology); Chapter 8 focuses on a Catholic cosmology as a hopeful outlook on life in the world and its epistemology of the engaged ways of knowing that it favors; Chapter 9 elaborates on the public nature of Christian faith and the responsibility of Catholic education to educate citizens who are committed to justice and the works of compassion in the public realm—consistent themes throughout the whole work. Chapter 10 offers reflections and a proposal to meet the particular challenge of religious education in Catholic schools with increasingly diverse faculty, staff, and students.

The Postlude draws together wisdom and insights from all the chapters to propose a *Catholic pedagogy*. Departing from the format of previous chapters, it summarizes their practical wisdom and insights as might be put to work in a spiritually grounded pedagogy, that is, approach to teaching.

A PEDAGOGY THROUGHOUT

The structure of the chapters will, in fact, reflect the overarching pedagogy that I recommend for Catholic education. I begin each chapter by establishing a general theme of importance to education *from* and *for* faith, and then invite readers to pause to reflect upon the theme from their own life experience and context. Then, drawing variously upon the scriptures, the curriculum of Jesus, and the tradition of Catholic education across two thousand years, I propose responses to the theme and suggest educational implications. I invite the reader to recognize how to take such spiritual wisdom to heart and to implement it as a Catholic educator. I end each chapter with curriculum implications and then invite what the chapter theme and proposals might mean for the educator's *soul*, for their teaching *style*, and for the educational *space*—all three being integral to implementing the spiritual foundations of Catholic education.

By way of language patterns, readers may already have noted that I often use a plural pronoun to refer to a singular noun, as in "every educator is to shape *their* own pedagogy," or as Shakespeare would have it, "May God send everyone *their* heart's desire." Indeed, this returns to the grammatical pattern of the Elizabethan era and has been approved by the US National Council of Teachers of English. My commitment is to promote gender inclusive language while avoiding the awkward "he/she" and "his/her" constructs.

On a similar note I avoid using male images and pronouns for God, except when quoting the original scriptures. Because human language is never sufficient for God, we simply cannot be fully *inclusive* of all that can be said of the Divine. But surely we can be more *expansive*, as the Bible is frequently, beyond male-only imagery for God (see Ps 18:1–2 for twelve different images, in just two verses). For some, this may be a new horizon. I respectfully invite you to consider it. Last, I avoid footnoting, recognizing the sources of direct quotations within the text. And now read on.

Part I

THE GOSPEL FOUNDATIONS
OF CATHOLIC EDUCATION

1

To Teach as Jesus Did

A caution: *"We who teach will be judged with greater strictness." (James 3:1)*
A promise: *Those who live rightly and teach others to so live "will be called greatest in the kingdom of heaven." (Matthew 5:19)*

THE CENTRALITY OF JESUS

What most distinguishes Christian faith is a historical person who lived in ancient Palestine some two thousand years ago and to whom his parents gave the name Jesus. Because Jesus constitutes the defining core of Christian faith—and thus its spirituality as such faith put to work—he should likewise shape the heart of Catholic education. Of course, there has been a two-thousand-year tradition since Jesus's time, and educators have much to learn and develop from that rich treasury. Yet Catholic education must ever find its cornerstone and guiding star in the person and teaching of Jesus—who he was, what he taught, and how he taught. The purposes that defined his life and the pedagogy he practiced should permeate what is done as education that is now identified with him.

His first disciples, having personally encountered Jesus, also became fully convinced that God had raised him up from death into a newness of life. This prompted their deep faith that this carpenter from Nazareth was also the Christ/Messiah long promised to the Jewish people. They referred to him as Lord—a sacred Hebrew name for God—and Son of God, convinced that Jesus uniquely embodied the divine presence. They embraced him as "the Savior of the world" (John 4:42) toward God's desire of fullness of life for all people (John 10:10). In time, early Christian disciples articulated their understanding of who he was by

3

recognizing two natures in one person, that Jesus, the Christ, was fully human and fully divine.

In Chapter 2 we review the nature, warrants, and educational implications of the Christian claim that God raised Jesus from the dead. Meanwhile, any person of good will, regardless of whether they embrace him as the *Christ of faith*, can look to the *Jesus of history* as an inspiring model for how to live one's life well, caring for oneself and for the common good of all. Furthermore, and as proposed throughout this text, the values that Jesus embodied in his public ministry are universal and lend the most positive of spiritual foundations for the work of education. All educators, of any or no particular faith persuasion, can be inspired by the values portrayed in Jesus and enhanced by putting them to work throughout their curriculum.

Such a proposal presumes upon the centrality of *teaching* in the public ministry of Jesus. What he did and achieved have been portrayed in varied ways throughout Christian history, as reflected in titles of faith like Savior, Redeemer, Liberator, or more historical descriptions, like wisdom figure, healer, prophet, righteous (just) one, or simply, Jesus of Nazareth. His most frequent title throughout all four Gospels is *huios tou anthropou*; though typically translated from the Greek as "son of man," it is more accurately rendered as "the human one" (*anthropos* refers to both genders), better capturing his deep solidarity with all humankind.

When we look, however, to what Jesus is portrayed as doing in his public ministry—his historical praxis—we can well describe his defining work as education and him, primarily, as a teacher. Over one hundred times the New Testament refers to Jesus's public ministry precisely as teaching and many times more with echoing portrayals like preaching, advising, counseling, correcting, outreaching, including, encouraging, affirming, and so on—all modes of educating. Yet New Testament scholars have paid comparatively little attention to the actual pedagogy of Jesus; such a hermeneutical lens here will help us recognize the richness of his educational approach, indeed of his whole curriculum, and how it might enhance our own.

Only in John's Gospel is Jesus described or addressed directly as *rabbi*, the term for teacher in his culture. For example, a Jewish leader named Nicodemus addressed Jesus, "Rabbi, we know that you are a teacher who has come from God" (John 3:2). Officially, however, it would seem that Jesus was not a rabbi in the traditional sense, which would have required years of intense study under the tutelage of a master rabbi, who would have been highly selective in choosing students. Jesus was more of a charismatic prophet, relying on his personal appeal and reaching out and welcoming all and sundry. Nevertheless, Jesus as teacher resembled something of the traditional rabbi role—to teach Torah, God's law of how best to live as people of God, and to do so by word and example. Jesus regularly interpreted and often reinterpreted Torah, always toward its fulfillment (see Matt 5:17–20).

Rather than dwelling on the minutiae, as the rabbis tended to do, Jesus preferred to summarize Torah into the law to love God by loving one's neighbor as oneself. He proposed that on this *greatest commandment* "hang all the law and the prophets" (Matt 22:40), as does the golden rule of "do to others as you would have them do to you" (Matt 7:12). Perhaps Mary Magdalene named him best; upon encountering the Risen Christ, she addressed him as "Rabboni," which was a more familiar and unofficial form of *rabbi*—as one might use of a favorite teacher (John 20:16), as Jesus was to her.

To be elaborated in detail later, Jesus's whole approach to teaching was marked by a deep engagement with people's everyday lives. Almost invariably he would begin to teach by focusing attention on some instance of people's own situation or concern or experience, or practice, and then teach his gospel of God's reign into the midst of their reality, all to encourage their embrace by choice of the *way of life* that he was proposing.

Furthermore, Jesus taught as much by his actions as by overt instruction (as do all teachers); his disciples learned constantly by what they saw him doing in varied circumstances. For example, his works of compassion for all in need was a central pedagogy of his life, with his praxis of care for the poor and suffering working hand in hand with explicit instruction (see Matt 4:23).

Importantly, from the beginning of his public ministry Jesus invited disciples *to share* in his work of teaching, and this in a culture where being teacher was a significant social role. Repeatedly throughout the Gospels Jesus invites people to "come follow me" and then makes clear that such following is not as a passive recipient but as an active participant in his teaching ministry. Disciples were to join in his work of educating for the reign of God, teaching people to embrace "the way and the truth and the life" (John 14:6) that he taught and embodied. The rabbis taught people to live by Torah but not necessarily to become formal teachers of Torah. Jesus, by contrast, wanted every disciple to share in his teaching mission, to join him in the work of educating people to embrace faith as a *way of life* for the reign of God.

This vocation, both to embrace his way and to participate actively in teaching it to others, is reflected in Jesus's initial call of disciples in all three Synoptic Gospels (Matthew, Mark, and Luke), and in his post-resurrection conversation with Peter in the Gospel of John. At the very beginning of Mark's Gospel we read of Jesus calling his first two disciples, the fishermen Simon (Peter) and his brother Andrew, with "follow me and I will make you fish for people" (1:17). Matthew's account (4:18–20) directly parallels Mark, while Luke has Jesus address a reluctant Peter with, "Do not be afraid; from now on you will be catching people" (5:11). John's Gospel portrays the Risen Christ instructing Peter three times to care for his "sheep" and concludes with "follow me" (21:15–19). Invited to walk in Jesus's footsteps, Peter had a renewed commission (having denied Jesus three times; see John 18:15–27) to lead and educate as Jesus did.

Midway through his ministry Jesus chose twelve special helpers, naming them apostles, and commissioned them to a leadership role of teaching and healing within his emerging community of disciples. Yet the teaching function was never limited to "the twelve." Soon thereafter, Jesus chose "seventy others" and sent them out "in pairs" to participate in his mission of teaching and healing—the two ever going hand in hand. In sum, they were both to "cure the sick" and teach that "the kingdom of God has come near to you" (Luke 10:1–12).

Note, too, that even as Jesus engaged *disciples* (the Greek *mathetes* can also be translated as "apprentice") to become teachers like him, he also warned them—at least six different times—not to "lord it over" those they taught (see Mark 10:41–45). Instead, they were to be like "servants" to all, apprenticing themselves to Jesus's own humility of life. Clearly, Jesus intended disciples to become educators like himself, teaching what he taught and how he taught it, for whom, and to what end.

All educators in Catholic schools, whether identifying themselves as disciples of Jesus or not, and regardless of their personal faith, can be inspired by Jesus's curriculum. To reiterate, this includes what, how, why, for whom, and where he taught. To appreciate all the more the contribution Jesus can make to Catholic education today, we briefly situate him in his historical context, noting how it shaped his teaching.

For Reflection and Conversation

- Look back over your experience of being educated; who stands out for you as an inspiring teacher? Why? What might you learn from that teacher for your own vocation?
- Whether drawing personally from Christian faith or just from popular culture (or from being "around" a Catholic school), what is your image

of Jesus as portrayed in the Gospels? How did you come by such an image? How might it inspire your teaching now?

THE SEARCH FOR JESUS

For almost two thousand years, people have been trying to get to *know* the historical Jesus. *Know* deserves italics here because it means much more than purely cognitive knowledge—as true for knowing any person. As elaborated in Chapter 8, to *know* Jesus and what he wants people to know is very holistic; it engages people's heads, hearts, and hands (will), and is to inform, form, and transform their whole way of *being* in the world. John's Gospel has Jesus pray to God for his disciples: "This is eternal life, that they may know you, the one true God, and Jesus Christ whom you sent" (John 17:3). In other words, to *know* God in Jesus fulfills the ultimate longings of the human heart; this surely reflects a very holistic kind of knowledge!

Furthermore, for individuals and the faith community, *knowing* Jesus continues to unfold as we find ourselves in new contexts and situations, with new questions and challenges. For example, we now readily recognize that Jesus and the Bible generally would encourage a deep respect and care for the natural environment, something rarely noticed until climate change and global warming became urgent historical issues. This is how Christian tradition has continued to evolve across the centuries, bringing fresh gospel wisdom to address the issues emerging in various times and contexts.

And so it will continue, as Vatican II said well, ever pressing on "toward the fullness of divine truth" and its "complete fulfillment" (*Dei Verbum*, no. 10). Christians believe that this deepening of the teachings of Jesus across the centuries—finding, as it were, "recessive genes" to address new situations—is guided by the Holy Spirit through the discernment of the Christian community. We can and will learn much from this long and still unfolding Christian tradition for how to educate *from* and *for* faith.

But even as we have much to learn from this two-thousand-year-old tradition, Catholic educators must constantly return to and be grounded first and foremost in Jesus as portrayed in the Gospels: that carpenter from Nazareth turned teacher. And, as noted in the Preface, getting to know the core values of Jesus is now all the more possible. Some two hundred years ago New Testament scholars began a "quest for the historical Jesus." This critical scriptural scholarship often draws upon other historical texts and sciences to discern what can be said reliably of the life and commitments of Jesus. After many waves of "questing," we now can be confident of at least the broad strokes and great themes in Jesus's life and teaching as reflected in the four Gospels, and then appropriated further in the other books of the New Testament.

Let us be clear that biblical texts cannot be treated as scientific or objective history (if there be such a possibility). However, the books of the New Testament are a reliable witness to the *faith* of the first Christian disciples, many of whom personally encountered Jesus, and of the communities that emerged around him and immediately after his death. Over time, as the first witnesses grew older, written fragments began to emerge, and so too did agreed-upon oral traditions. Eventually, beginning with Mark's Gospel around 70 CE and reflecting different cultural contexts, concerns, and audiences, the four Gospels emerged.

Note that all were crafted and shaped by people convinced that "God raised Jesus" from the dead (Acts 2:24), thus verifying that he was "the Son of God" (Rom 1:4). But rather than distorting their view of the historical person, this verification of him as the Christ/Messiah helped disciples to appreciate all the more the teachings and commitments that he embodied throughout his public life. They became rock-solid convinced that Jesus and what he taught was "of God" (Phil 2:6).

Likewise for us, situating Jesus in his historical context—the culture and politics that surrounded his life—helps to highlight the wisdom, truths, and values he taught, often in contrast to and in critique of his sociocultural situation. So, depending on the faith of his first and early disciples and their communities, what *can* we say reliably about this historical person, Jesus? Some initial background will heighten the significance of Jesus's pedagogy and what we can learn from him for the curriculum of Catholic education in our time. We elaborate further on the historical Jesus as relevant to the theme of each chapter that follows, but here we begin with an overview.

LOCATING JESUS OF NAZARETH

We know that Jesus was raised in the small town of Nazareth in Galilee, a backwater village in a backwater province. He was the son of Joseph, a carpenter, and his mother's name was Mary. They gave him the name Jeshua, which in Hebrew means "God saves." People from Galilee were darker skinned than those from Judea; most likely so was Jesus. They spoke with a heavy accent. Galileans experienced ethnic bias against them from both the Romans and their Jewish neighbors in Judea; they were viewed as "country bumpkins" when they went up to Jerusalem to celebrate holy days and pray in the Temple.

Jesus spoke Aramaic as a child, a forerunner of Hebrew. Besides the home instruction and good example of his parents, he would have been tutored in his Jewish faith at the local synagogue, a place of both education and worship. Based on the Gospels, it seems that he was well versed in both the Law and the Prophets, favoring Isaiah. Likewise, he was familiar with the Psalms and Wisdom literature; he is represented as quoting many passages from memory. Through his home and synagogue, then, Jesus was well grounded in his rich Jewish faith, which deeply shaped how he lived his life and taught others to live.

The Gospels attest that Jesus learned to be a carpenter from his father, Joseph; typically male sons took on the trade of their father. Having a trade might seem like providing economic security, but people in the Galilean villages would not have had the money for home furnishing except for the very basics. Knowing poverty from the inside was surely what gave Jesus his empathy for the poor and downtrodden.

During Jesus's lifetime Galilee was a province within the Roman territory of Syria. From about 60 BCE, and for two hundred years or so, the Romans ruled Galilee with an iron fist. They exacted exorbitant taxes, tributes, fees, and tithes from the people, who also had to pay a temple tax to the priests in Jerusalem. As a result of all the heavy taxation, most Galileans lived in dire poverty. Many people who once owned land lost it and went into debt, placing themselves in the hands of moneylenders, who exploited them further. Imagine how radical was Jesus's notion of simply forgiving debts in order to be forgiven (see Matt 6:12).

People who lost their lands and became poor day laborers also lost their dignity, incurring social shame. Honor and shame were powerful forces in Jesus's culture. Anything that diminished a person, like sickness or poverty, also reduced their social status. Against the grain of his culture, then, in Jesus's many miracles of feeding the hungry, curing the sick, and including marginalized persons, he not only relieved their personal suffering but erased their shame and restored their dignity in society.

The Galileans were brutalized by the Romans, who put down all forms of protest or resistance with terrifying cruelty. They regularly moved in and burned down whole villages that were failing to pay their taxes. That Jesus would push back against the oppression of the empire, championing the reign of God instead, was likely to bring his own destruction. He would have been well aware of the danger; his cousin, John the Baptist, had been beheaded for something similar.

The Jewish people often rose in revolt against the cruelty of Roman rule, and the Romans literally stopped at nothing to put them down. Quinctilius Varus, the Roman ruler around 4 BCE, put down a popular uprising in Jerusalem by crucifying some two thousand rebels and hanging them on a row of crosses that circled the city. Eventually the Romans even destroyed the beloved Temple in Jerusalem (70 CE), the very center of Jewish faith and identity.

As a child, Jesus must have heard such stories and experienced cruelty and social oppression firsthand. How amazing his first hearers must have been, then, when he declared, against all odds, that "the time is fulfilled" and announced the in-breaking "now" of God's reign of justice and peace and fullness of life for all (see Mark 1:15). What amazement such utopian sentiments would have elicited in the midst of a dire situation. No wonder that we read that his family "went out to restrain him, for people were saying, 'He has gone out of his mind'" (Mark 3:21). One can understand their suspicion of his mental health; for Jesus not to have recognized the risks he was taking *would* qualify him as insane.

Humanly speaking, one has to wonder why Jesus decided, at about the age of thirty (senior years in his culture), to leave his home at Nazareth to embark on the public work of teaching, beginning by traveling some seventy miles on foot to where his cousin, John the Baptist, was baptizing at the river Jordan, just outside of Jerusalem. By then, Joseph was most likely dead, and Jesus would have been the main support of his mother, Mary. Why did he up and leave home to go and *teach*? Most Christian scholars agree that as yet Jesus would not have had a clear sense of his identity as the promised Messiah; humanly speaking, this consciousness likely dawned gradually as his public ministry unfolded and people recognized him for who he was.

We also must wonder why a poor carpenter in a remote village would become convinced that he was called to be a teacher and educator of his whole people and beyond. As noted, teachers were expected to spend many years studying Torah under a master. He certainly surprised his neighbors. When Jesus journeyed home to teach in Nazareth, they wondered, "Where did he get all this. . . . Is this not the carpenter, the son of Mary?" (Mark 6:2–3). We can only surmise that Jesus felt an overwhelming sense of vocation to go and teach for the in-breaking of God's reign. Nothing less would have driven him to leave his family and village and strike out into the unknown—to do what would most likely lead to his own destruction.

John was "proclaiming a baptism of repentance for the forgiveness of sins," and "Jesus came from Nazareth of Galilee and was baptized by John in the Jordan" (Mark 1:4, 9). Then, upon being baptized, there followed an amazing theophany around Jesus. All three Synoptic Gospels attest to, as Mark puts it, "the Spirit descending like a dove on Jesus and a voice came from heaven, 'You are my Son, the Beloved; with you I am well pleased'" (Mark 1:10–11). Might Jesus have been as surprised as the people there present by such an extraordinary affirmation—and "from heaven"?

Whatever we imagine, Jesus's baptism marked the beginning of his public ministry and perhaps of his own as well as other people's gradual recognition of him as the promised Messiah. Though John's Gospel has no explicit baptism of Jesus, it recounts John the Baptist initially pointing to Jesus as "the Lamb of God who takes away the sin of the world," and testifying "that this is the Son of God" (John 1:29, 34).

After his baptism Jesus launched his public teaching, beginning, at least by Luke's account, at his hometown, Nazareth (see Luke 4:16ff.; Mark and Matthew simply say "in Galilee"). After John the Baptist was executed, it appears that Jesus relocated with his growing band of disciples to the house of the brothers Simon (later called Peter) and Andrew at Capernaum (see Matt 4:12–13), about thirty miles northeast of Nazareth. His ministry of teaching, which included healing, feeding, consoling, advising, forgiving, and driving out evil, took him throughout Galilee and the surrounding areas, and eventually to Jerusalem. If we accept John's chronology, Jesus's public ministry lasted for three years and included four visits to Jerusalem.

Tradition holds that Jesus was about thirty-three years old when Pontius Pilate, the Roman ruler of Judea (26–36 CE), had him crucified on a small hill outside the city of Jerusalem. Pilate acted in cahoots with Herod Antipas, vassal Roman ruler of Jesus's home province of Galilee, with both refusing to take responsibility for his sentencing. They did pin to his cross "the charge against him" as "the King of the Jews" (Mark 15:26). For the Romans, at least, Jesus was a political threat—he might cause the people to rise up against them—and thus the need to crucify him. But given the life he lived, the values he modeled, and the causes he championed, Jesus was not likely to die in bed. He died for what he lived for—the reign of God!

For Reflection and Conversation

- How might knowing some of Jesus's historical context shape what we can learn from him as educators today?

- What are some prime features of your own context that impinge upon your educating—both positive and negative?
- What practical wisdom have you learned already from the example of Jesus?

LIVING FOR THE REIGN OF GOD

Biblical scholars overwhelmingly agree that the reign of God was the central passion and purpose of Jesus's life. He appeared to understand his own *being* as centered on this great utopian vision of God reigning in people's lives and world, and for them to live into and experience the possibility of its realization as never before. The symbol represents hope for the best of everything for everyone and the well-being of all creation, precisely because this is what God desires as the ultimate outcome of human history. And because it is God's vision for us and for creation, it will be realized completely, if only in the end time, in time out of time. In the meantime, and for educators who look to Jesus for spiritual grounding, the reign of God poses the ultimate vision to guide our whole curriculum and the learning outcomes we are to effect in students' lives.

Traditionally and in most translations of the New Testament, the Greek *basileia tou theou* is rendered as "kingdom of God." However, because it is more of an unfolding process than a geographic location—as kingdom implies—the translation "reign of God" is more accurate. Also, Matthew's Gospel favors the language "kingdom of heaven." Rather than intending that God's reign is only for later in eternal time, however, scholars agree that Matthew, being an observant Jew, was simply reluctant to use the holy name and so inserted "heaven" as a synonym for God. Rather than a pie-in-the-sky hope to be achieved by and by, Jesus makes clear that the reign of God is to be realized *now* as God's will is "done on earth" as in heaven. Such "doing" of the divine will includes debts being forgiven and all having enough bread for the day—two key social concerns of the time, especially for the poor (Matt 6:9–13).

Compared to the Synoptic Gospels, where the phrase appears some one hundred and twenty times, John's Gospel has Jesus use reign-of-God language sparingly. Jesus does advise Nicodemus that "no one can see the kingdom of God without being born from above"; this requires being "born of water and the Spirit," and the Spirit, like the wind, "blows where it chooses" (John 3:3–8). The latter phrase is typically interpreted to mean that the Holy Spirit works freely and without borders to God's reign and is never confined to any particular people or religion. Then, at the end of Jesus's life, when John's Gospel recounts his trial before Pilate, the latter asks Jesus, "Are you the King of the Jews?" (John 18:33), reflecting the Roman concern in all four Gospels that Jesus was a political threat. In that context Jesus responds, "My kingdom is not from this world" (John 18:36).

This being said, the vision of God reigning over all is writ large in John's Gospel by its posing the image of "fullness of life" to summarize Jesus's divine intention for all people, sometimes coupled with the metaphor of light. In the prologue of the Fourth Gospel, when John reflects on Jesus as God's creating Word made flesh, it states, "In him was life, and the life was the light of the people" (John 1:4). Then, note the classic verse of John 3:16, which states that God sent God's own Son into the world in Jesus so that all "may have eternal life." Later, Jesus explains that he will give himself "for the life of the world" (John 6:51). Such life is not just for later but is to begin here and now. Combining the life and light metaphors, John records Jesus saying, "Whoever follows me will never walk in darkness but will have the light of life"—now (John 8:12).

Perhaps John's capstone statement, echoed just after Jesus claims to be like a good shepherd—a favorite image for God in the prophetic books of the Bible—is having Jesus declare, "I came so that they may have life, and have it abundantly" (John 10:10; some translations have "to the full"). Later still, John has Jesus refer to himself as "the way, and the truth, and the life" (John 14:6), posing his own praxis and teaching as how best to live as a person of God. Clearly, then, with the metaphor of life, John echoes the life-giving vision that the other gospel writers propose with the reign of God.

Luke provides an early summary of Jesus's understanding of what he felt commissioned to teach, "I must proclaim the good news of the kingdom of God . . . for I was sent for this purpose" (Luke 4:43). Matthew's earliest summary states, "Jesus went throughout Galilee, teaching in their synagogues and proclaiming the good news of the kingdom and curing every disease and every sickness among the people" (Matt 4:23). Note again that Jesus's teaching of God's reign included miracles of healing of every kind; imagine how loudly that must have taught!

Mark's Gospel, however, gives the earliest and classic summary of this core of Jesus's teaching. After Jesus's baptism by John the Baptist at the Jordan, he is submitted to a crucible of temptations "in the wilderness for forty days" (Mark 1:13). Mark continues: "After John was arrested, Jesus came to Galilee, proclaiming the good news of God, and saying, 'The time is fulfilled, and the kingdom of God has come near; repent, and believe in the good news'" (Mark 1:15).

Surely Jesus must have known the dangers he faced; his cousin John had already been arrested for teaching a similar message. Even in using the language *basileia thou theou*, "reign of God," Jesus was placing his Gospel in contrast to the Roman *basileia*—the word meant both "reign" and "empire." Beginning with Augustus (27 BCE to 14 CE), the Roman emperors proclaimed themselves as godlike, thus lending divine benediction to their conduct of the empire. Jesus must have known that his reign of God was in deep contrast with that of the Romans. Furthermore, he was passionately convinced that "the time is fulfilled," the waiting is over, and *now* is the moment for the in-breaking of God's reign. It calls people to repent (in Greek, *metanoia*); that is, to change their minds and hearts, and to believe and live "the good news"—the gospel (*evangelion*)—that God's reign is being realized *now* in a completely new way.

Though the notion that God is to rule all creation is a common theme in the Hebrew scriptures, the term *reign of God* was just coming into vogue in the Jewish faith of Jesus's time. Its summary description is *shalom*. Most often translated as "peace with justice," *shalom* means the best of everything for everybody and for all creation—with all the heart's hungers fully realized. The poet William Butler Yeats echoed it well as "the land of heart's desire."

For Jesus, then, God's reign means that God's best intentions for humankind will be completely realized eventually—in time out of time—but are to begin *now*. Here we can imagine beginning to fulfill all the deepest and wisest longings of the human heart, with them being God's desire for us as well. So, God's reign includes the practice of faith, hope, and love, of justice and peace, of compassion and mercy. It is to be marked by inclusion and hospitality in community; by fully recognizing the dignity and equality of all people; by putting an end to discrimination and prejudice, to injustice and oppression, to sickness and disease, to hunger and want, to environmental destruction; and the list goes on.

It is clear from Jesus's teaching that he understood the reign of God as a tensive symbol—a both/and hope. So it is for each person's soul *and* also a social challenge, to reach into and transform society. It will be realized in its fullness at an end time; indeed, only God knows "that day and hour" (Matt 24:36). Meanwhile, *now* is the time for its in-breaking—"the time (*kairos*) has come" (Mark 1:15). It is to shape people's prayers, as in "thy kingdom come," *and* likewise their politics, as in committing to do God's will "on earth as in heaven" (Matt 6:10).

Jesus told disciples that God must rule within their hearts (Luke 17:21) *and* that this demands outreach with compassion to people in need. In fact, doing the works of compassion and justice are an absolute require- ment for disciples if they are to "inherit the kingdom" (Matt 25:34).

It is also abundantly clear from how Jesus lived his life and his gospel that the reign of God means putting God at the center of one's existence. In a sense, promoting the reign of God is Jesus's proposal for how to obey the first commandment, which forbids false gods: "I am the Lord your God, who brought you out of the land of Egypt, out of the house of slavery, you shall have no other gods before me" (Exod 20:2–3). For God to truly reign, God must come first in people's lives—with "no other gods" allowed. In this light there is a deep logic to what Jesus proposed, building upon this first commandment, as the *greatest commandment* in the new covenant of God's reign and the imaging of God he was portraying.

As Jesus taught the reign of God, it became clear that he was por- traying God as covenant partner of unconditional love—from God's side—with us. God loves us unconditionally in the sense that we do not need to earn it; it is gratuitous, gracious—for free. And God loves us because love is the very nature of God. The classic summary of this aspect of Jesus's teaching is the simple statement that "God is love" (1 John 4:8). The text then adds that God "first loved us" (1 John 4:19); that is, God takes the initiative to love us without any earning or deserving on our part, unconditionally. This New Testament con- viction of God as love and as first loving us would come to its fullest expression in the Christian notion of the Blessed Trinity, portraying God as Triune Love both within Godself and ever toward us.

Following on, and given God's unconditional love for us, there is deep logic in Jesus making the greatest commandment of God's reign that we *love God by loving our neighbor as ourselves*. Our covenant response to God's unconditional love can be nothing less than to love God, others, and ourselves—even enemies (see Matt 5:44)—and to do so with every fiber of our being. So, when asked, "Which commandment is the first of all?" Jesus responds by drawing together two classic texts from his Jewish faith. These were the law to love God "with all your heart, and with all your soul, and with all your might," with everything we've got (Deut 6:4–5), and then, "You shall love your neighbor as yourself" (Lev 19:18). Jesus was the first Hebrew prophet to bring to- gether what was in effect three laws—love of God, neighbor, and self (we often forget that third leg)—and to weave them together as one.

In Mark's account (12:28–34), a scribe explicitly asked Jesus for the greatest *commandment*—singular. At first blush it would appear that

Jesus responded with threefold commands—love for God, neighbor, and self. So, "you shall love the Lord your God with all your heart, and with all your soul, and with all your mind, and with all your strength" (note the slightly different pattern from Deuteronomy to include "mind"). Jesus then adds, "You shall love your neighbor as yourself," and summarizes: "There is no other commandment (singular again) greater than these." In other words, the three aspects are symbiotic; for Jesus, our love for God is realized by loving neighbors as ourselves. When the scribe agrees, essentially repeating what Jesus had said, Jesus responds, "You are not far from *the kingdom of God*" (12:34, emphasis added). For Jesus's teaching, then, this radical law of love is the defining mode of our living into God's reign or, conversely, the more we live this greatest commandment, the more the reign of God is realized in our lives and world.

This greatest love commandment of God's reign—portraying God as unconditional love and inviting disciples to approximate as much—became the touchstone of Jesus's own life; he practiced what he taught. This prompted him to favor with loving kindness and mercy the poor, the hungry, the sick, the bereaved, those in the powers of evil, the excluded, the beggars, the sinners, the downtrodden, the oppressed, the despised, and the persecuted—the list goes on. Such liberating praxis was integral to Jesus's educating for God's reign; as Matthew summarizes, "Jesus went throughout Galilee, teaching in their synagogues and proclaiming the good news of the kingdom and curing every disease and sickness among the people" (Matt 4:23).

Recall, too, that not only was Jesus helping people in need, and teaching disciples to do likewise, but he was also erasing their social shame and lifting their exclusion from community. Jesus's reign of God was deeply *social* and *personal*. So his works of compassion were consciousness raising for his social context, pushing back against a fatalism that saw suffering as God's will or as a punishment for sin. He was working against cultural biases by reintegrating the people he helped back into their society, restoring their dignity.

Therefore, it is amply clear from Jesus's teaching and modeling that God's reign opposes all injustice, exclusion, oppression, and inequality. He was deeply convinced that God never approves of abuse or discrimination for any reason, but rather demands their opposite—respect for human dignity and justice for all. This commitment to the social values of God's reign prompted Jesus to make what contemporary scholars refer to as his preferential option for the poor. Simply stated, this means that he favored those who most needed the favor—the least, the lost, and the last.

There is no better gospel summary of how Jesus understood himself as the definitive agent and teacher of God's reign in human history than Luke 4:16–21. Luke situates this text at the beginning of Jesus's public ministry in Galilee. Jesus comes into his hometown, Nazareth, on the Sabbath and goes "according to his custom" to his village synagogue for worship. He is chosen or volunteers to read the scripture and is handed the "scroll of the prophet Isaiah"—his favorite. Jesus unrolls it and intentionally looks for and finds the text of Isaiah 61:1–2a. According to Luke's account, when Jesus reads it, he includes a phrase from Isaiah 58:6, referring to freeing the oppressed.

Jesus proclaims: "The Spirit of the Lord is upon me, because he has anointed me to bring glad tidings to the poor. He has sent me to proclaim release to the captives and recovery of sight to the blind, to let the oppressed go free, to proclaim the year of the Lord's favor" (Luke 4:18–19). The last verse is the hope for a Jubilee Year, the fiftieth year after seven times seven years. The jubilee was to be the ultimate Sabbath time when everything was given over to God—who owns it all to begin with. So, land was let lie fallow, debts forgiven, and all slaves and prisoners set free (see Lev 25:10–12).

After Jesus finished reading the Isaiah text and sat down, "the eyes of all in the synagogue were fixed upon him" (Luke 4:20). Then came a dramatic moment: Jesus said, "Today this scripture passage is fulfilled in your hearing" (Luke 4:21). Clearly he was claiming to be the Anointed One—the Messiah from God. With this as his "party platform," the remainder of Luke's Gospel unfolds, showing how Jesus fulfilled his defining role as the primary agent and teacher of God's reign within human history.

A most consoling aspect of Jesus's teaching for God's reign is his emphasis on the largess of God's mercy. Note that a central aspect of Jesus's public ministry was his forgiving sinners and welcoming them into his community of disciples—this surely taught loud and clear. Indeed, a frequent charge against him was that he was associating and eating with sinful people, the shared meal being a deep symbol of inclusion and hospitality in his culture.

An eminent instance was Jesus calling Matthew the tax collector to discipleship. All three Synoptic Gospels tell this story (Mark and Luke name him Levi) and as if there had been no prior encounter between them. Jesus simply says to Matthew, "Follow me," and Matthew "got up and followed him" (Matt 9:9). People had every reason to hate tax collectors; they were typically fellow Jews who were working for the enemy, the Romans, collecting high taxes with a generous commission for themselves. That Jesus would call such a person to become a disciple showed amazing inclusivity on his part, and Matthew's immediate acceptance reflects the charism of Jesus and the attractiveness of his teaching for God's reign.

Following on, Jesus goes to Matthew's house for dinner and "many tax collectors and sinners came and were sitting with him and his disciples" (Matt 9:10). That Jesus would include such people in his table fellowship taught loudly *and* brought an understandable protest. Some Pharisees present—committed and responsible interpreters of the Law, including avoidance of the nonobservant—asked a reasonable question of Jesus's disciples, "Why does your teacher eat with tax collectors and sinners?" (Matt 9:11). When Jesus overheard their concern, he intervened, saying, "Those who are well have no need of a physician, but those who are sick" (Matt 9:12). Then he gave his students a take-home assignment, "Go and learn what this means, 'I desire mercy, not sacrifice'" (Matt 9:13).

Here, Jesus was quoting (by heart again) from the prophet Hosea (6:6), who represented this injunction as spoken by Yahweh and as preferring *mercy* over cultic worship (the original Hebrew, *hesed,* is also translated as "loving kindness"). Just as God favors loving mercy over ritual purity, Jesus favors the same. Then he concluded by saying of himself, "For I have come to call not the righteous but sinners" (Matt 9:13). For Jesus God's reign heartily welcomes sinners.

So radical was Jesus's forgiveness that he even forgave people who, out of ignorance or hardness of heart, had not yet repented of their wrongdoing. He prayed on the cross for those who crucified him, "Father, forgive them; for they do not know what they are doing" (Luke 34:34). And he made the measure of disciples being forgiven our own forgiving of "those who trespass against us" (Matt 6:12). This reign of God as taught by Jesus is indeed a radical affair!

Another amazing instance of Jesus teaching the largess of God's reign is in the parable of the laborers in the vineyard (see Matt 20:1–16). Essentially, it represents a vineyard keeper as paying those who came "at the eleventh hour" the same wage as those who had borne the heat of the day, and from early morning. But why would any vineyard keeper be so absurdly generous? The only possible answer is not that the latecomers had earned their full wage but that they *needed* it to feed their families. Likewise, God gives us what we need even when we have not earned it. A people of God's reign and educators inspired by Jesus should be so munificent as well.

As Jesus gave over his whole being to the reign of God and was ultimately crucified for such commitment, disciples must give their all to what God intends. In two very brief parables Jesus encourages this "go for broke" commitment to God's reign—holding nothing back. Thus, the reign of God is like a person who finds "a treasure hidden in a field"; with "joy" they sell *everything* to buy the field (Matt 13:44). Or God's reign is like a merchant who finds a "pearl of great price"; likewise, the merchant sells off everything in order to purchase the pearl (Matt 13:45–46). As Catholic educators teach a personal and social ethic from the spiritual foundation of Jesus, whatever advances God's reign must be the ultimate criterion of what they propose.

The consoling aspect of Jesus's call to invest everything for the reign of God is that those two parables come immediately after two others where he teaches that even small efforts can make a difference. The tiny mustard seed can become a big tree, and a little yeast can cause a huge pile of dough to rise (see Matt 13:31–33). It is likewise regarding the reign of God. And every educator has experienced as much, when a word of kindness or a little extra help to a student in need can lend hope, maybe even turn a life around.

Educators especially need to see their work as a partnership in which every good effort is magnified by God's grace—and so can bear fruit a hundredfold (see Mark 4:20). We leave the story of the historical Jesus as educator here, for now. We will often refer to his teaching and modeling of God's reign throughout our review of the great exponents of the Catholic intellectual tradition (Chapters 3–6) and more explicitly again throughout Part III as what and how he taught pertains to all the foundational themes of Catholic education. The key takeaway from the reflections of this chapter is that the reign of God summarizes the great spiritual foundation and the utopian vision that Catholic educators are to teach and encourage in the lives of students.

For Reflection and Conversation

- Imagine making Jesus's portrayal of the reign of God the spiritual foundation of your own vocation as educator?
- What might be some core commitments and values to teach and live by?
- Name some concrete ways that you already encourage "learning outcomes" for the reign of God (most likely without using such language)?
- What are some new challenges you recognize to teach for God's reign as Jesus did?

FOR CATHOLIC EDUCATION

Educating for the reign of God. Each chapter of this book has a section (or sections) that reflect explicitly on how Catholic educators are to implement the spiritual foundation(s) that the chapter proposes. Here, we begin to reflect on what the centrality of God's reign in the teaching of Jesus and its law of radical love might mean for Catholic education today. Indeed, how to embrace the spiritual foundation of God's reign as taught by Jesus and to reflect it throughout the whole curriculum of a Catholic school is a central theme of this book. Here, we highlight some of the social implications, required especially by the communal nature of its greatest commandment.

Since the dawn of history, people of all cultures have recognized the significant social potential of education, even some grand public purpose. In the West the ancient Greeks had the notion of education as *paideia*, a holistic curriculum engaging the arts and sciences to prepare good citizens who would forge a virtuous society. Similarly, for the Romans, the intent of education was *humanitas,* as in preparing people to live into their full human potential and to contribute to the common good of the public realm. Since then, a consistent theme throughout Western history is that education is to promote the full development of people, shaping their very *being—who* they are and *how* they live. It should enable them to make and keep life human for themselves and others. In sum, education is to serve a noble and public vision for the well-*being* of people and of their societies.

Plato, for example, said that education is to engage and turn the soul of the person "toward the true, the good, and the beautiful." Aristotle proposes that education should encourage people toward happiness by inculcating practical and social virtues, and ultimately spiritual wisdom—the highest form of knowledge. The Book of Daniel proposed that the purpose of education is for people to live wisely, and that those who teach others such "righteousness" shall "shine like the stars of heaven, forever" (Dan 12:3).

In more recent times the great educator Maria Montessori (1878–1952) said that teaching is "the great art of companionship" to accompany students into their own boundless creativity and responsible freedom. John Dewey (1859–1952) portrayed education as the chief means of human development and social reform. The renowned Brazilian educator Paulo Freire (1921–97) proposed a utopian vision of education for our time as raising up the oppressed and promoting the liberation of all peoples. And the esteemed philosopher and mathematician Alfred North Whitehead (1861–1947) wrote that "the essence of education is that it be religious" and meant that it "inculcate duty and reverence" (*Aims of Education*, 3, 14).

As we elaborate in Chapter 8, much of public education in the Western democracies has lost all sense of such noble vision and social purpose. It is more interested in preparing people to "climb to the top" in our corporate world of unbridled capitalism, with no concern for "the neighbor"—beyond self-interest. Its intended learning outcome seems to be to produce what Canadian philospher Charles Taylor calls "buffered selves"—people who act only by and for themselves with self-sufficiency. It would be a dreadful failure for Catholic schools to follow suit. Instead, Jesus has given educators who walk in his footsteps the most inspiring and socially comprehensive vision of education—the reign of God with its mandate of radical love. What Catholic educators are to teach, how we are to teach it, and with what intent for our co-learners and the common good of all, must be constantly suffused with this spiritual foundation—Jesus's vision of God's reign of fullness of life for all people and creation (see John 10:10).

As the central commitment of Jesus's life and teaching, the reign of God calls Catholic educators, first and foremost, to teach for its radical law of love—of God and neighbor as oneself, even enemies. This is the ultimate mode of responding to God's unconditional love toward us. Paulo Freire, in crafting a socially liberating and personally humanizing education, insisted that its bedrock must be this *greatest* commandment of Jesus—radical love. Only by loving our students as ourselves and encouraging them to live likewise are we likely to render them an education that honors their full human potential and serves the common good of society.

Note that by its focus on *neighbor* as *oneself*, such love must be both personal and communal, encouraging authentic self-love *and* a radical love for others in the social and public realm. Consequently, and as we will echo often throughout, Catholic education is to promote the personal well-being of students and then the peace and justice of God's reign for their community and society. It should champion the human rights *and* the social responsibilities of its students, fostering the dignity and inclusion of all people. In sum, Catholic education should prepare its students to embrace the spiritual values that Jesus modeled and taught as his commitment to the reign of God. To encourage them to opt for anything less will not be Catholic education.

We might think about the reign of God, then, as the *meta-purpose* of Catholic education, the ultimate spiritual vision toward which we intend our educating to contribute. In day-to-day practice, of course, educators need to plan curricula for more immediate *learning* outcomes.

As teachers we choose what we want students to learn, craft our pedagogy accordingly, and then evaluate, somehow, if we have succeeded. But even in the needed everyday pragmatism of such lesson planning, the ultimate guide to the curriculum choices of Catholic educators is that they advance the reign of God—in these students' lives and in the life of the world.

Whether done implicitly or explicitly (much depends on the subject being taught), embracing the reign of God as the meta-purpose of Catholic education can make a rich contribution to the welfare of society. Likewise, it can greatly enrich the life of the students as having ultimate meaning, that they can live their lives into a Transcendent Horizon—our gracious God of unconditional love. And Catholic education should pose such living for God's reign as its own reward *now*. There is no surer path to happiness in life than to live for the reign of God as taught and modeled by Jesus. The Beatitudes (see Matt 5:3–11) epitomize such a *way*—but note, *makarios* can be translated as "happy" as well as the traditional "blessed." With integrity, we can promise our students that they will find the most happiness in life by living out the greatest commandment of radical love, and then by being peacemakers, by hungering and thirsting for justice, being merciful and compassionate, and so on—in other words, by living for the reign of God. And Catholic education inspired by Jesus's vision of God's reign suggests the kind of faith to encourage in students' lives and world.

For living faith as a way of life. Catholic education is to be conducted *from* and *for* faith. Patently, then, so much depends on what we mean by *faith*. Remembering that God's reign is to be realized "on earth" and "now," Catholic schools are to educate for an existential faith in people's lives, in other words, for a *living* faith that amounts to a *way of life* for the reign of God.

Note that this first requires a stretch far beyond the popular equation of faith with *belief*. Of course, there is a creedal aspect to faith, but belief alone would fall far short of *living* faith for the reign of God. To center the core of Christian faith on the reign of God as taught and modeled by Jesus calls forth a holistic faith that "gets done" in the everyday of life, and for education that is deeply formative of students in such *living* faith.

We begin by posing it as *living* faith into the truths and values of God's reign as taught by Jesus and, again, to be put to work at every level of existence—personal, communal, and social. Such *living* faith is an ultimate learning outcome to be intentionally promoted by Catholic education—the kind of faith *from* and *for* which we are to educate.

As suggested already, for Christian traditions faith is never realized alone but is always intertwined with the two other great virtues of hope and love. By making love of God and love of neighbor with all of one's being the greatest commandment of God's reign, Jesus makes such love constitutive to a life of Christian faith. Likewise, *living* faith is precisely what keeps hope alive and enables us to go on hoping, even in difficult times, not as naive optimism but as a commitment that inspires our own agency for our hopes.

In the Catholic intellectual tradition we elaborate Thomas Aquinas's proposal that the three great virtues are symbiotic, with each circling in both directions. So faith is the source of living with hope and love, and living with love nurtures the kind of hope that sustains our faith, and so on. Long before Aquinas, however, the symbiosis of faith, hope, and love is writ large in the life and teaching of Jesus for God's reign.

Furthermore, faith as a way of life is holistic in that it is to engage the whole person—their whole *being*. From its symbiosis with the greatest commandment of love, faith is to engage all of people's mind, heart, and strength. In other words, faith encourages us to embrace great creeds and convictions (our minds); it is to shape our relationships with God, others, and the world (our hearts); and it must be put to work—with the help of God's grace—in the values and ethic by which we live our lives (our strength/will).

Finally, the *living* faith to which Jesus invites us and for which Catholic education is to educate is to be *alive, lived,* and *life-giving.* Jesus's envisioning of God's reign invites people into a horizon of faith that is nurtured and grown throughout the journey of life; it is to be *alive* and vibrant, ever reaching into new horizons of faithfulness. Clearly, Christian faith is to be *lived*; as Jesus modeled and taught repeatedly, the reign of God is not simply by God's grace but is a gift (Latin, *gratia*) that engages our own agency; with God's help, Christian faith must get done! And clearly, Christian faith as a *way of life* toward God's reign should be *life-giving*, for oneself, others, and the world. What an inspiring spiritual foundation and ennobling horizon it is for Catholic education to educate *from* and *for* such *living* faith in students' lives.

Later, we will elaborate further on the explicit role of religious education in Catholic schools to educate all of its students *for* faith, in other words, to propose a Transcendent Horizon of unconditional love as the ground of human meaning, purpose, and ethic. As the description of faith above makes clear, it invites students to a whole way of *being* in the world; *living* faith is to define their *way of life*. It is to be integrated into who they are, who they become, and what they do with their lives. A Catholic school is to encourage and educate for such *living* faith in its students, albeit respecting their personal choice of a distinct identity within a particular faith tradition—or none!

RENEWING YOUR VOCATION AS CATHOLIC EDUCATOR

The conclusion of each chapter invites readers into more practical reflections on sustaining and renewing your vocation as educator, and helping to shape the life of your school. We name the three practical themes as for your *soul*, for your teaching *style*, and for the educational *space*. Note, however, that all three—not just the *soul*—invite you to take the foundational spirituality proposed in each chapter and implement it in the curriculum of your Catholic school. Note, too, that the educational *space* includes a teacher's classroom or laboratory and also the overall ethos that the school community mediates. It will be beneficial to pause with these reflections; the ideal is to have some conversation partners with whom to share your wisdom.

For the educator's soul. Servant of God Dorothy Day (1897–1980), the great Catholic social reformer and cofounder (with Peter Maurin) of the Catholic Worker Movement, once wrote that there is no greater blessing in life than to have worthwhile work. Given the life-giving potential and historical importance of this august vocation in the lives of students and society, educators have worthwhile work "in spades." Just imagine: Catholic educators are invited to be primary agents of the reign of God as taught by Jesus. And yet the humdrum of the everyday can lull us into a routine that forgets the vital importance of what we "do" in the lives and world of others—shaping their very *being* and thus our society.

- How might the horizon of God's reign inspire you to keep on in your own vital vocation, especially in challenging times and situations?
- Might you be encouraged by remembering that the proverbial sowing of a small seed or mixing in a pinch of leaven can be magnified by God's grace to produce "a hundredfold" (Mark 4:20)?

For your teaching style. We elaborate further on the pedagogy of Jesus in later chapters. Allowing for the historical, social, and cultural differences between his world and ours, all Catholic educators are, in a sense, to teach as Jesus did.

- From what you know already or learned in this chapter, what stands out for you about the pedagogy of Jesus? What might you find attractive? What might you learn from him?

- Looking to Jesus's defining passion as the reign of God, how might you describe the central passion of your own teaching? How can it inspire and sustain you, especially in challenging circumstances?

For the educational space. We noted a contemporary summary of Jesus's living for God's reign as his making an option for the poor. It simply means that Jesus favored those who most needed it—the least, the lost, and the last.

- How might you craft the environment of your classroom so that it makes an option for the poor? For example, how might you treat "academically poor" students, or rather, the ones who are "differently abled" and need extra time or tutoring, or the less popular ones?
- How might you encourage your students—within the classroom and outside it—to make an option of the poor?

No `utopias`!

2

To Educate for Hope

AN EMPOWERING HOPE

Though we may not advert to it often, a most significant function of education is to offer people *hope* for their lives in the world. Parents send their children, and youths and adults come to school out of hope that they will become something more than they are already. The common perception is that education lends hope for opportunities and possibilities that people would not have otherwise. The highest hope that education can offer people is to become more fully alive human beings, prepared to make an adequate living, to have a worthwhile life, and to contribute to the common good of all.

The hope of education, on the one hand, engages the learner's own agency and responsibility (for example, being willing to study); otherwise it is just wishful thinking that will likely disappoint. On the other hand, hope that depends entirely on ourselves and our personal efforts can become its own oppression rather than an empowering horizon. Our human condition needs a source of hope that is *gracious* to us, that comes as a gift and from beyond ourselves, especially to go on hoping in difficult times.

This means that the hope most likely to endure is grounded in *faith*, a faith that inspires and sustains people's own best efforts and yet lends a sense of gift from beyond our personal agency. All the great world religions are systems of faith that lend enduring hope and sources of hope that put faith to work. In this chapter we engage the particular symbiosis between faith and hope, though, as noted in the previous chapter, with the third great virtue, love, ever flowing back and forth with the other two to constitute *living* faith.

Different faith traditions have varied reasons for hope, and educators from other religious backgrounds can draw upon their own spiritual resources. Here I offer the ultimate Christian foundation for educating

27

with hope, encouraging all to imagine how their hope—whatever its grounding—can seed and harvest a humanizing education.

There are many particular symbols of Christian faith that lend hope; for example, that "God is love" (1 John 4:8); that God's mercy, as Mary said, "endures forever" (Luke 1:54–55), and the promise of "life everlasting" (the Apostles' Creed). However, the key symbol that grounds and permeates all Christian hope is faith in the resurrection of Jesus from the dead. Christian faith is that God raised up Jesus to new life on the third day after his crucifixion. This is the ultimate counter-symbol to what otherwise would have been Jesus's defeat—by death. By raising him from the dead, "God our Savior" has made "Christ Jesus our hope" (1 Tim 1:1). Christian faith is that the paschal mystery—Jesus's death and resurrection—released what Saint Paul repeatedly refers to as "an abundance of God's grace" into human history, empowering us to be agents of hope in our own lives and to others. Instead of encouraging naive optimism, however, Christian *faith for hope* needs, again, to be a *living* faith—faith put to work toward all our hopes and this with the help of God's grace.

We will do well to review the claims and implications of Jesus's resurrection as the key tenet of faith that most grounds the hope of Christians. To embrace such hope and put it to work can lend a powerful spiritual foundation for the work of Catholic education. Might the Christian conviction of God resurrecting Jesus inspire people from other faith traditions to reclaim their own cornerstone of hope; in substance if not in detail, it may well resemble the Christian source—our *gracious* God.

For Reflection and Conversation

- What are the primary sources of your own hope in the midst of life? How does your hope help you to "keep on," especially when faced with challenges and difficulties?
- What do you recognize as the correlation between hope and education? How is your own teaching a work of hope?
- What is the faith foundation that most sustains your hope?

QUESTIONS FOR THE RESURRECTION OF JESUS

The first Christian communities became rock-solid convinced "that ✳ God raised Jesus from the dead" (Acts 13:30). Furthermore, by his

✳ Except Thomas!?

rising, they believed that God affirmed the divinity of Jesus; as Paul writes, "Jesus was declared to be Son of God . . . by resurrection from the dead" (Rom 1:4). Then those first disciples were equally convinced that Jesus's dying and rising had changed the entire course of human history, that all of God's creation had been definitively oriented toward hope for realizing the reign of God. Because of what he had lived for and died for, "God raised up this Jesus" (Acts 2:32), and we can now "rejoice in hope" (Rom 12:12).

Jesus's being raised up from death to new life ensures the enduring hope that eventually good will triumph over evil, love over hate, justice over injustice, peace over violence, inclusion over discrimination, and so on, and that all people can begin "to walk in the newness of life" (Rom 6:4). For "the one who raised the Lord Jesus will raise us also" (2 Cor 4:14)—with all humanity being raised up by Jesus's rising. Because of the resurrection of Jesus, even death has lost its "sting" (1 Cor 15:55). For sure, we will all die, but just as surely "all will be made alive" (1 Cor 15:22) in God's eternal time, with our going home to God the Ultimate Horizon of hope for all people.

Lest the resurrection of Jesus and its hope for all be dismissed as wishful thinking, let us reflect briefly on the warrants that convince Christians of this central symbol of their faith. This will suggest how they and other partners might embrace the hope it symbolizes for Catholic education. The four most obvious questions about this faith-for-hope claim of Christians are *What resurrection? Is it believable? What does it promise? How does it work?*—especially for education.

May the responses prompt those educators who are confessing Catholics to embrace the hope reflected in Jesus's resurrection and to have this spiritual conviction permeate their vocation. For teachers from other or no faith tradition, may this Christian conviction inspire echoing sources of hope for their educating from their own spiritual resources. It is imperative that all Catholic educators educate for hope—hope for persons and for our world—and that our students put *living* faith to work as agents of hope for all.

What resurrection? Note, initially, that Christians recognize a great mystery here, something deeply of God and beyond human experience or full comprehension. The scriptures do not represent Jesus's rising as a resuscitation of his earthly body as if he returned to daily life. Nor was it a reanimation or reincarnation as if a soul rejoins its body or takes on a different one—as believed in some religions. And yet Christians are convinced that it was *real* for Jesus's earthly body.

On the one hand, the Gospels represent that the resurrected Jesus could eat breakfast with the disciples (see John 21:1–14) and invite "doubting Thomas" to put his hand into the bodily wounds from his crucifixion (see John 20:24–29). On the other hand, the Risen Christ could also pass through locked doors (see John 20:19) and could appear to disciples at will. So, while the earthly body of Jesus was not left to decay—his tomb was found empty—his risen body is of the divine realm that we have yet to experience ourselves.

So, what happened—at least as Christians claim? Scholars agree that Mark's account was the earliest Gospel, so let us follow his chronology. Mark relates that "when the Sabbath was over, Mary Magdalene, and Mary the mother of James, and Salome brought spices" to Jesus's tomb to anoint his body (now the third day since his crucifixion). They were wondering "who will roll away the stone" at the entrance, yet when they got there "they saw that the stone, which was very large, had already been rolled back." Within the tomb "they saw a young man, dressed in a white robe" and "they were alarmed" (Mark 16:1–5).

He tells them, "Do not be alarmed; you are looking for Jesus of Nazareth, who was crucified. He has been raised." He adds, "Go tell his disciples and Peter that he is going ahead of you to Galilee; there you will see him, just as he told you." Then, what is known as the shorter ending of Mark concludes with, "So they went out and fled from the tomb, for terror and amazement had seized them, and they said nothing to anyone, for they were afraid" (Mark 16:6–8).

In the longer ending that follows, we find three more resurrection snippets. The first states boldly that Jesus rose on the first day of the week and "appeared first to Mary Magdalene" (Mark 16:9). She went and told the other disciples "that Jesus was alive and had been seen by her" but "they would not believe it" (Mark 16:10–11). The second story states that Jesus appeared to two other disciples while walking in the country; "they went back and told the rest, but they did not believe them" (Mark 16:13). Last, Mark says that the Risen Christ Jesus "appeared to the eleven" and "upbraided them for their lack of faith and stubbornness, because they had not believed those (for example, the women) who saw him after he had risen." Then he gave them a commission to "go into all the world and proclaim the good news to the whole creation" (Mark 16:14–15).

The other three Gospels echo much of Mark, and yet they add their own accounts of disciples encountering the risen Jesus; we note some of their details below. For now, all four Gospels clearly claim that Jesus rose from the dead and that he was seen repeatedly by disciples, beginning with Mary Magdalene and other women. Indeed, Paul, in his first letter to the Corinthians, written as early as 53 CE (well before all four Gospels), states that Jesus "appeared to more than five hundred brothers and sisters at one time, most of whom are still alive, though some have died" (1 Cor 15:6).

Is it believable? Imagine for a moment that Jesus's resurrection *was* just a concocted story as some have claimed from the beginning (see Matt 28:11–15), or as if he rose only in the wishful hearts of disciples. This would have required a massive conspiracy and deep delusion among a huge number of people, many of whom would suffer persecution and give their lives in witness to Jesus's resurrection (see Acts 7:54—8:3; 9:1–2). Taking such a scam as at least highly unlikely, we can note three compelling reasons why it is credible to believe Jesus's resurrection was for real.

First, rather than conspiring to fabricate the story or being overly credulous, the above citations from Mark make abundantly clear that the disciples were not expecting Jesus to rise and were very reluctant to believe it. We find the same doubt and reluctance to believe it in the other three Gospels. For example, in Luke, when the women first tell the male disciples, the latter dismiss it as "an idle tale, and they did not believe them" (Luke 24:11). A subsequent account in Luke of the Risen Christ appearing to disciples notes that "they were startled and terrified and thought that they were seeing a ghost" (Luke 24:37). This was not an overly credulous community. ✳

Second, those male disciples who had "deserted Jesus and fled" (Mark 14:50) soon became fearless witnesses to his Gospel and resurrection. Mark says that "they went out and proclaimed the good news everywhere, while the Lord worked with them and confirmed the message by the signs that accompanied it" (Mark 16:20). This was because "Jesus presented himself alive to them by many convincing proofs, appearing to them during forty days and speaking about the kingdom of God" (Acts 1:3; note that the centrality of the reign of God continues for the Risen Christ). Later, the same Peter who had denied even knowing Jesus (see Mark 14:66–72), gave a mighty speech that boldly proclaimed that "God raised Jesus up" (Acts 2:24). Thereafter, having initially been a bunch of scaredy-cats, "with great power the apostles gave their testimony to the resurrection of the Lord Jesus" (Acts 4:33).

Third and perhaps most convincing, if Jesus's resurrection was a fabricated or make-believe story, given the patriarchal culture of the context and time women disciples would *never* have been cast as the star witnesses. All four Gospel accounts make clear that the women disciples were the first to see, believe in, and bear witness to the Risen Christ.

✳ But we are!

The most dramatic incident is the encounter of Mary Magdalene with the Risen One (see John 20:11–18). Rather than being overly credulous, Mary at first assumes that she has encountered the gardener and inquires where she might find the body of Jesus. After recognizing him and interacting with the risen Jesus, "Mary Magdalene went and announced to the disciples, 'I have seen the Lord'" (John 20:18). Because of her role of being the first to announce the resurrection of Jesus, later Christian tradition would hail Mary Magdalene as "the apostle to the apostles"—a title lost from history but recently restored to her by Pope Francis. (The popular portrayal of her as a "sinful woman" has no basis in the Gospels.)

All this lends credibility to Christian claims for the realness of Jesus's resurrection. Now, we ask, what does this mean for the course of human history and concomitantly for the agency of Catholic educators, both for those who believe in Jesus's resurrection and to encourage teachers from other traditions to find therein their own symbols of hope. What spiritual foundation might it lend to inspire Catholic educators and their mandate to educate for hope?

What does it promise? So what did the Irish poet William Butler Yeats mean when he wrote of Easter: "All changed, changed utterly: A terrible beauty is born." For Yeats, reflecting on the Irish Rising of 1916, and for the faith of all Christians, Easter has changed everything, definitively altering the course of human history toward the reign of God. But how to name this "terrible beauty" (by "terrible" Yeats meant "astonishing") has challenged Christians from when they first began to believe that God had raised up Jesus from death into newness of life on an Easter morning over two thousand years ago.

The challenge for the first disciples was to make sense out of the paradox of Jesus's horrible death and then the extraordinary reversal that God wrought by his resurrection. Why and to what end was this for all humankind—and thus a spiritual foundation to be put to work by Catholic educators and education? Saint Paul, the greatest interpreter of Jesus's resurrection, got us started with multiple metaphors; let us sample a few. While they have varied emphases, that Jesus's dying and rising lends *hope* for every person and indeed for all creation was a constant promise of them all.

One of Paul's often repeated metaphors was that God in Christ has set all humankind free: *free from* personal enslavement to sin; *free to* oppose sinful social structures; and *free for* becoming the best people and society that we can be. With confidence, Paul wrote to the Romans, "The Spirit of life in Christ Jesus has set you free from the law of sin and of death" (Rom 8:2). Because of Jesus's dying and rising, all people can live into "the glorious freedom of the children of God" (Rom 8:21). And to the Galatians, Paul wrote, "For freedom Christ has set us free. Stand firm, therefore, and do not submit again to a yoke of slavery" (Gal 5:1). Instead of living captive to some personal slavery or having simply to accept unjust social structures or oppressive cultural patterns, the Risen Christ empowers Christians to stand for freedom at all levels. Catholic education should represent the hope of such freedom to students, encouraging them to accept and be agents of God's work of liberation through their own ways of living.

Another classic text is 1 Corinthians 15 where Paul portrays Jesus's resurrection as raising up all humankind—not just Christian disciples. He begins by reiterating that God verified Jesus and what he lived and died for by raising him from the dead; the resurrection is God's unqualified endorsement of Jesus and his teaching. Paul then avers that faith in the raising of Jesus lends hope for *our* rising as well because of his solidarity with all humankind. Indeed, for Paul, such hope is the make-or-break feature of Christian faith, for "if there is no resurrection of the dead, then Christ has not been raised; and if Christ has not been raised, then our proclamation has been in vain and your faith has been in vain" (1 Cor 15:13–14).

Rather than such faith-for-hope being in vain, however, Paul claims that Jesus's rising has even "destroyed death" (1 Cor 15:26), offsetting our greatest and ultimate loss—of life to death. By God raising Jesus from the dead, now for all people death has "lost its sting" (1 Cor 15:55); we can have "victory [over death] through our Lord Jesus Christ" (1 Cor 15:57). While this does not erase the reality of our own eventual demise, it transforms death as rebirth into eternal life. Catholic education is to offer such final hope to its students, posing the potential to live into eternal life in God's presence as life's ultimate horizon.

To capture the hope lent by Jesus's death and resurrection, sometimes Paul used multiple metaphors, even in the same verse. So the risen Jesus "became for us *wisdom* from God, and *righteousness* and *sanctification* and *redemption*" (1 Cor 1:30, emphasis added). Likewise, Jesus is the one "in whom we have *redemption* and the *forgiveness* of sins" (Col 1:14, emphasis added). As if summarizing all the metaphors, Paul says that we "have come to *fullness* in Jesus" (Col 2:10, emphasis added). Catholic education is to portray a horizon of fullness of life for its students; according to John's Gospel, that is exactly what the historical Jesus promised (10:10) and then made possible by his dying and rising.

And lest Paul be thought the only metaphor maker about the effects for all people of the paschal mystery, consider an inspiring summary text from 1 Peter: "Blessed be the God and Father of our Lord Jesus Christ! By his great mercy he has given us a new birth into a living hope through the resurrection of Jesus Christ from the dead, and into an inheritance that is imperishable, undefiled, and unfading, kept in heaven for you" (1 Pet 1:3–4). Education grounded in faith toward such an ultimate horizon must surely offer tremendous hope to its students.

Over Christian history three dominant metaphors have emerged for capturing the historical hope catalyzed by the paschal mystery: *salvation*, *redemption*, and *divinization* (or *theosis*—becoming God-like). *Salvation* and Jesus as Savior portrays a sense of being made safe, secure, and whole, of being delivered from danger, of enjoying good health (Latin, *salus*). Paul wrote often of "the salvation that is in Christ Jesus" (2 Tim 2:10) and named him "our Savior" (Titus 1:4).

Redemption, and Jesus as the Redeemer of humankind, responds to our need for forgiveness and mercy, and for God's help to counteract the effects of human sinfulness, our own and our society's. As Paul suggests, all people can find "redemption . . . in Christ Jesus" (Rom 3:24), making him our Redeemer, who mediates "forgiveness of our trespasses" (Eph 1:7). Might we say boldly, then, that Catholic education should help to *redeem* people's lives, assuring that they need never be bound by mistakes and shortcomings but can always repent and renew. What amazing hope!

The *divinization* metaphor may be the ultimate expression of hope for humankind. It proposes that Jesus's dying and rising enable all people to grow into divine likeness (echoing Genesis 1:26–27), ever more reflecting in our being our own divine potential. As Paul asked rhetorically of the Corinthians, "Do you not know that you are God's temple and that God's Spirit dwells in you," and added, "God's temple is holy, and you are that temple" (1 Cor 3:16–17). Through Jesus's human bond with all people and his divine bond with God, now all people "may become participants of the divine nature" (2 Pet 1:4). This divinization or *theosis* model is much favored by Eastern Orthodox and Eastern Catholic traditions, famously summarized by their great theologian Athanasius (296–373) as "God became human [in Jesus] so that humans could become more like God." What amazing hope this could lend to educators in imagining the positive potential of their students—it would seem nigh limitless!

How does it work? Such positive metaphors for what God achieved in the life, death, and resurrection of Jesus—and there are many more in the New Testament—are inspiring, and yet we can wonder, how do they actually work in our day-to-day life, how can people experience and live with the hope that the paschal mystery represents? And how can Catholic educators so educate? Are all these metaphors and their hopes no more than wishful thinking?

The summary response is that all the metaphors are realized and made effective through the power of God's *grace*. While God's grace has been operative in the world since God's very act of creation (with a Big Bang some fourteen billion years ago), through Jesus's life, death, and resurrection, grace has been augmented all the more. Now people are ever in receipt of what Paul repeatedly refers to as "an abundance of God's grace" (Rom 5:17), which God now pours out "in overflowing measure" (1 Tim 1:14). Echoing, God's "grace and peace" are now ours "in abundance . . . in Jesus our Lord" (2 Pet 1:2).

Certainly, *grace* is not an easy term to pin down, though it is repeated over one hundred and fifty times in the New Testament writings—clearly a central theme. We have hinted at it before, and, as we review in Chapter 7, what grace is and how it *works* have often been at the center of Christian controversies. A key is to remember Jesus's ultimate revelation that "God is love" (1 John 4:8) and has unconditional love for humankind (1 John 4:19). Furthermore, God's love is not simply a good-will sentiment from a remote heaven but reaches out and into our lives with constant support, help, encouragement, and whatever we need to live as people of God.

God's grace, then, is well summarized (echoing theologian Karl Rahner, 1904–84) as *God's effective love ever at work in people's lives*. We can receive and respond to God's grace precisely because of the soul within us, that animating and defining spirit by which each person is alive with the life of God (see Gen 2:7). And grace works from within our souls not by dispensing with our agency but by engaging it all the more; grace empowers and sustains our own best efforts.

In the age-old formulation from the Catholic intellectual tradition "grace works through and enhances nature," meaning that God prompts and augments our own best efforts. While God's grace is "free" (*gratia*), as we said before, it comes to us as a responsibility, or better a "response-ability." The Bible's image is of a *covenant* partnership between ourselves and God; the biblical covenant always holds both sides to account for their commitment. God's grace both empowers and expects our own agency.

As the New Testament writings make clear, God's grace is available to *all* people, not just to Christians. This is because God's *liberating salvation* (my favorite metaphor) that began in Jesus now continues through the Holy Spirit; and the Spirit, like the wind, "blows where it chooses" (John 3:8). The Second Vatican Council was summarizing a two-thousand-year-old tradition when it noted that through his humanity, Jesus was united with all humankind. As a result, "not only Christians" but "all people of good will in whose hearts grace works in an unseen way" have the capacity "in a manner known only to God" to benefit from "the paschal mystery"—that is, all people can be empowered by God's saving grace in Jesus Christ (*The Church in the Modern World*, no. 22).

Note how people in recovery from addiction speak of the great challenge involved, and yet typically they also pay tribute to a Higher Power—God's grace at work through their own efforts. Now all people can "approach the throne of grace with boldness, so that we may receive mercy and find grace to help in time of need" (Heb 12:16). Even for ecological concerns, God's grace assures—with our collaboration—that eventually "creation itself will be set free from its bondage to decay and will obtain the glorious freedom of the children of God" (Rom 8:21).

Perhaps *the* most hopeful spiritual foundation of Catholic faith, to be intensely put to work in Catholic education, is to assure students that they always have the help of God's grace, especially in difficult times. Students can always make their own best efforts with God's grace empowering them to keep on with hope. In sum, because of Jesus's dying and rising and the grace of God that this paschal mystery releases into human history with abundance, all people can live with hope, come what may.

As Catholic educators we can constantly encourage our students to be confident that ultimately no falsehood can become true, no tyranny endure, no oppression triumph, no injustice prevail, no slavery remain, no discrimination become just, no cross be too heavy, no addiction be beyond recovery, no bad habit be unbreakable, and the list goes on. What a spiritual foundation of faith-based hope this is for all people, and one in which to ground Catholic education. Let us imagine now and throughout subsequent chapters what such hope might mean in practice for Catholic educators.

For Reflection and Conversation

- Think of a time when you experienced God's grace at work in your life—in some vivid and explicit way. What might you learn from that memory?
- How might the notion of God's constant help—grace—sustain your hope now? The hope you have for your students? How can you put such hope to work through your teaching?

FOR CATHOLIC EDUCATION

What does it mean for the curriculum of Catholic schools and its educators if we embrace the faith-with-hope that God's abundant grace is ever available and at work for all—and for Christian faith through the dying and rising of Jesus? What if we embrace the spiritual foundation that life in the world is the theater of God's grace with us to be agents of grace within it?

We have already said much about grace, and the theme recurs, especially in reference to a Catholic anthropology (Chapter 7) and a Catholic cosmology (outlook on life) and its principle of sacramentality (Chapter 8). For now, let me summarize that always having the help of God's grace to empower and sustain our own agency for good is among the most positive spiritual foundations of Catholic faith that Catholic education can mediate to its students.

Let's focus first on how a Catholic theology of grace encourages our educating *from* and *for* faith that lends *hope* for all, and then on the *possibilities* and *responsibilities* of such hope. As suggested earlier, educators who do not share Christian faith and its theology of grace might be inspired by it to reach into their own spiritual resources and traditions to find a resonant source of hope to permeate their educating.

From and for faith for hope. In the Preface we cited the summary statement by the *Catechism of the Catholic Church*: "At the heart (of Christian faith) we find a Person, the Person of Jesus of Nazareth, the only Son from the Father" (§426). Now that we have both emphases on the table, the historical person of Jesus whom God raised up as the Christ of faith, we have a more complete sense of the "heart" that is to ground Catholic education. Given Jesus's centrality of the reign of God (Chapter 1) and now God's abundant grace through the Risen Christ, we are to educate boldly in these postmodern times *from* and *for* faith that lends *hope*. Having begun the description of *living* faith in the first chapter, here we focus on the challenge of our postmodern context, where faith is to lend hope for all, *much* against the grain of our secular age.

First, and to state the obvious, the very fact that a school presents itself to the world as Catholic is a declaration of its commitment to educate *from* and *for* a particular faith perspective on life and to encourage as much in its students. Catholic schools, surely, are to prepare people for the realities and challenges of their lives in the world, an *immanent* concern. Then equally, they are to propose a *transcendent* take on life that encourages students to have faith in themselves, in others, and in an Ultimate Horizon. To name this Mystery, believers say "God," and Christians refer to a personal God as revealed in Jesus, who loves us unconditionally and draws us into covenant partnership, thus lending meaning, help (grace), and ethic for our lives.

Catholic education, then, is to ground itself in and encourage both a horizontal and a vertical perspective on life, preparing people to live well in the world with faith that lends hope, immediately and ultimately, for their lives. But is faith-based and hope-encouraging education even plausible in our postmodern context? Can such a spiritual foundation for an educational system be effective and persuasive in our time and place? We must be realistic about this challenge and yet keep hope alive for faith, and faith alive for hope.

To appreciate the challenge and opportunity of faith-based education for hope, it will help to situate this in our historical context. The dominant assumption now is that we live in a secular age—largely absent of faith or religious influence, especially in the public realm. Many contemporary people embrace "an exclusive humanism" by which they function as "buffered selves," closed off from the Transcendent and, indeed, from the neighbor, providing by and for the "self" alone (Canadian philosopher Charles Taylor). They presume that faith is passé, soon to pass away entirely. So, why encourage a faith-based educational system that seems so outdated to the sociocultural reality of a secular world? Might proposing such faith as a source of hope be at best deluded and at worst dangerous in that it might diminish our human responsibility, relying upon God to solve our problems for us rather than facing them ourselves—alone?

While secularization can be understood in varied ways (fall off of religious practice, demise of religious influence in the public square), Taylor argues that the most threatening aspect of secularity in our era is that social conditions have changed to now be adverse to faith. There was a time—not so long ago—when Western culture encouraged faith, mostly through enculturation, whereas now the sociocultural conditions work against it. This secularity is the legacy of *modernity*—the emergence of what we might call the modern world with its emphasis on critical and technical rationality that saw faith as simply wishful thinking. Can Catholic education swim against such a powerful tide?

The typical attitude of modernity and its major thought leaders (Feuerbach, Nietzsche, Marx, Freud—all atheists) was that "enlightenment" would *subtract* religious faith out of society, that educated people would simply recognize it as the superstition of their grandparents.

But this has not transpired; some 85 percent of people in the world today continue to claim a faith stance. When one wonders why faith endures, the Christian and Jewish response, of course, is that all people are made in the image and likeness of God (see Gen 1:27), and are alive by the very life-breath of God (see Gen 2:7). In other words, we are innately spiritual beings, created to live with faith. As the French mathematician Blaise Pascal (1623–62) summarized this biblical truth, "There is a God-shaped hollow in the human heart that nothing else can fill" (see Pascal, *Pensées*).

Modernity dismissed such faith sentiments as simply uninformed, even irrational. By contrast, there are significant signs now that Western consciousness is shifting away from a modern into a *postmodern* age that rejects the rational elitism and presumed atheism of modernity and is more open to a faith perspective on life. In contrast to modernity's claim that faith is irrational, many postmodern thought leaders, often believers themselves (for example, Ricoeur, Gadamer, Levinas, Kristeva, Taylor, Keller), see belief as just as reasonable as unbelief, placing theism and atheism on level ground—at least by way of reason. This newly emerging sentiment has echoed through the Catholic intellectual tradition for nigh two thousand years—a tradition that has championed the partnership of faith and reason, claiming that each is needed to enhance the other.

There is also an irony here: a faith perspective may actually be *more* reasonable than an atheistic one that claims to be purely "scientific." The latter, as a strictly rationalist/empirical approach, can be effective in addressing the *what* and *how* questions regarding life in the world but assiduously avoids the *why* questions. The ultimate *why* question, of course, is why there is anything rather than nothing. And then we can wonder about the intelligent design and order of creation, and why there is beauty that we can experience, and why people have an innate sense of ethic, and why we can think and then think about our thinking, and the list of *why* questions goes on. Facing them openly can make a faith stance seem more reasonable than a purely rational explanation—there is none!

Taylor and other social commentators now argue that our postmodern age shows significant signs of a new openness toward faith compared to the antagonistic attitude of modernity. They propose that faith by conviction—what some authors are calling a *well-reasoned* faith (beyond inherited)—is urgently needed in the public realm if our societies are to have the spiritual grounding to function for the common good of all. Likewise, such authors contend, and there is empirical data to support their claim, people seem to live more humanly with a convicted faith and spiritual grounding in comparison to living with a totally immanent frame of life.

Perhaps significant is that it is common for young people now to claim to be "spiritual," albeit often adding, "but not religious." At least they are recognizing and embracing their souls' and their need for a spirituality. Likewise, of those who declare their religion as "none," some 90 percent claim to believe in God (somehow) and 75 percent admit to praying regularly. As sociologist Grace Davie argues, there may well be as many believers as ever, though often without belonging to a specific faith community. Surely this emerging era, more friendly and open to the spiritual, can be well served by educating boldly *from* and *for* faith that lends hope to the human condition. It would seem so!

Let us focus specifically now on the mandate of Catholic education to educate *from* faith. As noted at the outset, this signals an education that is more grounded in a spirituality than a philosophy. Its spiritual foundations should reflect all the central convictions and values of Christian faith, putting them to work throughout its curriculum. The defining core, of course, is Jesus's vision of the reign of God, now lent hope by God's abundant grace through the Risen Christ.

Furthermore, Catholic education *from* faith should draw upon and reflect the two-thousand-year-old Catholic intellectual tradition and its various partnerships of faith and reason, revelation and science, knowledge and formation, and so on, as relevant to education. Likewise, educating *from* faith should reflect a contemporary Catholic theology around issues that are foundational for education; this would include its understanding of the person and of community (Chapter 7), its perspective on the meaning of life and favor for formative ways of knowing (Chapter 8), and its embrace of a public faith that encourages compassion and justice for all (Chapter 9).

In educating *for* faith, I reiterate that a Catholic school, while favoring a Catholic faith stance toward life, must totally respect the particular spiritual identity of its students, whether firmly in place or just emerging. It must never proselytize its non-Catholic students, respecting their own faith traditions and discernment. On the other hand, a Catholic school must not offer a faithless education; that would violate its covenant with its students and parents—and with God. At a minimum, the whole curriculum of a Catholic school, with all its administrators and teachers collaborating, is to educate students in a faith foundation for life. And here we now add that such educating be done with confidence in God's grace that lends hope and empowers students' own agency. The Transcendent Horizon that a Catholic school proposes to its students should not be the impersonal and indifferent god of deism or the energy of the universe, or, more colloquially, "the Force." Instead, it must propose a personal God of loving kindness as Jesus imaged, whose effective love is ever at work in their lives, empowering their lived response of faith, hope, and love.

Being explicit about educating *from* and *for* faith seems to be a particular challenge for Catholic institutions of higher education, at least in the United States. One "straw in the mind" is that when one reads the vision statement of our Catholic universities and colleges, they rarely mention God explicitly and Jesus even more rarely. Oh, they find humanistic language to reflect the school's values—spiritual development, finding purpose and meaning, commitment to compassion and justice, and so on—but most often without naming the faith foundation and Ultimate Horizon of their educating, namely God as revealed in Jesus Christ. They are possibly apprehensive that any explicit mention of God or Jesus will be a "turn off" to potential students—and faculty. Catholic colleges and universities need to move beyond such *✝* biases and concerns of modernity and explicitly embrace their faith in God as revealed in Jesus Christ as the cornerstone of their educating.

The possibilities and responsibilities of Christian faith for hope. Note that these are two sides of the same coin and that we have already intimated much about them. Education that has confidence in God's grace must surely pose extraordinary possibilities to its students, and then, that same grace brings great responsibilities as well. For clarity, let us set them out separately here. First, the *possibilities*.

Saint Irenaeus, a great scholar of the early church (writing in the second century) proposed a visionary description of God's desire for us and our human potential. A contemporary translation runs, "The glory of God is the human person fully alive." In other words, God's intent is that all people blossom into fullness of life, and the more we do so, the more God is glorified. Rather than limiting us, faith and hope in God enhance our human potential.

Catholic education, grounded in the vision of God's reign and the assurance of God's grace, must be a catalyst of such hope for all students. We must enable them to develop all of their gifts and talents, regardless of how they are differently abled, convinced that the more they do so, the more God is praised and glorified. In the Catholic intellectual tradition Saint Ignatius of Loyola champions this sentiment, some fifteen hundred years after Irenaeus, with his notion of the *magis*; this means that Catholic education must enable everyone to excel according to their own gifts and potential.

✱ Xtian educ. better be good!

Then, regarding our *responsibilities* as people of faith for hope, note again that even our English word *grace*—from the Latin *gratia* meaning "for free"—reminds us that God's effective love in our lives is gratuitous, unearned by us, and mediated as gift through God's work of liberating salvation in Jesus. This being said, and in the immortal words of the great Lutheran theologian Dietrich Bonhoeffer (1906–45; executed by the Nazis), "There is no cheap grace." Or as the letter of James summarizes, "Just as the body without the spirit is dead, so faith without works is also dead" (Jas 2:26).

So, God's grace empowers our own agency and deepens our responsibility. One can hear Christian preachers (especially on Sunday morning TV), making it sound as if faith means simply to trust in God to do good things for us, even make us rich—without any responsibility on our part other than blind faith. In Catholic theology, however, this is only half the story; as stated already, all of God's grace comes to us as a responsibility—an ability to respond. God's grace and human agency are to function in partnership, even as grace prompts and sustains our side of the covenant.

Reflecting again on the symbiosis of the three great virtues, to put faith to work with love is the source of our hope. Unless rising up from *living* faith, hope is only wishful thinking, a false rather than a well-grounded optimism. By grace, we are to work for our hopes, and by *living* faith with love we can be confident in our hoping. This spiritual foundation encourages Catholic educators to nurture their students in such hope for themselves and for others, and to embrace their responsibilities, by God's grace, to work toward their hopes with love by *living* faith.

RENEWING YOUR VOCATION AS CATHOLIC EDUCATOR

God's raising up of Jesus from the dead is a powerful symbol of hope for all people and for human history. Though central to Christian faith, there has been little written on its import for Catholic education—what does resurrection hope and its abundant grace mean for what teachers do every day. Surely our educating is to be a work of faith for hope with love—all sustained by God's grace.

For the educator's soul. With confidence in God's grace, Catholic educators have an amazing opportunity to lend hope to their students, preparing them also to be agents of hope for others. For hope, then, educators are to be instruments of God's grace in the lives of students.

However, it can be a challenge at times—for both teacher and students—to keep on hoping.

- To be an instrument of God's grace for hope you need to have hope yourself. This requires some spiritual practices that sustain your own hope, ever asking God's help, especially in challenging situations. What are some present practices that help to sustain your hope? How might you deepen them?

- Referring to sowing the seeds of God's word, Saint Paul used the analogy that while some plant, and others water, "only God gives the growth" (1 Cor 3:7). In other words, as teachers we must do our best by our students and then leave the rest to God. How might you embrace this wise spiritual practice? (Hint: God's grace assures that everything does not depend solely on *us*!)

For the teaching style. Most likely, we have all experienced teaching styles that were encouraging and likewise ones that were dispiriting. The pedagogy of Catholic educators, confident in God's grace, should be most encouraging of all students, lending hope across the spectrum of student gifts.

- Review your own teaching style by how it *encourages* students; on a scale of 1 to 10 (very encouraging), how do you score yourself?

- How might you adjust or renew your teaching style to foster hope in your students, and to make them agents of hope to others?

For the educational space. We noted that many Catholic universities in the United States seem reluctant to use "God language" in their mission statement. Surely all Catholic schools should have a clear, explicit, and persuasive articulation of the school's Catholic identity and its commitment to educate *from* and *for* faith.

- Does your school have a clear mission statement that reflects its Christian faith-for-hope foundations? Has it been reviewed recently?

- If the mission statement needs revision, how might this be engaged? What might be one great suggestion *you* would make?

Part II

FROM THE DEPTHS
OF TRADITION

3

The *Didache*, Augustine, and Benedict

A PASSION FOR EDUCATION

There are deep faith-based reasons why the early Christian church cane to embrace education as one of its central ministries, and not just to teach what Jesus taught but offering general education as well—what we might call the four Rs of reading, 'riting, 'rithmetic, and rhetoric.

From the beginning the mandate to live for the reign of God as Jesus taught gave disciples a sense of responsibility for the common good of all—and not just of fellow Christians. They sensed that the liberating salvation that God effected in Jesus, and which continues now by the power of the Holy Spirit, is not simply for the personal benefit of individual disciples. They were clear that Christians are to "work out their salvation" (Phil 2:12) by contributing to the well-being of others and the common good of all—Christians and non-Christians alike. Indeed, they could not have been disciples of Jesus and thought otherwise.

Living Christian faith for the reign of God has always demanded that disciples and the Christian community do good works in the world. As the church became established, it began to recognize that a much-needed way of contributing to the common good was to offer people an education. However, this aspiration did not enjoy immediate consensus. Some were hesitant about getting the church involved in general education and the exposure to secular learning that this would require, the latter often seen as a danger to Christian faith. That it was to teach the gospel of Jesus was certainly agreed as integral to its mission in the world. But one can reasonably understand why some church leaders and theologians questioned engaging in general education—the four Rs. Didn't the church have enough work in evangelizing for Christian faith?

The apprehension that the Greco-Roman intellectual life of the surrounding culture could be a threat to the high moral standards of the gospel was well founded. The Greek approach to education, known as *paideia*, and the Roman *humanitas*, while holistic were also aristocratic, intended for a small minority of "full citizens"—10 percent of the population, at most. This was contrary to the egalitarian spirit of the Christian faith, where there was to be "no longer Jew or Greek . . . slave or free . . . male or female" but "all to be one in Christ Jesus" (Gal 3:28).

Greco-Roman education included what we now call the liberal arts (philosophy, history, languages), and the sciences (physics, biology, astronomy), all accompanied by in-depth formation in civic virtues through poetry, music, and reading good (pagan) literature. However, its moral code fell short of what Christians perceived as demanded by the gospel.

The civil *paideia* demanded worship of the gods as essential to being a loyal citizen and for moral formation. Christians, like their Jewish neighbors, rejected all forms of idolatry and committed to worshiping "the only true God" whom they had come to "know" especially through Jesus Christ (see John 17:3). The ways of knowing for secular learning were by human reason alone, to embrace the right ideas (Plato), and to practice the right virtues (Aristotle) by rational discernment and reasoned persuasion. Christians, however, took their primary truth and moral imperatives from the divine revelation reflected in Jesus and their scriptures. In many ways the make-or-break issue came down to whether faith and reason could be reconciled and work as partners in Christian faith-based education.

Might we find a hint of favor for such a dual emphasis within the Great Commission that Christians believed they had received from the Risen Christ? Mark's Gospel has Jesus say simply, "Go into all the world and proclaim the good news" (16:15), a commission to evangelize (make disciples) and share the gospel of Jesus. Matthew, however, broadens beyond evangelizing specifically to include teaching as well, and as Jesus had taught. So the Risen Christ directed them to "go make disciples," and also "to teach them to obey everything that I have commanded you." The Greek verb used is *didaskontes*, as for regular teaching. Was that a hint that forming disciples—evangelization—might also work hand in hand with education?

For the first few centuries Christians continued to be wary of engaging in general education, keeping their focus on proclaiming the good news and forming disciples. Gradually, however, some Christian scholars began to propose that access to secular learning might actually enhance peoples' understanding and living of the gospel. At first this proposal met with some deep skepticism.

For example, a great Christian theologian named Tertullian (160–240) argued that "Jerusalem" (that is, the gospel) should have nothing to do with "Athens" (that is, secular learning), nor "the church with the academy." What more could people need after the fullness of divine revelation in Jesus, he wondered: "After Jesus we have no need of speculation, after the gospel no need of research." He even likened "a concord between the academy and the church" as a dangerous bonding between "heretics and Christians" (Tertullian, *Prescription against Heretics*, VII).

Wiser voices prevailed, however, recognizing the need to forge a *Christian paideia*; this meant integrating the best of secular scholarship and the gifts of the culture with the wisdom of the gospel, all to encourage *living* faith and the flourishing of the human person. A significant voice for such partnership was Clement of Alexandria (150–215), a leading Christian theologian who was well educated in classical Greek learning before his conversion. Clement readily recognized that his academic scholarship and critical reasoning background were assets to his Christian faith; in fact, he claimed, his background had prepared him to recognize the truth of the gospel. For this reason Clement was convinced that Greek philosophy was a gift from God's providence as a preparation for Christ; it "exercises the mind, rouses the intelligence" so that when people encounter "Truth itself" in Christ Jesus, they can more readily recognize it.

Clement went on to argue that education is, in fact, a *work of salvation* that begins with "the desire for eternal life aroused by an intelligent response to it laid in the ground of our minds." Note the partnership of desire and reason that prompts people in the quest for eternal life—through education. He then proposed that "the Teacher" par excellence, who combines desire and learning, faith and reason, and prompts us toward eternal life "is called Jesus . . . the good shepherd."

For Clement, Jesus's pedagogy began with *persuasion*, by engaging people's felt desires with the intent "to guide to a life of virtue, not merely to one of knowledge." And yet, insisted Clement, Christ the teacher teaches "to guide and develop (the soul's) capacity for knowledge." For Clement, then, good education is an asset for persuasion and formation in Christian faith. Echoing John 8:32, he summarized, "Knowledge is light . . . and sets free" (*Christ the Educator*).

Clement became a leading teacher and eventually head of a great Christian center of learning at Alexandria—perhaps the first formal Catholic school. He was succeeded by Origen (182–254 CE), another Christian scholar who looked upon secular forms of study as "stirrups to reach the sky" of biblical wisdom. Soon other Christian schools emerged at Ephesus, Rome, Jerusalem, Antioch, Edessa, and elsewhere, all intent to combine the best of secular scholarship and its reasoning with the teachings and practices of Christian faith—that is, to forge a *Christian paideia*. This marked the beginning of formal Catholic education and likewise its bedrock over ensuing centuries—the Catholic intellectual tradition. ✳

So the Catholic intellectual tradition might be said to have begun with that both/and commission from the Risen Christ on a hillside in Galilee—to evangelize *and* teach. From the debates that ensued, Christian educators gradually appreciated the needed partnership of divine revelation with secular learning, or, shall we say, of faith and reason. This conviction became well established across the centuries: faith needs reason to ground, monitor, develop, and persuade thereto; reason can be enlightened and guided by faith toward ultimate truths and great moral values. As subsequent centuries attest, faith without the censor of critical reason can be dangerous (approving and practicing slavery, the Crusades, witch trials, and so on), whereas reason without the Transcendent Horizon of faith—God—can persuade to deadly ideologies and falsehoods (for example, Nazism).

Having early forged this foundational bond between faith and reason, the Catholic intellectual tradition and the education it encouraged gradually embraced all kinds of related or echoing partnerships to distinguish Catholic education across the centuries. Though never achieved perfectly, often poorly, and sometimes more sinned against than honored (for example, the condemnation of Galileo), yet in its better realization the Catholic intellectual tradition suggested a thread of partnerships that endure to this day: between faith and reason; revelation and science; the spiritual and academic; wisdom and knowledge; formation in virtue and education in ideas; personal development and academic excellence; tradition and new horizons, the immanent and the Transcendent, the horizontal and vertical, nature and grace—ultimately reflecting the covenant partnership between God and humankind.

So, though sometimes more honored in the breach than in observance, the partnership of faith and reason suggests many other such partnerships. When woven into Catholic education, these partnerships offer a rich possibility for a holistic and humanizing curriculum, one with deep potential to serve the well-being of students and the common good of society. Instead of limiting the horizon of education, as often claimed, a faith and reason partnership—and its echoing instances as listed above—can greatly enrich its potential to educate people to live well and wisely. An instance from the partnership of revelation and science may exemplify this point.

✳ CIT only as good as its representatives/ practitioners

In its religion curriculum a Catholic school can well teach the story of creation as recounted in Genesis 1, reflecting the myth (i.e., of *truth*, though not to be taken literally) that God created everything in six days and on the seventh day God rested. Likewise, in its science curriculum, it can teach cosmogenesis as a Big Bang" of energy some fourteen billion years ago that gave rise to the universe. And there is no contradiction between the two accounts; they are simply two different ways of knowing great truths—mythical and scientific—and of engaging the mystery of creation that ever remains. Indeed, the faith story enriches the scientific one with spiritual wisdom; it proposes that all people are made in the divine image—and emphasizes male and female (Gen 1:26–27), that humans are to be responsible stewards of the earth (Gen 1:28), and that all of creation, including ourselves, is "very good" (Gen 1:31). Science alone could never know or teach such wisdom!

Reflecting the Catholic intellectual tradition with varying success, those early schools led on to the Celtic and Benedictine monastic schools that began to flourish in the sixth century, to the Carolingian schools of the ninth century, to the cathedral schools of the twelfth century. Many of the cathedral schools developed into the first great universities, such as Bologna (1088), Paris (1150), Oxford (1167), Cambridge (1209), Lisbon (1213), Salamanca (1218), and so on. The universities writ large the partnership between faith and reason, with theology enthroned as *queen of the sciences*. It is worth noting that those first great universities were founded by papal charter—that is, commissioned by the church—reflecting that even the most academic education and scholarly research are integral to the church's mission to the world. And those early universities were staffed by the emerging religious orders, especially the Augustinians and Dominicans.

As worldwide evangelization emerged and the Christian faith became a universal presence, so too did Catholic schools—now spread throughout the world. The network of Catholic schools differs greatly from one sociocultural context to another. Some are funded exclusively by the church, others by student tuition; some have government sponsorship and church cum elected school-board management. Indeed, all the Catholic schools throughout some two hundred countries probably amount to the largest single system of education in the world. As noted already, they increasingly serve a large non-Catholic student population and have an often growing percentage of non-Catholic teachers. But as noted in the Preface, Pope Francis encourages rather than laments such situations; he does not see open enrollment as a threat to the Catholic identity of the schools. Instead, this is an opportune moment to renew

Reveals confidence, not fear

commitment that all Catholic schools render what they promise—a truly *Catholic* education.

One rich resource to help maintain the integrity of Catholic schools—that they provide what they propose—is the rich two-thousand-year-old tradition of the Catholic intellectual tradition. Being highly selective here, we can raise up in this Part II some tidbits of historical wisdom that seem particularly germane to the challenges of our time and that can nurture the vision of Catholic education today. We begin, in this chapter, by reclaiming some old-but-wise memories, highlighting the *Didache*, Augustine of Hippo, and Benedict of Nursia.

The next chapter gleans wisdom for Catholic education today from Thomas Aquinas and Julian of Norwich. Chapter 5 reflects on the Reformation era and its aftermath, with Ignatius of Loyola. Chapter 6 highlights two of the greatest women pioneers in the history of Catholic education, Angela Merici and Mary Ward. Though only a select few of primary proponents of Catholic education across the centuries, and all well predating our own time, these great forebears represent a "cloud of witnesses" (Heb 12:1); they offer rich and life-giving memories for the present and future of Catholic education.

For Reflection and Conversation

- From your own experience, what do you recognize as the potential of Catholic education to contribute to the lives of students today and to the common good of society?
- What do you perceive as the assets of the Catholic intellectual tradition partnership between faith and reason, revelation and science, and so forth? Might there be limitations?

THE *DIDACHE*

We begin with a brief but foundational reflection on this fascinating teaching document from the very early church; its wisdom needs to be embraced by Catholic educators in every age.

Outside the canon of the New Testament, the *Didache* is likely the earliest statement of what and how Christians were to teach as their faith. Scholars disagree on its date of origin, but some place it from the end of the first century, and it would appear that at least some of its pericopes are that early. Its opening line identifies it as "the Lord's teaching to the nations by the twelve apostles"—thus claiming apostolic status.

Most often referred to as "The Teaching" (literally, *didache*), for a long time there was no known version of its text. Many early Christian authors appeared to quote or refer to it, but without an actual text some scholars presumed that it simply referred generically to the corpus of Christian teachings. There was great excitement, then, when a Greek copy was discovered in 1873 at Constantinople by a bishop named Philotheos Bryennios. Thereafter, other copies and fragments were discovered—in Latin, Coptic, Syriac, and Arabic—signaling its widespread use and status in the early centuries of the church.

We might summarize the *Didache* as having three parts: an inspiring summary of the demands of Christian discipleship (Part 1); locating Christian discipleship within a community of disciples that is sustained by prayer and worship—it has a full version of the Lord's Prayer and two early fragments of eucharistic prayers (Part 2); and describing the Christian community as led by apostles, teachers, bishops and deacons, all of whom, it would appear, both teach and can preside at Eucharist, and whose authenticity was to be ever evaluated by their faithfulness to "the way" of Jesus (Part 3). The life-giving memory I highlight here is from the *Didache*'s description of *living* Christian faith that is focused in its first part and reflected throughout.

The first verse begins with a bold summary statement of the whole document: "There are two ways, one of life and one of death; and between the two ways there is a great difference" (1:1). It then proceeds to summarize these two ways, beginning with, "Now this is the way of life: First you must love God who made you, and second, your neighbor as yourself" (1:2).

It then proceeds to outline the most life-giving way for Christians to live, beginning with a gloss on the greatest commandment and emphasizing love even of enemies, "for what credit is it to you if you love those who love you?" (1:3). As might be expected, it goes on to list familiar sins to avoid in every age (murder, adultery, fornication, theft, and so on) and some more contextual to its time (sorcery, magic, astrology). The clear proposal is that this *way of life* is not only demanded by Christian faith but is also its gift, portraying the best possible way to live our lives for our own good and equally for the good of others.

It then describes the *way of death*, repeating much of what the *way of life* is to avoid and adding specifically social sins. So, people who embrace the way of death have "no pity for the poor, do not exert themselves for the oppressed . . . turn their backs on the needy, oppress the afflicted, defend the rich, unjustly condemn the poor, are thoroughly wicked" (5:2). With a general exhortation to all, it urges: "See that no one leads you astray from the way of *the teaching*" (6:1). Part I ends with an endearing note of compassion—"If you can bear the Lord's full yoke, you will be perfect. But if you cannot, then do what you can" (6:2)—heartening for us all.

The Didache *for Catholic education.* The key wisdom from the *Didache* for Catholic education across the ages is that we are to educate people to live for what brings *life* for ourselves and others, and to avoid what is "deadly" for any or all. The entire curriculum of a Catholic school is to be crafted to inform, form, and transform people into a *way* that is life-giving for themselves and, as for Jesus's aspiration, "for the life of the world" (John 6:51). Catholic education should educate from and for a spiritual foundation that encourages all its participants with a very positive outlook on life and their responsible participation in the world—regardless of their particular identity in faith.

Some scholars commenting on the *Didache* opine that even presenting a *choice* to people—posing every person as capable of choosing between a way of life and a way of death—was countercultural for its time. In that era and context people generally presumed that their lives were determined by the gods, or by the movements of the stars, or by their social circumstances—that they had little choice in shaping their own destiny. But Christian faith attests that by God's grace, which is available to all, every person can avoid the way of death and embrace instead the way that enhances our own life and that of others. That we partner with God in such agency is a most life-giving spiritual foundation for us to put to work in our lives.

The *Didache* witnesses that we have such agency, over against the fatalism of its time—and perhaps ours. As a memory from the earliest centuries, then, the *Didache* invites Catholic educators to teach all students in a way that is *life-enhancing* for themselves and for others, with the gentling note that while never perfect, we are ever invited "to do what we can."

AUGUSTINE OF HIPPO (354–430)

After Saint Paul, no one has been more influential in shaping the understanding of Christian faith than Saint Augustine. Likewise, there has been no more significant architect in crafting the "both/and" of the Catholic intellectual tradition. Augustine's summary way of knowing for educators is that all knowledge originates from the human desire for truth (from the heart), placing its primary source within the affections of the knower. And yet, for reliable knowledge, the heart must engage the faculties of the mind as well.

As Augustine recounted in his *Confessions*, around the age of eighteen he read a text by the Roman philosopher Cicero and was "aroused to pursue wisdom." This became a central philosophical passion of his life, leading him eventually to embrace Christian faith to satisfy his "restless heart." That encounter with the thought of Cicero also encouraged Augustine to use his critical thinking in his own agency for knowing, drawing particularly upon the philosophy of Plato.

Significantly and contrary to the later Enlightenment, which treated the mind as if limited to reason, Augustine emphasized the functions of memory and imagination as well, with the three capacities of mind working much like the one and Triune God—his analogy. From his intellectual conversion upon reading Cicero, pursuing the truth became Augustine's driving passion; he was convinced that only thus can we live well and wisely. Eventually, he came to realize and embrace that the most ultimate and defining truth to be known is that God loves us.

At age thirty-three, after a wayward youth, Augustine embraced the Christian faith. Now he became fully convinced that reason—ever coupled with memory and imagination—could be enriched by faith in their common quest for truth, and conversely, that faith could deepen and develop from the monitor and persuasion of reason. Indeed, he sometimes used the adjective *catholic* to signal being open to the truth wherever it can be found, convinced that all truth is ultimately of God.

For Augustine, the human desire and longing for truth reflects our hunger for God. As he summarized on the first page of his *Confessions*, "You have made us for yourself alone, O Lord, and our hearts are restless until they rest in you." Theologically, then, our hunger for knowledge can be explicitly named as hungering for God. And, for Augustine, coming to "know" God is to grow evermore into experiencing God's love. Within that Transcendent Horizon, all the disciplines of learning and ways of knowing are fueled by the heart's desire for such ultimate truth, guided by the whole mind. For Augustine, then, all of our quests for knowledge—in all of the disciplines of learning—can lead us to "know" God and God's unconditional love for us.

Augustine was born in Tagaste, North Africa (present day Algeria), to a pagan father, Patricius, and a devout Christian mother, Monica (later sainted). He had the typical education in Greco-Roman *paideia* of the day and became a teacher himself of grammar and rhetoric. After his conversion to the Christian faith he became a priest and was elected by the people of Hippo (people had such a voice in those days!) to be their bishop (396 CE). He founded a monastic community there and lived out his life in Hippo as scholar and bishop, teaching, preaching, and writing—voluminously. His greatest classic, *The City of God*, was written over fifteen years and completed shortly before he died. He never forgot the waywardness of his youth, ever insisting that the church must welcome both saints and sinners alike.

While Augustine is most renowned for his contribution to Christian theology, his writings on education, all reflecting the Catholic intellectual tradition, are also a rich resource. Here, we must be selective and will treat only two of his most insightful educational works, namely, *The First Catechetical Instruction* (its Latin title, *De Catechizandis Rudibus*, literally means "the catechizing of country folk"), and his text, *The Teacher* (most often called by its Latin title, *De Magistro*). The first, as the title suggests, is focused on catechesis—education in Christian faith; the second is on general education. Both works reflect Augustine's core emphasis on the defining human desire for truth and ultimately for God that prompts all of our hungers for knowledge.

Augustine the educator. From an overall reading of his *First Catechetical Instruction*, Augustine proposes a rather amazing and progressive pedagogy—even by today's standards. Great contemporary educators like John Dewey, Maria Montessori, Nel Noddings, and Paulo Freire echo many of Augustine's sentiments.

Augustine counsels teachers to gain the confidence and trust of their students, always showing loving care for their well-being; to begin teaching by first arousing the students' interests in what is to be taught (a big emphasis in Dewey); to employ various teaching methods to maintain student engagement; to pitch the academic level to the learning capacities of the participants; to explain a little at a time, and clearly; to offer engaging presentations, often pausing to summarize; to create a pleasant learning environment and show care for students' bodily comfort; and to create a welcoming space that invites the contributions of all. He points out that teachers must maintain their own enthusiasm (*hilaritas*) for what they are teaching, and that they should never resort to corporal punishment—a revolutionary idea in schools of his time, and indeed, until comparatively recently.

In *The First Catechetical Instruction* Augustine proposed the core conviction that "the chief reason for Christ's coming was to manifest and to teach God's love for us." Indeed, the catechist is to access all the content of Christian faith by crafting it as "a narration of God's dealings with man from the creation of the world down to the present period of church history; they should all be referred to love as their final cause." Then, by way of learning outcome, Augustine advises the catechist: "With this [God's] love set before you as an end to which you may refer all that you say, so give all your instructions that (they) to whom you speak by hearing may believe, and by believing may hope, and by hoping may love." For Augustine, our human vocation is to live a loving life in response to God's love for us; this is the ultimate wisdom to be taught and learned within Christian religious education (13–27).

In the latter part of *The City of God*, written some twenty-five years after *The First Catechetical Instruction* and further developing the original idea found in the latter, Augustine crafted the whole story of humankind in a narrative framework, posing the history of the world as the history of God's saving love at work within it. Despite human suffering and sinfulness, Augustine was convinced that God is at work within human history and for our salvation; this earthly city is to merge into our eternal home. Such is the ultimate Truth, and all education, in whatever discipline of learning, can be crafted to enable people to live into such a horizon of meaning and purpose, enlightening their minds and satisfying the hungers of their hearts.

Turning to Augustine's general education text, *The Teacher*, note, ironically, that it is a relentless exercise in downplaying the teacher's role and establishing the student as the primary agent in the teaching/learning process. Indeed, some of Augustine's critics—for example, Aquinas in a similar treatise on the teacher some eight hundred years later (reviewed in the next chapter)—would say that he exaggerated the student's role as if the teacher is unnecessary. Yet Augustine's proposal will forever challenge Catholic educators to actively engage students as the primary agents of their own learning, encouraging them to think for themselves, to see for themselves, rather than telling them what to think and what to see.

The first ten chapters of *The Teacher* are an analysis of language, anticipating some of the focus on linguistic philosophy and semiotics in our contemporary era. Then, drawing upon that foundation, Augustine insists that the primary purpose of words in teaching is to draw out "the truth that presides already within" students themselves. Echoing a theme noted above, the truth within each person is a sharing in "God's everlasting wisdom" (177). Augustine explains that this "*wisdom of God*, which every rational soul does consult" is accessed through their own "interior light of truth" (179). For this reason, and as if speaking directly to a student, Augustine reasons, "I should question you in a way adapted to your capacity for hearing that Teacher *within* you" (180, emphasis added).

So, the teacher's essential role for Augustine is to engage the agency of the students in the teaching/learning dynamic; note in particular the crucial role of questioning (a Socratic echo). As a punchline of his central proposal, Augustine asks rhetorically, "For who would be so absurdly curious as to send his child to school to learn what the teacher thinks" (185). In other words, don't send young people to school to learn what the teachers think but to learn to think for themselves (175–186).

Augustine for Catholic education. I can think of three valuable assets from Augustine for Catholic education today; they will echo in subsequent authors, but let us credit them here from Augustine. The first is his proposal that *the whole curriculum is to have a unifying core*, with all the disciplines of learning working together within and toward a horizon of ultimate truth. The later Enlightenment period will deliberately sever the disciplines of learning from a grounding in faith, as if the latter would compromise their academic freedom and rigor, but robbing them of a unifying horizon. Augustine reflects the conviction that faith and reason can be mutually enriching in a unified curriculum, bonded by the common quest of people's hearts and minds to know and live the truth and this into an ultimate Horizon—of God's love for us and the hope it lends.

A second legacy of Augustine for Catholic education is his emphasis on the *agency of the knower*. Though possibly overstated, let there be no doubt that good education fully engages students as active participants in the teaching/learning process. Instead of being passive recipients who simply feed back to teachers what has been fed to them, students must be actively involved in accessing whatever discipline of learning is being taught, invited to think for themselves about it, and encouraged to come to their own understanding, judgments, and decisions. Augustine would insist that Catholic education should be the antithesis of what Paulo Freire called "banking education," as if teachers are simply to "deposit" information in passive receptacles, expecting them to recall it for exams.

Third, we need to learn from the central pedagogy of each of Augustine's texts and to hold them in fruitful tension rather than collapsing in favor of either one. In *The Teacher*, Augustine emphasizes the absolute agency of the student in coming to knowledge. It appears as if all knowledge must come from within, with the teacher simply prompting and drawing it out with good questions. But this would appear to downplay the role of the teacher and of traditions of learning.

However, in *The First Catechetical Instruction,* expanded in his magnum opus, *The City of God*, Augustine nuances his emphasis on the knower, making clear that teachers ought to teach the great story of what God has done and is doing throughout human history. Placed together in a fruitful tension, the two texts reflect the need for a pedagogy that honors what comes both from within *and* from without.

In religious education this will mean honoring people's own stories and spiritual wisdom from life and yet also accessing for them the Christian Story—the overarching narrative of God's saving work within human history, as Augustine cast it—encouraging them to learn from and integrate the two sources. In general education it will mean actively engaging students as agents of their own knowing and from their own experience while also lending them ready access to what John Dewey called "the funded capital of civilization"—all the arts, sciences, and disciplines of learning that have emerged as our human legacy from across the ages. Embracing both convictions, knowing from within and from without—one from each of Augustine's texts on education—is important for all educators. Later authors will make both commitments more explicit, but we can note the seeds here in Augustine's paradoxical positions.

For Reflection and Conversation

- Reflecting the wisdom of the *Didache*, what would you list as *ways of life* in our time and context? The *ways of death*? How can your educating encourage students toward the first and discourage the second?
- What of Augustine's proposal that the deepest desire of humankind is to know the Truth, which, ultimately, is that God loves us? How would this spiritual foundation shape how you teach? How can *you* witness to God's love for your students?

SAINT BENEDICT (480–547) AND MONASTIC SCHOOLS

As Augustine lay dying (431), the barbarian tribes were at the gates of Hippo; they had already taken Rome (410). These were any peoples outside the control and culture of the Roman Empire—Huns, Franks, Vandals, Saxons, Goths, Celts, and so on. They seemed intent on the destruction of the empire and to avail themselves of its spoils. There followed an era throughout Europe, well named the Dark Ages, when much of Western culture and the Greco-Roman *paideia* of its schools, including the Christian ones, were wiped out. They would not revive again until those tribes were converted (somewhat) to the Christian faith and the founding of monastic schools, beginning in the sixth century.

Monasticism emerged in response to the loss of rigor among Christians in living their faith. In the early centuries of the church, and even up to Augustine's time in some cultures, there was a rigorous catechumenal process for admitting newcomers to the Christian faith. The process lasted for up to three years, with an emphasis on forming people in Christian discipleship—*living* Christian faith. However, as Christianity became the official religion of the Roman Empire—beginning with Constantine's Edict of Milan of 313—new converts poured in, but without formation or adequate catechesis in the Christian faith. For example, when the Emperor Constantine declared that only Christians could be officers in the Roman army, guess what many soldiers did! Eventually there were mass conversions of whole tribes to Christianity (whenever a ruler embraced it) without any real preparation or formation in gospel living.

Monasticism was an institutionalized expression of radical Christian living, bonding participants in community with an ordered rule of daily life, and embracing vows of poverty, chastity, and obedience. It emerged in response to the breakdown of Christian discipline, determined to return to the radical values of the gospel and to put these to work for the public welfare. The monks embraced Jesus's invitation to the rich young man to "go, sell what you have, and give to the poor and you will have treasure in heaven; then come, follow me" (Mark 10:21).

So, the vocation to the monastic life was not to be embraced simply to save one's own soul—"treasure in heaven"—but to live the gospel values of Jesus in order to be of service in the public realm and to advance the reign of God in the world, especially to "give to the poor." It was deeply convinced of the sociopolitical nature of Christian faith and its responsibility to work for the common good of all. The physical labors of the monks were sustained by their "work" of prayer.

One of the primary social services that the monasteries took on was to provide education. Likewise, they were committed to conserving learning by transcribing cultural manuscripts—especially the Bible—in danger of being destroyed by those barbarians. A most significant instance was the educational work and copying of the early Irish monasteries, beginning in the late fifth century. They provided a beacon of light in the Dark Ages, at first in Ireland and then throughout Europe. Here, however, we focus on the worthy instance of Benedictine monasticism and its contribution to the educational mission of the church through its monastic schools (a little more on Celtic monasticism in Chapter 4).

Benedict of Nursia was born into a noble family and was well educated, as was still the privilege of Roman nobility. At around twenty, having sowed some wild oats and fallen in love a few times, he determined to embrace the radical thrust of the gospel—loving enemies, giving all to help the poor, and so on. Benedict set off to become a hermit and after three years joined a monastery. Eventually he founded the monastic order that bears his name, with its headquarters at Monte Cassino (established in 529), about eighty miles southeast of Rome.

Benedictine monasticism invites its followers to a rich spirituality, enhancing and respecting the person within community, embracing manual labor (at that time considered the work of slaves), as well as a life of daily prayer in common and contemplative reflection on the scriptures. The monasteries had a huge social outreach in caring for the poor, the sick, and the needy; they helped to develop better farming practices and professional services, including in law and medicine.

Most significant for our interest here, however, Benedictine monasteries became primary agents of education in the Western world for the next three hundred years and continue to have a significant influence to this day. Along with instruction in Christian faith, their schools taught the seven liberal arts made up of the *trivium* of grammar, rhetoric, and logic (all to enable a person to speak well and persuasively) and the *quadrivium* of arithmetic, geometry, astronomy and music. This whole curriculum was a classic instance of the Catholic intellectual tradition, constantly engaging faith and reason, revelation and science, formation and information, and so on. The ultimate intended learning outcome of monastic education was not simply knowledge but spiritual wisdom for life.

Drawing upon previous resources and from his own experience of monastic life, Benedict wrote a *Rule* for his communities. He intended it "for beginners" who wished to live the radicalness of the gospel in a vowed and stable community, one that holds all goods in common. The Benedictine Rule is one of the great classic texts of Western civilization and education—for both how it educated its monks and then the education they brought to the general population.

There is a strong tradition that throughout his life Benedict was close to his sister Scholastica (480–547), who is said to have located near Monte Cassino; apparently, the siblings had regular visits and conversations. With his encouragement Scholastica founded a monastery close to Monte Cassino, modeled on her brother's *Rule,* originating Benedictine monasticism for women. They died just a few days apart and by Benedict's instruction were buried in the same grave at Monte

Cassino. In effect, they were cofounders of Benedictine monasticism—for men and women.

Benedict the educator. There are at least three aspects of the Benedictine charism that inspired its educational mission and offer great wisdom for Catholic education today: its commitment to *a public faith*—to be a resource for the betterment of society; its embrace of a *spiritual way of knowing,* as well as a more reasoned and discursive one; and its tradition of *welcome and inclusivity*. While these three overlap, let us briefly note each one. They suggest spiritual foundations that Catholic educators should put to work in our time.

Educating for a public faith. At first, the monastic life might look like a withdrawal from the world. As noted already, however, Christian monasticism, epitomized in the Benedictine charism, was an expression of deep care for the world. There are monastic traditions in other faiths that can seem like a form of escape, but in Christian monasticism one entered the monastery not to evade the world but precisely to embrace and serve it. Even the monastic life of regular prayer throughout the day had the primary intention of advancing God's reign.

Benedict's *Rule* called all of the monks to daily manual labor, placing it alongside of prayer as equally "the work of God." Only by their own labor could the monks have the resources needed, as Benedict insisted in the name of Jesus, to feed and protect the poor, to care for the sick, to console the bereaved, and to bury the dead (a favorite listing of his).

That the monasteries were to educate arose at first out of necessity; the monks needed to be able to read in order to participate in the Divine Office, praying the psalms together at regular intervals throughout the day. And likewise, they had to be literate for their copying of manuscripts. Soon, however, their schooling reached out to the children of the local villages as well, at least incipiently recognizing the need for universal education. Their educating, like their monastic life, was "to set aright the course of our lives in doing what is good" (*Rule* 1:5). Here, Benedict names, at the top of the list, the greatest commandment to love God and neighbor as oneself, and then the golden rule, which he states negatively as "do not inflict on someone else what you would resent if it were done to yourself" (*Rule* 3:1). Benedict promises that this is the way of life and of education that can "change us into the likeness of God" (*Rule* 1:3), convinced as he was of our *theosis*—divine potential. Note the very positive anthropology in Benedict's proposal.

A spiritual way of knowing. Though constantly combined with manual labor and shared prayer, the *Rule* of Benedict also invited monks into a contemplative life, to listen and respond to the spirit within them. The epitome of their contemplative practice was their *lectio divina*. Literally, "divine reading," this is a practice of reading a selection from scripture over and over, going ever deeper, listening to the spirit within as the text speaks to the heart and calls one to holiness of life.

The usual pattern begins with an introductory reading of a Bible text simply to notice its initial aspects and what immediately engages the reader. There follows a second reading that goes deeper and meditates upon the text (mediation as *talking* to God), followed by a third reading and pause to contemplate the text in-depth (contemplation as *listening* to God). *Lectio divina* concludes with the prayer that arises from the heart to move readers forward in Christian living.

This contemplative mode of prayer was to be interspersed throughout the daily work and rhythm of monastic life. The *Rule* advises that "all the community must be occupied at definite times in manual labor and at other times in *lectio divina*" (*Rule* 48:1), and the latter with heightened practice on Sundays (*Rule* 48:6). Not only was *lectio divina* to nurture the spiritual life of the monks, but when done in common and with conversation, it also became, in effect, the monastic way of "doing" theology. Its theologizing was grounded in deep thinking, and yet its distinguishing feature was to begin with the heart, listening to the wisdom emerging from the sacred texts through one's soul and the souls of other community members as they shared together.

Benedict cautions that in listening to the spirit within a person must be careful "to recognize the bitter spirit of wickedness which creates a barrier to God's grace and opens the way to evil." One must listen instead to "a good spirit which frees us from evil ways and brings us closer to God." It is the "good spirit" that all "should strive to cultivate" (*Rule* 72:1). We will encounter this discernment of spirits again with Ignatius of Loyola and examine what it might mean for Catholic education. Here, some thousand years prior to Ignatius, we find it central to the soul-engaging "ways of knowing" in the Benedictine monastery. *Lectio divina* and its contemplative mode of knowing became a distinctive aspect of Benedictine spirituality and of its educating.

Welcome and inclusivity. The Benedictine monastery was amazingly democratic—long before democracy was a common political practice. For example, the abbot (or abbess in Benedictine convents) was elected by popular vote. Furthermore, all the leaders, rather than lording it over others, "should follow the loving example of the Good Shepherd" with particular care for community members who stray (*Rule* 27:2). All important decisions were made by communal discernment. For this, the abbot "should call the whole community together and personally

[handwritten marginal note:] ✗ 'spirit w/in' some as truth inside ? students ?

explain to them the agenda that lies before them" (*Rule* 3:1); and then, amazingly, the youngest monk was to be the first to speak and be heard.

This inclusivity was reflected in that all aspirants of good intention were to be welcomed to join the community—regardless of their social status. Inclusivity was also reflected in the warm welcoming of guests, with hospitality for all a particular mark of the Benedictine charism. The *Rule* insisted that "any guest who happens to arrive at the monastery should be received just as we would receive Christ himself" (*Rule* 53:1). Indeed, "as soon as anyone knocks on the door or one of the poor calls out, the response, uttered at once with gentle piety and warm charity should be 'Thanks be to God' or 'Give me your blessing'" (*Rule* 66:1); guests were to be treated as "other Christs." In imitation of Jesus at the Last Supper as found in John's Gospel (John 13:1–15), the Abbot was to wash the feet of guests "with the whole community involved in the ceremony" (*Rule* 53:3).

Benedict for Catholic education. For Catholic schools and their accessing of this monastic aspect of the Catholic intellectual tradition, the Benedictine charism calls for education toward *a public faith,* to educate for a social ethic that reaches out into the world with compassion for those in need and justice for all. In our day, too, this requires encouraging in students the kind of critical social consciousness that uncovers the sources of injustice and works to change the public realm for the common good. Such sociopolitical formation should be integral to a Catholic education. We will develop further the notion of a public and political faith in Chapter 9, but let us recognize the seeds of it here in the Benedictine charism.

Likewise, and faithful to the Catholic intellectual tradition reflected in the Benedictine tradition, the epistemology encouraged in a Catholic school should include a contemplative and meditative way of knowing as well as a more discursive and reasoned one. This means encouraging and prompting students to listen to themselves and to their own hearts as well as to their heads. This spiritual mode, well discerned, can be a rich and empowering way of knowing. It has been lost, in large part, to all education, including Catholic, in favor of logical reasoning alone. It is past time for Catholic education to reclaim this rich tradition of soul-engaging spiritual reflection as a formative and humanizing way of knowing. Despite the rationalist bias against it, it may be far more reliable than the cognitive alone.

Furthermore, a Catholic school should be marked by welcome and unqualified inclusivity. We will return to this spiritual foundation again because even the very etymology of the word *catholic* (from the Greek

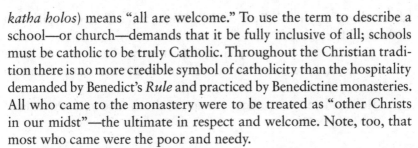

katha holos) means "all are welcome." To use the term to describe a
school—or church—demands that it be fully inclusive of all; schools
must be catholic to be truly Catholic. Throughout the Christian tradition there is no more credible symbol of catholicity than the hospitality
demanded by Benedict's *Rule* and practiced by Benedictine monasteries.
All who came to the monastery were to be treated as "other Christs
in our midst"—the ultimate in respect and welcome. Note, too, that
most who came were the poor and needy.

Finally, the Benedictine tradition of giving every monk a voice in
communal discernment, beginning with the youngest, was also an instance of its catholicity. It would surely suggest a courageous modus
operandi for the governance of a Catholic school today. Might we
solicit and welcome the opinions of students, as well as of faculty and
staff, taking seriously their concerns and giving them voice in caring
for the common good of the school community?

For Reflection and Conversation

- What do you find most inspiring about the Benedictine charism for your
  own journey in faith? For your vocation as an educator?
- Imagine how to incorporate a meditative/contemplative way of knowing into your pedagogy. How might you encourage students to listen
  to their souls?

RENEWING YOUR VOCATION AS CATHOLIC EDUCATOR

The *Didache*, Augustine, and Benedict have much wisdom for the *soul*,
style, and *space* of Catholic educators and for education in our time.
They represent some deep spiritual foundations, including a commitment to *living* faith for life, to engaging the agency of students in the
teaching/learning dynamic, and to welcoming all "to the table" with
hospitality.

For the educator's soul. Catholic education is surely to encourage
people to make good foundational choices in life, to develop a sound
conscience, to seek paths that are life-giving for self and others. The
Didache boiled this down to choosing between two ways—a way
of life and a way of death. This echoes the Book of Deuteronomy,
where Yahweh God speaks through Moses, "I have set before you
life and death, blessings and curses. Choose life so that you and your

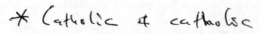
* Catholic & catholic

descendants may live" (Deut 30:19). Might this still be our stark and
either/or life choice.

- As you look at your own journey in faith, recognize some of the major
  turns you have made toward *life* at its best? How can you deepen
  those turns?
- How can you encourage, prompt, and convince your students to
  "choose life"?

For the teaching style. It is imperative that Catholic educators employ
a pedagogy that actively engages students in the teaching/learning
dynamic; besides Augustine, we will see this writ large in Aquinas and
Mary Ward. Yet, in the past at least, Catholic education was often ste-
reotyped as being didactic and authoritarian. This is clearly contrary
to the commitments of the Catholic intellectual tradition and truly
Catholic schools.

- Recognize the ways that you already engage students, as agents
  of their own knowing, to participate actively in the teaching/learning
  dynamic?
- How might you consistently invite students to think for themselves (so
  much depends on the questions we raise—the need to move beyond
  pure recall).

For the educational space. By its very definition, a Catholic school
should be a place of hospitality and welcome for all—faculty, staff,
and students—regardless of faith, background, race, economics, gender,
ethnicity, sexual orientation, ability, and so on.

- Looking at your school, note the ways that it says to the world that
  "all are welcome." How might it improve its hospitality and inclusivity?
- How might *you* contribute to the catholicity of your school?

4

Celtic Monasticism,
Thomas Aquinas,
and Julian of Norwich

CELTIC MONASTICISM

After the death of Benedict (547) the Benedictine monasteries and their schools mushroomed throughout Europe, playing a major part in evangelizing and educating the many barbarian tribes that had overrun the Roman Empire. They were well partnered in this good work by the major outreach across Europe of Celtic monks and monasteries. From the sixth century onward, the Irish church, itself based on a monastic structure and spirituality (with abbots leading rather than bishops), reached into Europe with multiple foundations. In addition to prayer and manual labor to support themselves, Celtic monasteries emphasized education and not simply of their own monks. They became a second major influence throughout Europe in turning the tide from the "Dark Ages" to a more enlightened time.

Likely the leading exponent and exporter of Irish monasticism was Saint Columba (521–97), also known as Colum Cille, who began as a monk at the monastery of Clonard in central Ireland. Columba is credited with founding ten monasteries, most notably the great monastic center on the Scottish island of Iona. From Iona, the major monastery of Lindisfarne was founded, and then great Celtic monasteries spread out across Europe—at Bobbio in Northern Italy, Saint Gall in Switzerland, and numerous other locations. For Catholic education and its spiritual foundations, Celtic monasticism offers three important memories.

First, it had a strong commitment to preserving the legacy and learning of the past. The invading tribes across Europe seemed to relish destroying ancient manuscripts, not only of the Bible but the writings of Greek and Roman scholars like Plato and Aristotle, Cicero and Philo. Because Ireland is an island, removed from the European mainland, the invading tribes did not often reach there, and the Irish monasteries preserved many valuable manuscripts. And they had a wise instinct to begin to make copies.

Typically, Irish monasteries had a scriptorium where the monks copied the ancient texts. Often they transcribed the scriptures with artistic illustrations and flourishes; one thinks of the *Book of Kells*, or the *Book of Durrow* or the *Lindisfarne Gospels,* all beautifully illuminated copies of the four Gospels. The manuscripts copied in Irish monasteries later became a major resource in the revival of learning throughout Europe (prompting at least one author, Thomas Cahill, to write a book entitled *How the Irish Saved Civilization*). Might Catholic educators today learn a lesson from those old Irish monks? Without simply repeating the past, we must always conserve its wisdom for the present. This is an important service to human well-being—particularly in a throw-away culture where the new is ever presumed better than the old.

Second, Irish monasticism had a deep missionary commitment, encouraging its monks to travel out from their monasteries and across the seas in order to spread the gospel among the barbarian tribes. They called their missionaries *peregrini pro Christo*—"travelers for Christ"—and they reached into the farthest corners of the then-known world. (There is even a legend that Abbot Brendan of Clonfert (484–577) and a group of his monks, sailing in a *currach*—a sturdy Irish boat—reached what was later "discovered" as America.) Furthermore, the Irish missionary monks laid emphasis on God's mercy and forgiveness, allowing people to celebrate the sacrament of reconciliation repeatedly; at that time the Roman church allowed it only once in a lifetime. Those Celtic monks can inspire Catholic education today to invite students to share their faith intentionally and ever to have confidence in God's mercy.

Third was what we would call today an environmental consciousness. Celtic spirituality had (and still has) a deep sense of the presence of God in nature and of our responsibility to care for the earth and all its creatures. It imagines that there is only a thin veil between creation and the Creator, and the veil is thinnest of all in the midst of nature. Catholic education today must instill in students a sense of responsibility for the environment. Reading some of the prayers and practices from Celtic spirituality can inspire an environmental consciousness in our time.

THE CAROLINGIAN RENAISSANCE

The Benedictine and Celtic schools continued to spread across Europe and yet were reaching only a small percentage of the people—the ones who lived near a monastery or those aspiring to be monks or sisters. Most often, too, rulers saw to it that their children got the limited places in such schools. Indeed, a typical attitude was that the general population did not need an education. Unless one was going to work in civil service or enter a monastery or convent, education was considered an unnecessary luxury. A more inclusive attitude began to emerge, though slowly, with the rise of the Emperor Charlemagne (747–814).

Charlemagne, also known as Charles the Great, was born at Aachen (present-day Germany) into the royal household of the Frankish kingdom (present-day France and more). He became emperor of the Franks in 771, and soon thereafter conquered most of the other regional tribes (Saxons, Lombards, and so on). On Christmas Day, 800, in Saint Peter's Basilica in Rome, Pope Leo III crowned Charlemagne as Holy Roman Emperor—in effect, ruler of the Western world. Pope Leo gave him the special title Defender of the Faith.

This event and title marked the beginning of what has been described as the marriage of throne and altar. The symbiosis of the spiritual and temporal powers—often dubbed Christendom, with pope and emperor working hand in hand (though not always happily)—remained in place until the Protestant Reformation. Christendom endured for well over seven hundred years, with the church functioning as educator and often dictator of the realm.

With the help of his chief adviser, Alcuin, a learned deacon from the cathedral school at York, which had been founded from the Celtic monastery at Lindisfarne, Charlemagne launched a major renaissance of culture and learning throughout the Holy Roman Empire. The "Educational Proclamation" he issued in 787 directed bishops to found cathedral schools for the local youth and for all monasteries to conduct schools for their monks so that these "soldiers of the church" would be able to break open for the common people "the wisdom of Holy Scripture" (in Cully, 89–91).

Charles appointed Alcuin as head of his palace school at Aachen, and Alcuin made it a model to be imitated throughout the empire. It retrieved much of the Christian *paideia* lost during the Dark Ages. Its curriculum included the earlier *trivium*—grammar, rhetoric and dialectics, all studied by reading classical authors like Homer, Sophocles, or more recent Christian authors like the Venerable Bede and Boethius.

This was accompanied by the *quadrivium* of arithmetic, geometry, astronomy, and music—with music often a means of Christian catechesis through singing hymns and psalms.

All those liberal arts were to enable students to function well in society and be able to read and study the sacred scriptures to nourish their faith. Alcuin's writings emphasize, however, that the ultimate intent of formal education is to reach beyond knowledge and "to flourish in the beauty of wisdom." Becoming wise is the learning outcome of embracing "Our Lord Jesus Christ, who is the virtue and wisdom of God." Alcuin was convinced that only spiritual *wisdom* would make for better citizens, a more peaceful empire, and lead into eternal life. Most likely this is still true! ("Alcuin Letter to Charlemagne," in Cully, 85–87).

Then, two years later, in 789, Charlemagne made the first major step toward universal education in the Western world; though not realized until long after his time, he at least sowed the seed with his "Proclamation of Universal Education." It decreed: "Let schools be established in which boys and girls may learn to read" (in Cully, 91–92). The statement made clear that all monastic and cathedral schools were to admit the local children as well as aspiring candidates for religious life.

Charlemagne's motivation was not entirely altruistic; he recognized the political potential of education and how an educated populace would make for a better society—and perhaps fewer wars! The emerging bureaucracy of his enormous empire also needed huge numbers of civil servants who could read and write. Then, in 802, explicitly concerned for Christian catechesis, Charlemagne promulgated: "We will and command that lay people shall learn thoroughly the Creed and the Lord's Prayer" (in Cully, 92). Indeed, it was Charlemagne who ordered that the Apostles' Creed be prayed at mass every Sunday, hoping that a shared faith among the very diverse tribes would be a source of unity for the empire.

These initiatives gave rise to what historians call the Carolingian Renaissance, helping to reclaim much of what was lost following the barbarian invasions (many of those invaders were now at least nominally Christian). As noted already, the great cathedral and monastic schools that emerged from the Charlemagne era lead to the founding of the first great universities in the late eleventh and twelfth centuries—Bologna, Salamanca, Oxford, Paris, Cambridge, and so on. That the church would sponsor universities and locate theology within them as the queen of the sciences is the epitome of the Catholic intellectual tradition. Undoubtedly the greatest scholar and exponent of the Catholic intellectual tradition to emerge in the new millennium was Thomas Aquinas.

For Reflection and Conversation

- We may think that we have universal education today, but in fact there are huge numbers of young people throughout the world who don't have access to this fundamental human right (girls being excluded more often than boys). How can Catholic schools work to promote universal education—where everyone, girls and boys, and those differently abled—have ready access to a good education?
- Celtic monasticism had a keen ecological consciousness. What is the responsibility of Catholic schools regarding this issue today? How might we promote a deep commitment to environmental stewardship?

THOMAS AQUINAS (1225–74)

No one has been more committed to the partnership of faith and reason and to the correlative expressions of the Catholic intellectual tradition (wisdom and knowledge, formation and scholarship, and so on) than Thomas Aquinas. Thomas was convinced that, while faith is a gift from God, it must seek understanding in order to be personally appropriated and lived with conviction. Aquinas was also convinced that reason can aid theology in establishing first principles, like the existence of God, and to defend, elaborate, explain, and develop Christian faith as history unfolds for different times and cultures.

Indeed, the definition of theology as "faith seeking understanding," coined by Anselm of Canterbury (1033–1109), became the main agenda of this era and is still much favored today. Thomas and other scholars who joined in this more academic approach to theology became known as the Scholastics (from *schola,* meaning "scholar"). This Scholastic movement marked a transition from the monastic approach to theology as contemplative reading of scripture to grow in holiness—the dominant mode of the first thousand years—to theology as rational discourse about theological truth claims. Surely Christian faith needs both the monastic and scholastic!

Thomas was born in the principality of Aquino, central Italy, just a few miles from Monte Cassino, the youngest son of the Count and Countess of Aquino. At five, his parents enrolled him at Monte Cassino, fully intending that he become a Benedictine monk (religious life was not unusual for the youngest son in aristocratic families). However, for college studies Thomas was sent to a Dominican college in Naples and fell in love with their still new ministry (founded by Saint Dominic in

1216) of public preaching of the gospel as well as intellectual study. Much against his parents' wishes, Thomas joined the Dominicans, who sent him to study at the University of Paris. There his teacher was Albertus Magnus (1200–1280), the leading Scholastic theologian of his day; he introduced Aquinas to the writings of Aristotle.

Lost during the Dark Ages, the study of Aristotle was revived first at the great Muslim center of learning at Cordoba, Spain, led by its Islamic scholars Avicenna (980–1037) and later Averroes (1126–98); the latter also collaborated with the Jewish scholar Maimonides (1135–1204). Inspired by them, Albertus Magnus led the Christian retrieval of Aristotle and so taught his star student, Thomas, who would outdo his master. Aristotelian philosophy became the bedrock of Thomas's theologizing. Eventually, he was appointed a professor at the University of Paris (gaining tenure over much opposition). Though he taught in other colleges across the years, the University of Paris remained his academic home.

Thomas wrote copiously (in very illegible handwriting), with his greatest works being the *Summa Contra Gentiles*, a manual for missionaries to make persuasive argument for Christian faith, and his magnum opus, *Summa Theologica*, meaning a "theological summary." Thomas began writing the *Summa* in 1265; he died (1274) just shy of its completion.

Aquinas's Pedagogy. Being very selective, I raise up three insights from Thomas's practice of the Catholic intellectual tradition that are particularly relevant to Catholic education in any age: his conviction that knowing originates from human experience; his use of probing questions (that is, not just for recall) as integral to the dynamic of teaching; and his conviction that education includes moral formation. As we focused on Augustine's text *The Teacher*, here we focus on Aquinas's text of the same title, and in which Augustine is often Thomas's foil. Though it is only a small excerpt (and seldom studied) within the huge corpus of Aquinas's writings, *The Teacher* reflects much of what educators can learn from him.

Knowing originates from human experience. Though renowned for his commitment to critical reasoning, Aquinas was convinced that knowledge begins from the sense data of our experience. Echoing Aristotle, he insists that "nothing is ever in the mind that was not first in the senses." So, all knowing begins with sense perception that the mind then reflects upon and appropriates as knowledge. His pithy summary in "Reply to Objection 4" in *The Teacher* runs: "From the sensible symbols, which are received in the sense faculty, the intellect takes the essence which it uses in producing knowledge" (in Cully, 111).

So knowledge begins with a kind of sensual intellect that collects and organizes the data from experience that our rational intellect then proceeds to understand, and, for authentic cognition, moves on to make judgments and decisions about. The decisions can be cognitive, affective, or behavioral, and can reach from particular to universal ideas, and also to ethical principles and wisdom to guide moral action.

When Aquinas brought this understanding of the knowing process into education, he explicitly disagreed with Augustine's claim that all truth is already within us from God—only needing to be drawn out. Yet, while knowledge itself is not already within, our capacity for it is indeed innate and native to the human condition. Thomas emphasized that knowing begins from our own experience, which is then brought to explicit knowledge with the help of the inner capacities of the mind that God gave us.

Somewhat agreeing with Augustine, the student is to be an active agent in this process, uncovering truth and figuring things out rather than receiving from a teacher "on high." For Aquinas, it is true that "to know something by discovery is more perfect than to learn from another" (ibid., 116–17). However, rather than minimizing the role of the teacher—as he understood Augustine to have done in *his* treatise *The Teacher*—Aquinas goes on to say that while "the acquisition of knowledge through discovery is more perfect" on the part of the student, there is need for the teacher as well. He writes, "through instruction, the teacher who has the knowledge as a whole can lead to knowledge more quickly and easily than anyone can be led by (them)selves" (ibid., 118).

In summary, for Aquinas, promoting knowledge—and virtue, as below—should engage students in reflecting on their own experiences of life in the world. Likewise, they need instruction in ways that lend ready access to the disciplines of learning, connecting them and integrating them with students' own experiences—an ongoing cycle. This both/and of *experiential* learning and instruction in *tradition* in a constant cycle is what Aquinas would recommend for Catholic education.

Use of probing questions. A distinguishing mark of Scholastic pedagogy was always to begin with an engaging question (in Latin, the *quaestio*). This could vary from the very esoteric (an old joke is of Scholastic scholars debating "how many angels can fit on the head of a pin") to intensely personal questions that deeply engaged the everyday lives and concerns of students—their own experience. Far beyond recall questions that simply invite students to repeat what teachers have taught, teaching, for Aquinas, should begin with questions that invite students to be agents of their own knowing and to think rigorously for themselves.

After posing the question and inviting students to think deeply, the Scholastic pedagogy was to offer a series of wrong answers to the *quaestio*, often quoting scripture or Christian tradition and sounding very convincing. The next step, then, was to refute those plausible but wrong answers, and then to pose what might be the more correct ones, all intending to prompt students to continue to think critically for themselves. Even as a predictable pattern, it served to deeply engage the agency of the students in the teaching/learning dynamic.

For example, in *The Teacher*, the first *quaestio* asks whether a person can teach another (and thus be called a teacher) or whether God alone teaches. His first response (wrong) is to say that God alone teaches (citing Augustine seven times). He then debunks this by arguing that God makes us active agents in our own knowing process, and yet we can well be instructed by a teacher—a both/and response and explicitly pushing back against Augustine's overemphasis on the agency of the student alone.

Historians allege that some of the questions posed by Scholastic professors at the University of Paris led to riots by students in the streets, so intense were the debates that ensued. Those Scholastics clearly understood that crafting great and small questions and inviting students to think deeply about them were imperative to engage them actively in the pedagogy.

Such intense questioning in matters of faith clearly reflects that faith must be brought to understanding and embraced by conviction; this engages critical thinking to examine data and then to move to understanding, judgment, and decision. Aquinas was convinced that faith devoid of personal conviction is less likely to be lived out as one's own. Add to this the evidence from across the ages that faith without the monitor of critical thinking can be downright dangerous. There is, then, a central place in all Catholic education for critical reflection by students and for questions that prompt it.

Education for moral formation. This theme is not so present in Aquinas's *The Teacher*, though he notes in "Reply to Objection 1" that because we are "of God's likeness . . . we are able to judge concerning all things," and he clearly included moral issues (in Cully, 111). He makes very explicit elsewhere, however, that the process of cognition should lead to moral values as well as to sound ideas. A central conviction of Aquinas is that God has implanted in every person a "natural law" by which we are capable of knowing right from wrong, moral from immoral. Furthermore, recognizing and then doing what is right is encouraged by our own reflection on the daily experiences of life. His entire dynamic of cognition—which begins by paying attention to sense experience and then moves to understanding, judgment, and decision—is to lead the person, disposed by the natural law within each one, to recognize and embrace not just the truths but the moral imperatives of life. Besides knowledge, Aquinas's way of knowing was to lead to moral discernment and decision-making, which, in turn, would be formative of people's character and values.

Now so disregarded and even opposed in general education, a rich legacy of the Catholic intellectual tradition *a la* Aquinas (and other strong voices) is to insist on the integration of education with moral formation. Aquinas advises that education which honors the full dynamics of cognition—and especially that pushes beyond understanding to judgment and decision—will encourage moral formation as well as insight as the learning outcome. Indeed, the entire dynamic of cognition is to merge into wisdom for life.

Note here, too, that for Aquinas—as for Aristotle—moral formation does not come by clarity of thought alone (Aquinas was more influenced by Aristotle than Plato). To become virtuous and to acquire the good habits of right living require that people embrace the actual practice of virtue. We become truthful by telling and living the truth; we become kind and loving by doing acts of kindness and love; and so on. In a sense, this again reflects Aquinas's fundamental conviction that we are to learn from reflection upon our own experience. The more our well-reasoned moral actions become a habit, the more we become virtuous people. (Aquinas undoubtedly would enthusiastically support programs of outreach and service learning in modern Catholic schools as integral to the curriculum and essential to formation in social values.)

Aquinas for Catholic education. To inherit a little of Aquinas's contribution to the Catholic intellectual tradition and echoing the points above for Catholic education, our pedagogy must (1) encourage students to attend to and reflect upon their own experiences of life in the world; (2) pose good questions that encourage such reflection; and (3) nurture the moral formation of students. ✳

First, engaging students' lives and inviting their reflection upon them should be an integral aspect of a Catholic pedagogy. (Note that Paulo Freire, a great contemporary exponent of this praxis way of knowing, was much influenced by Aquinas.) In fact, students may learn little from their own experiences unless we invite their reflection upon them.

✳ call for explicit formation buts
up against pref. for indirection

Furthermore, whatever traditions of learning we wish to teach, we must try to connect with students' own lives—their experiences and interests. This is how they are most likely to see for themselves and make their own what we want them to know from what Dewey called "the funded capital of civilization." Information transferred without integration into people's lives and their own recognition through personal reflection is soon forgotten and has little to no impact on who people become.

Second, Aquinas and the rich Scholastic tradition encouraged educators to *pose great questions* to students, questions that engage them as agents of learning from their own experiences as well as from teacher instruction. We should spend as much time creating engaging questions and reflective activities as we do in preparing what to access from traditions of learning. Teachers need to pose generative themes that engage students' lives and invite critical (discerning) reflection on their daily experiences in the world. And while inviting students to understand, our questions should prompt them onward into their own recognitions and decisions.

Third, Aquinas would insist that Catholic education have *formation as integral* to its intended learning outcomes. Because authentic cognition unites the theoretical and practical for Aquinas, education should enable people to both embrace the truth and choose the good. As we elaborate later, the Enlightenment era argued to separate theoretical from practical reasoning, and thus education from formation. Education that neglects formation is an aberration to our human condition and overlooks the fact that no education is morally neutral; it encourages either values or disvalues.

For sure and overtly, Catholic education should be value laden, proposing the universal values epitomized in the life of Jesus of Nazareth and inviting their practice and then reflection upon them—the ultimate source of formation. The Enlightenment legacy now prompts Western government-sponsored education to overlook the moral formation of its students; it is no wonder there is so much falsehood and lying in the public realm. The formative aspect of Catholic education was never more needed! Let Aquinas encourage us to imagine how to meet this crucial challenge more effectively; the future of our world depends on it.

For Reflection and Conversation

- What might you learn from Aquinas about crafting questions and reflective activities to engage both the experiences of your students and the disciplines of learning?

*But how didactic?

• What do you see as the formative aspect of Catholic education? Imagine how ethical formation can be deliberately structured throughout the entire curriculum of a school, regardless of the subject being taught.

JULIAN OF NORWICH (1342–AFTER 1416)

After Aquinas, the Scholastic approach to theology became dominant; the Catholic Church even declared Thomas its official theologian. There were some alternative voices, for example, the Franciscans Bonaventure (1217–74) and Duns Scotus (1265–1308). They continued to put emphasis on the monastic notion of theology as seeking spiritual wisdom rather than rational understanding. The Scholastics largely won out and continue to have significant influence to the present day on the Catholic intellectual tradition. However, a new resource, holding to the union of theology and spirituality, also began to emerge in this era, namely, the voices of women scholars.

As the reader will note, we have not yet heard women's voices in the Catholic intellectual tradition, and this is only because education was largely closed to women up to this time. The few women who received an education were from ruling families with the resources to hire tutors, and they were schooled to fulfill what were seen as their domestic responsibilities—homemaking and raising children—and certainly not for doing theology. Jesus, as we noted in the first chapter, practiced full inclusivity of women in his public ministry and inner circle of disciples. Likewise, the story of Pentecost makes clear that all present "were filled with the Holy Spirit" (Acts 2:4), having previously noted that the awaiting community included women disciples "and Mary the mother of Jesus" (Acts 1:14). This commitment to gender inclusivity, however, did not withstand the overwhelmingly male chauvinism of the cultures that received Christian faith.

In the Scholastic era a new phenomenon emerged against that male-dominating grain, namely, a number of accomplished women scholars who somehow found a way to gain a higher education, even in theology. The growing litany of their names would include Hildegard of Bingen (1098–1179), Mechtild of Madgeburgh (1212–82), Mechtild of Hackerborn (1241–99), Margery Kempe (1373–1438), and a host of others only now being discovered. A few managed to find a voice in the life of the church of their time, like Catherine of Sienna (1347–80), and a little later Catherine of Genoa (1447–1510) and Teresa of Avila (1515–82). Such women represent what revisionist historians now call the hidden history of women—meaning that such leaders and scholars were present throughout but their voices were silenced or kept hidden. Today they are finally being discovered and heard.

Historians opine, too, that these medieval women scholars strategically presented their work as being in spirituality rather than theology, with a method more of prayerful reflection than critical reasoning alone; such a spiritual approach seemed less likely to draw negative attention from the official church. The times were dangerous for anyone doing theology; suspected heretics were burned at the stake. We have only begun to reclaim the depths and richness of the theology-cum-spirituality of the brave women pioneers. Perhaps the most notable, and with particular wisdom for Catholic education, was Julian of Norwich.

Julian referred to herself as a recluse, or an anchorite, who lived alone in an anchorage—cloistered cell—attached to the Church of Saint Julian and Saint Edward in Norwich, England; we don't even know if Julian was her real name. For livelihood, she depended on the charity of the local people. Yet her writings reflect an in-depth knowledge of theology, including the writings of Augustine and perhaps Aquinas; clearly she had been well educated with competence in Latin. She refused to identify as a teacher (probably for safety), insisting instead that "Jesus is everyone's teacher." She developed a reputation as a spiritual mentor; there are historical records of other leading women coming to her for spiritual counsel.

Julian would have been a child at the time of the bubonic plague (also known as the Black Death) from 1347 to 1351, a devastating illness that wiped out some one-third to one-half of the population of Europe. The suffering was horrendous and continued long after; this puts into amazing relief Julian's relentless note of hope and confidence in God's love. Then, on May 13, 1373, when she was about thirty years old and during a serious personal illness, Julian claimed to have experienced "sixteen revelations" centered on a vivid experience of Jesus's passion and death on the cross.

Julian soon wrote a short reflection on her mystical experience that she called "Comforting Words for Christ's Lovers." Then, after some twenty years of further prayer and reflection on her experience, she wrote *Revelations of Divine Love*—completed in 1395, and typically called *Showings*. This was the first book by a woman to be published in the English language. Both the shorter and longer texts reflect a theological method of prayerful reflection as in *lectio divina*. Her focus, however, was not exclusively on the scriptures but also on her own spiritual experiences in the "showings" and in the life and nature around her, all intended to promote Christian holiness of life. Julian's writings, reclaimed in more recent years, are a rich and enduring resource for Christian theology and spirituality—and also for Catholic education.

Julian as educator. Again needing to be very selective, I raise up three overlapping spiritual foundations from Julian's writings that seem particularly relevant to the practice of Catholic education today: her *spiritual courage* and the role of personal convictions in matters of faith; her insistence upon *hope for all people* because of God's love and their own innate goodness; and her awareness that God is literally "beyond all names"—calling us to be more *expansive in imaging the Divine.*

Spiritual courage. To say that Julian had extraordinary courage is an understatement. First, she had to trust that her mystical experiences were valid, that God was truly communicating with her through her own life and her reflection upon it (a core conviction of the Catholic intellectual tradition). This trust arose from her constantly testing out and praying over what God was revealing to her heart. Yet it took great courage for her to believe what she was hearing from her own life and prayer, which sometimes appeared to be in contrast to the official positions of the church. Her relentless courage was grounded in her amazing understanding of God. The church of her time presented God as distant, harsh, and judgmental; Julian, by contrast, became convinced that "God is all goodness and loves me tenderly" and literally put that in writing (*Showings*, chap. 77).

Furthermore, Julian had the courage to embrace her convictions and make them public. In contrast, the church of the time would have insisted that it alone spoke on behalf of God and Christian faith, and the duty of Christians was simply to listen and obey. Having to tread very carefully, Julian would often protest her loyalty to the teachings of the church and yet say things that were much in contrast to the "party line" of her day.

For example, the church of the time commonly preached that most people would be lost to damnation and only a select few be saved—those who "earn" God's love by following exactly the church's directives. Julian, by contrast, became convinced that "before God made us, God loved us, which love has never abated and never will" (chap. 86). And because of such unconditional divine love, she had the courage to insist, in what is likely her most quoted line, that for everyone "all will be well, and in the end, all will be well" (chap. 12); in other words, all people will be saved.

Hope for all. Based on those convictions, Julian held out hope for all people, for here and hereafter, precisely because of God's unconditional love for *every* person. Furthermore, she was convinced that all people are essentially good and are empowered by God's grace to live into their potential goodness. That God loves all people unconditionally, and is full of mercy and compassion for all, without exception, is repeated myriad times throughout *Showings* and went against the grain of the church and its teachings at that time.

For example, Julian reflects little of what the church was teaching about "original sin" and "the fall" of Adam and Eve, for which we are still being punished. Instead, Julian imaged Jesus, God's own Son, as "falling into humanity" with his incarnation into the womb of Mary to take on our human estate. Then, even as Adam sinned as we do, when God looks upon us now, instead of seeing only sinful Adam or people like ourselves, God sees God's own Son, Jesus—who is in solidarity with our human estate—and has mercy on us (see chap. 51). So God forgives and loves us regardless of our sins, yet ever calls us, as Jesus did, to "sin no more" (John 8:11).

While she is not naive to people's capacity for sin, Julian's defining image of the person is as essentially good, certainly more good than evil. Our innate goodness arises from the presence of God's life within us: "Greatly ought we to rejoice that God dwells in our soul; and greatly ought we to rejoice that our soul dwells in God" (chap. 54). The whole person is good—including the sensuality of our body: "So are we, soul and body, clad and enclosed in the goodness of God" (chap. 6). For this reason, "we are called to be partners in God's good will and work" (chap. 43) and, by the help of God's grace, we can respond.

So, "nature is all good and fair in itself and grace was sent out to save nature and destroy sin" (chap. 63). In lovely imagery she writes, "We have come out of God by nature . . . to be brought back into God by grace" (chap. 64). Because of God's love at work in our lives as grace, and our own innate goodness, there is always hope for every person: "For our God is so good, so gentle and courteous that he can never assign final failure to those in whom he will always be blessed and praised" (chap 53).

Imaging the Divine. Julian is keenly conscious that God is Ultimate Mystery and that all names for God inevitably fall short. Most amazing is her realization that God is beyond gender; she uses both male and female imagery for God. This has been a slowly emerging awareness in our own time—that to name God constantly as male is to favor men over women, in society as well as church. In Julian, some seven hundred years ago and arising out of her own spirituality and prayer, we find a similar consciousness and care around language and imagery for God.

Throughout both scripture and Christian tradition, God is predominantly (though not exclusively) portrayed with male imagery, yet Julian simply refused this total male gendering of God. So, "God rejoices that he is our Father and God rejoices that he is our Mother" (chap. 52). And again, "As truly as God is our Father, so truly is God our Mother" (chap. 59). Reflecting upon the triune nature of God's love for us, traditionally represented as Father, Son, and Holy Spirit, Julian writes, "God almighty is our loving Father and God all wisdom is our loving Mother (in Jesus), with the love and the goodness of the Holy Spirit which is all one God" (chap. 58).

Following on, the challenge to use inclusive and expansive imagery for God is particularly reflected in Julian's description of the Blessed Trinity. Beyond the traditional imagery she uses varied trinitarian formulas to capture the "Threeness" of God. So, the trinitarian nature of God is power, wisdom, and love; nature, mercy, and grace; creation, recreation, and sanctification; maker, protector, and lover—and Julian's imagery goes on.

Perhaps most amazing is that Julian often names Jesus in feminine terms, convinced that the Risen Christ is now above gender specificity. She frequently refers to "our mother Jesus" and, with lovely imagery of the Eucharist, writes, "The mother can give her child suck of her milk, but our precious Mother Jesus can feed us with himself" (chap. 60). For all of our claims to "know" God, Julian reminds us that God is Ultimate Mystery and always "beyond all names."

For Catholic education. Julian of Norwich encourages Catholic educators to invite students: to reflect upon their own spiritual experiences to nurture their personal relationship with God; to be confident of their own goodness, and God's mercy; and to be expansive in their imaging of God.

Personal spiritual experience as revelatory. To paraphrase the great Catholic theologian Karl Rahner, "The devout Christian of the future will be a 'mystic' or will cease to be anything." By 'mystic,' Rahner meant one open to how God reaches out to us through our ordinary and everyday experiences. This is how we can encounter God's presence and grace to us personally—in the mysticism of the everyday. In a sense, and again paraphrasing Rahner, God's most personal and intimate revelation to our lives is through our own story.

Julian of Norwich, seven hundred years before Rahner, had the same insight—and the courage to trust in her own spiritual experiences of God's presence in her life. From such courage she came to deep personal convictions and commitments, often against the grain of her time and church. Catholic religious education in particular should encourage students to reflect with confidence upon their own life experiences in the light of faith and come to their own spiritual wisdom for life—that they then live out with courage and with confidence in God's unconditional love for them.

To be confident of their own goodness and God's mercy. Julian would recommend that Catholic education encourage in students a very positive self-imaging, emphasizing and encouraging their potential goodness, and giving them hope that they can continue growing as good people. When students are so treated and respected, they are more likely to act and become so. No matter what background students come from, or what personal or social challenges they may experience, there is always hope for their goodness, not just by their own efforts but by the grace of God. As we say often throughout, God's grace prompts and augments our own best efforts, and we *are* ever capable of responding.

Furthermore, all people are likely to sin occasionally and fall short of *living* faith. Yet, in Christian tradition there is no unforgivable sin; the largess of God's mercy is greater than any of our sins. Julian constantly reminded people that God's mercy is ever on offer. Likewise, regarding the challenges and suffering that come our way—as they did for Julian—we will address them differently if we have faith in God's grace, God's effective love at work in our lives. Julian's insight encourages Catholic educators always to inspire hope in their students, especially in difficult circumstances.

Expansiveness in imagining God. Regarding our language and imaging of God, because we educate from and for a faith stance toward life, Catholic educators are inevitably drawn into "God-talk." As public and influential figures, we must be particularly careful in how we speak of God to our students. We must ever acknowledge the Mystery of which we speak, and how limited is all of our God language and imaging. We can know enough to live as people of God; after that, God is Mystery, infinitely beyond our ken.

For example, rather than using language patterns that limit God to being male, we must try to speak of God in more expansive terms—as the Bible does. It has masculine and feminine images for God, neutral and impersonal ones, and myriad images besides. Just the first two verses of Psalm 18 have *twelve* different images for God, with the Psalmist struggling to name the Holy One who is beyond all names. Surely we can expand our language a little, as Julian would encourage, and avoid God-talk that effectively favors men over women in church and society. This can be a challenge, because in addition to much traditional biblical imagery, many of our prayer patterns favor God as male.

In particular, Christians take for granted the prayer which Jesus himself taught us as beginning with "Our Father." While the Greek is *Pater* ("Father"; Matt 6:9), we know that Jesus spoke Aramaic, a Hebrew dialect, and there the word is "Abba." Some New Testament scholars suggest that Jesus may have favored this term regularly; he used it explicitly at least once (see Mark 14:36). They also point out that the etymology of *Abba* refers to both the heart of a father and the womb of a mother. Might Jesus have intended such inclusivity? Regardless, might one consider, at least in personal praying, using "Our Loving Parent, who art in heaven," or something similar? Whatever we decide, let Julian encourage us to be imaginative and perhaps a little adventuresome in how we speak of God—always Ultimate Mystery. ✳

RENEWING YOUR VOCATION AS CATHOLIC EDUCATOR

As we reflect upon the educator's *soul*, the teaching *style*, and educational *space*, we have much to learn from Thomas Aquinas; we return to his insights in Chapter 8 on epistemology and through the work of the great Thomistic scholar Bernard Lonergan. Here, given how women's voices have been suppressed across the ages in both church and society, let us give primary focus to appropriating the rich spiritual foundations offered by Julian of Norwich for our soul, style, and space, raising her extraordinary voice a little louder.

For the educator's soul. Julian would surely urge Catholic educators to be representatives of God's love to their students, to reflect to them, and especially to those who need loving assurance most, that they are unconditionally loved by God, who is full of mercy for them. A favorite exercise I have engaged across the years is to invite my graduate students to recall a great teacher they have experienced in their schooling. When I ask participants why they chose the particular person they did, invariably, in one way or another, it is a teacher who somehow showed them love, care, and respect.

- Recognize the ways that you already show love for your students. How might you deepen and recommit to being such a loving educator-witness to them?
- How can you encourage your students to love and care for themselves? To be confident in God's love and mercy toward them? To be loving and merciful toward each other?

For the teaching style. Both Aquinas and Julian were committed to reflective ways of knowing, with Aquinas being more rational and Julian being more contemplative and prayerful. While the rational mode is

✳ Refreshing/ opes to diff ways of talking about God

certainly needed, so too is the prayerful and spiritual. Though thriving throughout much of the first thousand years (we saw the Benedictines as primary exponents), a spiritual way of knowing has been greatly diminished in the West. It is ironic that Eastern traditions like Buddhist meditation and Zen mindfulness are now bringing Christians back to our forgotten tradition of contemplative knowing. Julian of Norwich can help as well.

- How might you invite your students to be more contemplative, to listen to their own "deep heart's core" (Yeats)—their souls? What kinds of questions might encourage this?
- Imagine a specific exercise that would bring young people into a contemplative mode. (One of Julian's most famous contemplations focused on a simple hazel nut that she was holding in her hand; as she "listened" to it, even that little nut spoke to her of God's love.)

For the educational space. We don't immediately think about the words and the language we use as shaping the ethos of our communal space, as in a school or classroom. Yet assuredly they do. Martin Heidegger, the great German philosopher, proposed in his "Letter on Humanism" that "language is the house of being." He meant that we live and dwell in language, which has the power to shape our very identity as *human beings.* Furthermore, teachers in a Catholic school most likely engage regularly in God-talk—even if they are not designated religious educators. We can be inspired by Julian and her constantly expanding language for God to reach beyond male only imagery.

- Might you develop—if you do not already do so—the habit of using language patterns that include all people, for example, *humankind* instead of *mankind, people* instead of *men, person* instead of *man,* and so on.
- Might Julian encourage you to use more expansive language for God, going beyond male-only imagery? What might be a good alternative for you? Might you consider, "Our Loving Parent," or "Our Mother and Father," or some other alternative wording?

5

Ignatius of Loyola
and the Society of Jesus (Jesuits)

From the twelfth century to the sixteenth century the church continued to be the primary educator in the Western world. Many of its monastic and cathedral schools flourished, as did its chartered universities and a growing number of parish schools. Whether implicit or explicitly stated, the assumption was that offering education *from* and *for* faith is integral to the church's mission to the world. It advances God's work of liberating salvation within human history precisely because it contributes to the personal good of students and the common good of society.

The church's dominance in education began to wane, however, with the Protestant Reformation. Martin Luther (1483–1546) is credited with initiating the Reformation. It began when he posted his "ninety-five theses," calling for much needed church reform, to the door of the church in Wittenberg, Germany, on October 31, 1517. The Christian community had experienced its first structural divide in the separation of Eastern Orthodox churches and the Western Catholic church, the division usually dated to the year 1054. This separation, however, was more cultural than doctrinal; in large part, Christian faith in both the East and West continued with shared beliefs and sacraments. The Reformation launched by Luther, however, led to a deeper division; while theologians usually focus on the doctrinal nature of the divide, I highlight here its consequences for education.

That the church of the time was riddled with scandals and corruption and in urgent need of reform is beyond dispute (what else is new!). Indeed, in 1983, on the five hundredth anniversary of Luther's birth, Pope John Paul II, speaking at the Lutheran church in Rome, publicly thanked Luther for three great gifts to the life of the whole church, Protestant and Catholic: (1) returning the Bible to the core of Christian faith and insisting that all have ready access to God's word through sacred scripture; (2) restoring a radical theology of baptism that constitutes all the baptized as a "priestly people"; and (3) reminding Christians of our constant need of God's grace to live our faith, beginning with the grace of faith itself. In the polemics of the Reformation era, however, and with poor means of communication, the Christian church suffered its second major division, now into Catholic and Protestant.

Luther soon realized that as long as the church controlled the schools, the traditional faith would continue to be taught to the rising generations and his Reformation would fail. He was also anxious to broaden access to education for all, convinced that all Christians need to read and understand the scriptures in order to fulfill their baptismal responsibility as "the priesthood of all believers." Indeed, the Reformation was the greatest stimulus toward universal literacy in the history of the Western world—so that all could read their Bible.

In his "Letter to the Councilmen of All Cities in Germany" (1524) Luther urged them to "establish and maintain Christian schools" in their municipalities. Note well, he intended them to continue as truly *Christian*. Indeed, Luther told the rulers that such state-sponsored schools are "the command of God" and are needed "both for the understanding of Scripture and for the conduct of good government" (Cully, 141). Note the dual purpose that Luther wisely intended—spiritual and social.

Luther's letter was a major catalyst for founding what we know now in the West as public education, a school system sponsored exclusively by the state. Though Luther was adamant that such schools remain Christian, quite quickly state-sponsored education lost its commitment to the both/and of the Catholic intellectual tradition. This was augmented by the Enlightenment movement in philosophy that followed soon after and which was distinctly opposed to all religious faith, and certainly in government-sponsored schools. The Enlightenment, considering faith simply unenlightened, forged exclusively rationalist and empirical ways of knowing (the legacies of René Descartes and Francis Bacon, respectively) that came to dominate the modern era—especially in education.

So, instead of faith and reason, the public schools soon favored reason alone; instead of revelation and science, they favored science alone; instead of the spiritual and the academic, they favored the academic alone; instead of formation and knowledge, they favored knowledge alone; instead of transcendent and immanent perspectives, they favored the immanent alone; and so on. Thus, the public schools rejected the partnerships that mark the Catholic intellectual tradition.

Catholic schools, however, continued in their both/and approach to education, and none more effectively than those conducted by the Jesuits, inspired by their founder Saint Ignatius of Loyola. Ignatius was the leading exponent of Catholic education in the immediate post-

Reformation era. Indeed, in my opinion, Ignatius and the Jesuit education he crafted is the epitome of Catholic education across the centuries and to the present day, ever deeply grounded in spiritual foundations.

For Reflection and Conversation

- What is your own sense of the place of formation in education—Catholic or public? Why is this of growing concern for postmodern societies? How do you imagine honoring the formative aspect in your own teaching?
- Luther rightly quoted Saint Augustine, who proposed that the church must be *semper reformanda* (always reforming) itself. What are some issues or practices in the Catholic Church today that you see as needing reform? How might Catholic schools contribute to reforming the church?

SAINT IGNATIUS OF LOYOLA (1491–1556)

Ignatius of Loyola founded the Society of Jesus, better known as the Jesuits. It was the first non-cloistered (outside of a monastery) Catholic religious order to undertake the founding, managing, and staffing of schools as its primary mission. The Jesuits also became enormously influential and can be well said to subsume the best of Catholic education and the Catholic intellectual tradition that grounds it. It is worthwhile, then, to spend a little extra time with Ignatius, given his importance for Catholic education in every age thereafter and throughout the world today. First, let us situate him in his historical context—at the height of the Reformation.

Ignatius was from the royal house of Loyola, a principality within the Basque province of northern Spain. He was the youngest of thirteen children. As a young man he enjoyed all the pleasures that came with being a member of the ruling class and fancied himself as a courageous knight-at-arms, given to saving maidens in distress. At the age of thirty, while defending the Spanish city of Pamplona against French invaders (1521), Ignatius was struck by a cannon ball that injured one leg and broke the other. During his lengthy recuperation Ignatius asked for some reading to help pass his time. The only books available were a life of Jesus and some lives of the saints. Ignatius noticed that those readings brought him great peace, whereas when he dwelt on his ambitions for power and romance, he became unhappy. Gradually, he began to recognize his calling to follow Jesus, and instead of being a knight-at-arms, he chose to become a knight for the reign of God—in holy chivalry.

Ignatius left Loyola for a pilgrimage to the Holy Land, wishing to experience personally where Jesus had lived and died. Along the way he paused and dwelt in a cave outside the city of Manresa for ten months (March 1522–February 1523). There, from reflecting on his own spiritual journey and conversing with people who came to him for spiritual mentoring, Ignatius mapped out the beginning of his *Spiritual Exercises*. These would profoundly shape not only the spirituality of the Jesuits but also their work of education.

Ignatius was convinced that his experience of conversion was not unique because God is similarly at work in the life of every person, inviting us to respond. So, he crafted this "way to converse about the things of God" (his own description of the *Exercises*) so that people might see and respond to God's loving invitation in their lives. Considering our language pattern here, we can summarize that, for Ignatius, God's invitation in every person's life is to embrace *living* faith for the *reign of God*.

THE SOCIETY OF JESUS (JESUITS)

Convinced that he needed a good education himself to fulfill his life mission, Ignatius eventually made his way to the University of Paris, earned a master's degree, and was ordained a priest. Gradually he began to gather friends with whom he shared his *Spiritual Exercises*. On August 15, 1534, he and six companions chose to bond into a vowed religious order and to call themselves the Society of Jesus. Indeed, some claim that they spoke of Jesus so often that they were given the nickname Jesuits, intended as ridicule but they embraced it happily. Their core commitment was to follow in the footsteps of Jesus, empowered by the Risen Christ, and always for the reign of God. In 1540, the Society received papal approval and Ignatius was elected the first father general.

Though reluctant at first to make education their chief apostolate, the Society opened its first school for non-Jesuit students at Messina, Sicily, in 1548. By the time of Ignatius's death, July 31, 1556, there were a thousand Jesuits and seventy-four schools throughout Europe and even into India and Brazil. By 1773, when the order was suppressed by Pope Clement XIV (mostly out of envy for its success; it was restored in 1814), the number of Jesuit schools reached as high as eight hundred throughout the world.

Ignatius and the Jesuits as educators. We turn now to some of the life-giving memories that the Jesuit tradition, especially its spirituality, carry for Catholic education. Note, too, that this spirituality is often referred to as Ignatian to signal that this charism is open to all educators—not just Jesuits. There are three significant documents in the early history of the Jesuits that help integrate their spirituality into their educational charism. It can be said that their practice of education was their spirituality put to work.

The three documents are the *Constitutions of the Society of Jesus*, the *Ratio Studiorum* (literally, plan of studies) for Jesuit schools, and the *Spiritual Exercises*. We draw at least one life-giving memory for Catholic education from the *Constitutions* and *Ratio*, and then dwell at greater length on the *Spiritual Exercises*, simply because it is Ignatius's spirituality that most shapes the purpose and process of Jesuit education.

From the Constitutions. Ignatius began writing the *Constitutions of the Society of Jesus* in 1541, shortly after receiving papal approval, and continued revising them until they were officially adopted by the Society in 1554. The English translation has been through one revision since then, mostly to update the language for modern use. The *Constitutions* are concerned with the overall governance and functioning of the Society; they say little explicitly about education, which emerged only gradually as the Jesuits' central ministry. Yet the *Constitutions* are inspired throughout by the motto and sense of purpose that Ignatius chose for the Society, *ad maiorem Dei gloriam* (for the greater glory of God). This defining motto, often abbreviated AMDG, would flow into and shape the educational mission of the Society as well.

And how would education give greater glory to God? By being a means of holistic salvation in people's lives; God is glorified by human flourishing. In sum, the *Constitutions* state, all education is "to aid people to the knowledge and love of God and to the salvation of their souls" (chap. 5); this is the purpose that "constitutes" the Society and thus its members' educating of themselves and, increasingly, of others. Ignatius and the early Jesuits came to recognize education as the chief means for helping people to live lives that glorify God and find salvation—lending it a transcendent potential. Thus, the *Constitutions* reflect the spiritual foundation that education is ultimately about *saving souls*—for living well and humanly now and into eternal life hereafter.

That everything can and should be done for the greater glory of God also encouraged the Jesuit openness to pursue multiple and varied disciplines of learning, convinced that every aspect of creation is an expression of God, and thus to study it, gives God glory; no object or field of study is considered profane. While the *Constitutions* position theology at the pinnacle of the curriculum of Jesuit schools, the positive attitude toward life and all of God's creation led Jesuits into multiple disciplines of study. Even today, there are Jesuit scholars engaged in study from astrophysics to zoology (from A to Z), and in every field in between. And by high-pointing theology as the pinnacle of the curriculum, the *Constitutions* encouraged what we might call a fusion of horizons, with all the disciplines rising upward to quest and recognize the Transcendent Horizon of creation, thus enabling all study and research to be pursued *ad maiorem Dei gloriam*—AMDG.

From the Ratio Studiorum. Inspired by their own rigorous experience as students at the University of Paris, Ignatius and his early companions insisted that the Society's schools reflect a broad sweep of learning, all marked by academic excellence. Even in the earliest Jesuit schools the curriculum reflected both breadth and depth of scholarship. They honored the traditional *trivium* of grammar, rhetoric, and logic, and the *quadrivium* of arithmetic, geometry, astronomy, and music. Jesuit schools then broadened these subjects into the liberal arts (history, literature, philosophy, theology, and so on), the sciences (biology, chemistry, physics, and so forth), and the performing arts (drama, opera, and music). Jesuit schools emphasized reading the classics of the humanist tradition, Homer, Cicero, Seneca, and others; they saw conversation around good literature as a prime resource, especially for the moral formation of students.

These academic subjects stretched across the grades, beginning with teaching the youngest students to read and write and culminating with the study of theology, with a faith perspective suffusing the whole curriculum. The overall intent was to prepare graduates for *living* faith, to be good citizens in society, and to save their eternal souls.

In time, the Jesuits working in schools recognized the need for an overall and consistent plan of studies that would craft the school curriculum to be appropriate to age level, be cumulative across the grades, and be consistent throughout the growing network of Jesuit schools. Work on such a *Ratio* began in 1586, with a first draft circulated for comment and improvement, and was finally issued in 1599. It became the primary resource for the curriculum planning of Jesuit schools throughout the world, with its influence lasting into the present era.

The *Ratio* echoes the sentiments of the *Constitutions* that all Jesuit education is to be conducted "for the good of souls" (no. 40; in Farrell, 14). This requires that education "lead (people) to the knowledge and love of our Creator and Redeemer" (no. 1; in ibid., 1). Such a faith stance, then, prepares students for "the loving service of God" in the world (no. 1; in ibid., 62). So, beyond ensuring a grade appropriate, cumulative, and comprehensive curriculum, the *Ratio* proposed a faith-inspired vision toward which all the disciplines of learning could contribute, bonded in common purpose because of their shared Transcendent Horizon—God and God's reign as revealed in Jesus Christ.

While its language of "saving souls" sounds dated to its time, it can be heard now as the enhancement of people's lives and world by lending a spiritual foundation for living well and wisely. Might it invite our reflection on all the modern ways that people can lose their souls (to the market, to consumerism, to addictions, to the self alone, to the internet)? Allowing for the dated language of the *Ratio*, might Catholic education still be well considered as aiding the *salvation of souls*—empowering the hearts and spirits of students today to live well and wisely for self and others?

The second aspect is the pedagogy that was recommended for implementing the *Ratio*. Though more implied than explicitly summarized in the text, the first Jesuits championed and passed on the approach to teaching they had experienced at the University of Paris—the *modus Parisiensis* (the Paris method). The method invited teachers in Jesuit schools to employ a very participative style of teaching that actively engaged the students in the teaching/learning dynamic.

Varying as appropriate to age level and from one discipline to another, a typical learning unit would begin with the *lectio* (lesson), which was subdivided into three parts: *prelectio,* an introduction designed to actively engage student interest in the topic for study; the *lectio,* which laid out clearly the *core* or summary of what was to be taught and learned; and after these opening movements the *expositio,* a thorough explanation of the material of focus and its implications.

Even in educational systems that favor such an intentional and participative pedagogy, this is usually presumed to be the end point—when whatever is to be taught has been taught clearly and students appear to understand it. However, in the Parisian/Ignatian method this was only about halfway; students had yet to integrate the lesson into their own knowing and to make good decisions about it. So there followed a *repetitio,* in which the students, most often working in groups, reviewed the core lesson *for one another.* Thereafter, they engaged in a *disputatio,* a lively conversation and often debate around the lesson theme. The unit ended with an *exercitatio,* in which students imagined how to put their newfound learning to use and subsume it into what they already knew.

Such a participative pedagogy—in which students are actively engaged as agents of their own learning, are encouraged to understand, to "see for themselves," and to make judgments and decisions about

Does every lecture have to end w/ a christian lesson?

what is learned—would be championed later by great pedagogues like John Dewey, Paulo Freire, and Maria Montessori. It is inspiring to find it here as a constitutive feature of early Jesuit education.

From the Spiritual Exercises. As noted above, Ignatius first began to craft his *Spiritual Exercises* when he lived as a hermit in a cave near Manresa. The contemporary experience of the *Exercises* is now spread over thirty days of intense spiritual discernment and conversation with a well-trained guide. The first week encourages recognition of the reality of sin in one's life and world, but knowing that God's love and grace are more powerful than all evil. The second week focuses on the historical life of Jesus and the values he modeled. The third week meditates on Jesus's pouring out his life for others through his passion and death. And the fourth week invites the exercitant to embrace the hope offered by Jesus's resurrection and commit to living for the reign of God in the world.

Ignatius published the first edition of the *Exercises* in 1548 and continued to revise them throughout his life. At one point he came under suspicion from church authorities and was imprisoned briefly by the Inquisition; he was suspect for inviting people to a direct personal relationship with God, not one mediated exclusively through the institutional church. Ignatius certainly affirmed the role of the faith community in people's spirituality, yet he also insisted that God is present in the life of every person, inviting their personal discernment and response.

From his own experience, which he did not consider unique, Ignatius was convinced that by listening deeply to the movements of one's own heart and soul, we can discern the promptings of the Holy Spirit toward how best to live for the greater glory of God—fulfilling our ultimate purpose in life. As he notes in the "First Annotation," the *Exercises* are "methods of preparing and disposing the soul to free itself from disordered attachments . . . seeking and discovering God's will regarding the disposition of one's life for salvation" (in Tetlow, 3).

While the full experience of the *Exercises* unfolds over four weeks of intense prayer and with deep "converse about the things of God," enabled by a well-trained guide, its dynamic of spiritual discernment can be a regular practice throughout one's daily life. It is especially appropriate in moments of life decision about how best to choose for the greater glory of God. Indeed, a favorite Ignatian practice now is a daily *examen*. This amounts to taking a little time (usually at day's end) to review with God the events of a given day and to discern how one responded or failed to respond to the movements of God's Spirit at work, ending by asking for Gods mercy and grace as needed.

With the principal focus on the spiritual life, its practice of discernment and the whole dynamic of the *Exercises* lent a rich grounding for Ignatian pedagogy and for all Catholic education. For example, one can readily imagine how such careful discernment in the spiritual life would encourage an educational process of critical thinking and personal decision-making. The following five core aspects of the spirituality of the *Exercises* have particular import for the curriculum of not only Jesuit but all Catholic schools.

1. *Personal agency and responsible freedom.* The entire dynamic of the *Exercises* reflects the conviction that God engages each person as a responsible agent of their own life and invites them to discern freely how best to live it. True discernment resists false desires and social expectations and, instead, embraces one's own personal calling from God with real freedom. This requires the person to evaluate "the spirit" that may be moving them in making life-choices, being alert for true and false spirits—the latter intent to lead them astray. In this counsel Ignatius was inspired by the scripture text: "Beloved, do not believe every spirit, but test the spirits to see whether they are from God" (1 John 4:1). It is only in following the good spirits that we discern what to do with our lives and choose with true freedom.

A pointer for such discernment is that following the good spirit brings *consolation* and a sense of being true to oneself, whereas following the bad spirit brings a feeling of *desolation* and alienation from one's true self. Note well, however, that such discernment is never for one's own self-interest alone; it always has the overarching horizon of realizing the reign of God—the personal and common good of all. Indeed, we are ever faced with choosing between what the *Exercises* call "the two standards," that of Jesus and God's reign, which enhances the self and others, and the ways of the world, which do the opposite.

Such spirituality encourages a Catholic education that empowers all students to be agents in their lives and context, to choose and make their unique contribution to their own well-being and to the public realm, and to do so with responsible freedom. Instead of preparing dependent recipients or people who simply "fit in" with social expectations, or, conversely, people who just "do their own thing" regardless, Catholic education is to encourage students to embrace and develop their talents as free historical agents who can do great things with their lives, never for themselves alone, but for the common good of all.

2. *To see God in all things.* Though not explicitly stated in the *Exercises,* the intent of this favorite Ignatian phrase is writ large throughout

their dynamic and is now cited frequently to summarize the overall outlook on life that the *Exercises* encourage. Such spiritual "seeing" is to be one's dominant perspective on life in the world. Indeed, the whole spiritual dynamic of the *Exercises* encourages such a sacramental outlook in participants. The principle of sacramentality, so core to Catholic faith and high pointed in seven formal sacraments, recognizes that God is present, revealing God's will, mediating God's grace in the ordinary and everyday of life, and inviting people's lived response toward the reign of God. Catholic education is to nurture students in such sacramental consciousness and commitment.

For Ignatius, the world is the theater of God's grace. In other words, *this* is where we encounter God's initiative in our lives and are empowered to respond toward realizing our ultimate calling, what Ignatius simply calls "saving our souls." Such recognition invites us to look at everything—"wealth, fame, health, power, even life itself"—as having the potential to bring us to God and to our true selves or likewise away from God and our very selves, alienating us from whom God calls us to be (in Tetlow, 35). Again, so much depends on good discernment. To "see God in all things" logically requires beginning with what Ignatius calls the "application of the senses." By this he means an intense looking at *the real* in our lives, including the physical world around us and our daily experiences within creation; the more we "see" and recognize *the real*, the more likely we are to "see God in all things."

Ignatius would strongly encourage Catholic education that nurtures in students this sacramental outlook on life in the world. In educational terms it calls for a pedagogy that deeply engages students own lived experiences and their reflection upon them. Beyond simply "looking at" life, an Ignatian-inspired Catholic pedagogy is to nurture an outlook that sees the more in the midst of the everyday, the Ultimate in the ordinary, the Transcendent in the immanent, the Creator in the created order—again, to see God in all things and to discern how best to respond.

Ignatius insightfully notes that the key to nurturing such a sacramental consciousness is "to see with the imagination" (in Tetlow, 35). This begins, as noted above, with an "application of the senses" and taking note of one's own sensory data from the life and world around. To reflect on that data surely engages our reason and memory, and then it seems that Ignatius particularly emphasizes the imagination—most likely the least used of our three capacities of mind. The *Exercises* often propose reflections that rely heavily on imagination, for example, to imagine being in the presence of the historical Jesus, to imagine his location, what he looks like, the tone of his voice, what he might say, and so on. We elaborate such pedagogy further in the Postlude of this work. For now, note that asking imaginative questions or posing exercises that invite students to use their imagination (as well as their reason and memory) should be a hallmark of Catholic education.

3. *To engage the whole person.* It is already clear that discernment is central to Ignatian spirituality so that we live according to what God desires for us, and this to our own benefit, to that of others, and to the glory of God. Here we emphasize that for education, such discernment is to engage the whole person—reason, memory, and imagination, and then our emotions and heart as well. Remember the ultimate Ignatian guideline to right discernment is whether our hearts experience *consolation* and a felt sense of peace from the decisions we make. On the contrary, we are alerted to poor decisions by the *desolation* they bring to our hearts and emotional well-being.

Western education and its academic life in general has become colonized by the disengaged and technical rationality of modernity, as if critical reasoning about empirical data is the only reliable way of knowing. Such reasoning takes little or no account of memory or imagination, and never of one's feelings and affections; indeed, the latter are to be avoided as if they are likely to lead astray. By contrast, the *Exercises* encourage Catholic education to engage the whole person, all of students' faculties and abilities for knowing and relating in the world. The intent is to invite students toward spiritual wisdom for life as the ultimate learning outcome. Formation in such wisdom requires engaging students' hearts and hands as well as their heads.

4. *Care for the whole person who is ever to excel.* The spirituality of the *Exercises* has encouraged an emphasis in Jesuit—and Catholic—education to care for and develop the talents of the whole person. Such care entails encouraging each student "ever to excel" according to their personal gifts and toward what is "of greatest value" to their lives (no. 97; in Tetlow, 36). In Ignatian-parlance, the dual values here are often referred to by their Latin expressions *cura personalis,* "care of person," and *magis,* literally, "the more."

Cura personalis calls for education that reflects deep care for each student as a person made in the divine image and likeness, helping them to develop their particular gifts and their sense of vocation in life (what to do with their gifts). Such *care* entails developing students' academic and intellectual gifts, and likewise their spiritual, emotional, aesthetic, and physical ones. Recalling the breadth of the *Ratio* curriculum and how it reached beyond the academic, Catholic education is to develop students' aesthetic gifts through drama, art, and music, and to encourage their physical and relational development through sports and games. Therefore, *cura personalis* encourages a holistic education that cares for the whole person.

The *magis* suggests that Catholic education challenge students to reach for their best, and to settle for nothing less than excellence—whatever *their* potential. Students are to become the best possible persons they can be, according to their gifts and talents, and how they are abled or differently abled. Such encouraging of excellence is for students' own benefit and so that they put their talents to the service of others—all *ad maiorem Dei gloriam*.

5. *Community, compassion, and social justice.* Clearly, the *Exercises* encourage each person to discern and embrace their particular vocation to live for the greater glory of God. That personal spiritual journey, however, is best traveled and nurtured in and through a supportive faith community. While a Catholic school is not a parish, still, as a community grounded in the spiritual principles of Christian faith, it should provide for all participants who so desire some explicit opportunities for shared prayer, worship, and spiritual nurture—while encouraging their active participation in a "base" faith community. And Ignatius would echo the spiritual conviction of Benedict—that a Catholic school be truly catholic in its inclusivity of all students, faculty, and staff.

Furthermore, both the students and the whole school community are to be distinguished for their compassion and care for people in need. This should not be limited to a school's local context but, picking up another traditional sense of *catholic* as "universal," its care is to be without borders—reaching out far and wide. Such inclusive compassion for all, and especially for the poor of every kind, is what most gives glory to God, as the *Exercises* encourage, and, of course, as mandated by the teachings of Jesus.

In more recent times there is keener awareness in Jesuit and all Catholic education that this commitment to compassion flows into works of social justice, to address the social structures and cultural mores that cause oppression and suffering. All three of these faith-based commitments—to community, to compassion, and to social justice—are well captured in a popular Jesuit slogan that encourages students to become "men and women for and with others." That phrase originated with Fr. Pedro Arrupe, then superior general of the Jesuits, in 1973.

Ignatian spirituality indeed is a very rich tradition and with deep implications for all Catholic education—not just that of Jesuit schools. We could say much more, but it is to be hoped that these reflections have raised up some of the more distinctive aspects of the Ignatian foundations that can enrich the spiritual grounding and then the practice of all Catholic education.

For Reflection and Conversation

- What aspects of Ignatian spirituality and pedagogy do you find most attractive and why?
- What insights might you put to work in your own vocation now? Imagine some concrete steps toward their implementation?

RENEWING YOUR VOCATION AS CATHOLIC EDUCATOR

As suggested already, Jesuit education, instead of being unique, is the epitome of Catholic education. It particularly reflects the spiritual principles that put Catholic faith to work through education. For this reason much of its implications for *soul, style,* and *space* will be echoed in Part III on contemporary foundations and practices of Catholic education. Given how Jesuit pedagogy is so grounded in the spirituality of Ignatius of Loyola, let us focus here on what it might suggest for all educators.

For the educator's soul. A wisdom to be learned from Ignatius, surely, is how vital it is that educators have a spiritual foundation for their vocation and work; indeed, this is the overall aspiration of this book. Undoubtedly, we can learn much from philosophy and from social scientific research on education. Yet for Catholic education to be true to its name and its grounding in faith, its teachers and administrators need to nurture their own spirituality and put it into practice throughout their vocation as educators.

- Looking to the spirituality of Ignatius, might you consider practicing a regular *examen*, focused on your daily life? This would amount to a brief end-of-day reflection, with God as conversation partner, in which you look back over what you did that day and how it went. Then, try to recognize where the Spirit was moving and how well you responded— or not. Close with whatever prayer rises from your heart and with some resolve for the next day.

For the teaching style. There is a strong contemporary image of the spiritual as something esoteric and exclusively personal, simply a search for self-fulfillment. By contrast, Catholic spirituality, epitomized in

Ignatius of Loyola, is about putting our faith to work so as to become the best person we can be for ourselves and for the life of the world, thus living lives that give glory to God.

- How might you reflect such a humanizing spirituality in your teaching style? Consider posing exercises and questions that engage the hungers of students' hearts—their souls.
- How might you encourage students, with or without using spiritual language, to be alert for good and bad spirits in their lives, positive and negative social influences, and how to know the difference and to make wise choices between them?

For the educational space. Catholic schools typically have the outward trappings of being faith based—usually in their name, in statues or wall hangings (for example, a crucifix in the class room), in celebrating Christian holidays, in options for prayer and worship, and so on.

- Going beyond the outward trappings, imagine ways that your school can reflect more effectively its Catholic spiritual foundations and implement faith throughout the curriculum.
- How might you help to create a conversation with colleagues around your school's Catholic identity and what might need deepening or renewal?

6

Angela Merici and Mary Ward

Part II promised to raise up a few of the most life-giving memories and practitioners of the Catholic intellectual tradition that are relevant for Catholic education today. Of course, we can only touch the tips of the icebergs—though we have encountered some big ones. And there is no richer legacy for Catholic education than the witness and courage of the first women pioneers in this good work, great and brave leaders who insisted not only that women be educated but that they be educators as well. They represent a long line of great women educators who were to follow in their footsteps. Inspired by their spiritual foundations, they took educational leadership at great risk to themselves, challenging the culture of their time. And they stood against the law of the church, which continued to forbid such an active apostolate to women.

From a great host of women educators, two that we will consider in some depth here are Saint Angela Merici (1475–1540), founder of the Company of Saint Ursula in 1535 (better known as the Ursulines), and Venerable Mary Ward (1585–1645), who founded the Institute of the Blessed Virgin Mary in 1615 (also known as the IBVMs or Loreto Sisters). Joined across the years by literally hundreds of other women's orders, the Ursulines and IBVMs reflect the courageous witness of them all to the dignity and equality of women—against the grain of both church and culture.

First a parenthetical note. During the Counter-Reformation, which followed the Protestant Reformation, a host of vowed religious orders of women and men emerged and were dedicated to a variety of public ministries—to work with the sick, the poor, the blind, the orphaned, the disabled, and so on. Each order tends to have a particular *charism* that suggests the kind of work it renders and the gospel spirit it brings to doing so. An order's charism functions as a kind of "canon within the canon" of its ministry, suggesting a particular service and emphasis that it embraces for living out the gospel of God's reign in the world. Of course, many of the orders have a charism for Catholic education.

The Ursulines were the first non-cloistered religious order of women educators, and they, along with the Jesuits, were soon joined by a host of other orders of both women and men; their educational apostolate has continued to the present day. Indeed, since that era and until the recent past, Catholic education has been carried forward almost exclusively by vowed religious orders of priests, brothers, and sisters—by far too many to enumerate here. A well-known Catholic joke is that not even God can remember all of the initials for all the Catholic religious orders and what they stand for—CSJ, RSM, SDB, RSCJ, OP, and so on.

That women, especially mothers, were the mainstay to educate children in Christian faith has been true from the beginning of the church and across the centuries. Regarding more formal education, women could embrace the vowed religious life of the cloister at least since the days of leaders like Saint Brigid of Kildare (451–525) and Saint Scholastica (480–543). The sisters in such monasteries would have been taught to read in order to participate in the divine office. When young women from the ruling class received an education, the curriculum focused exclusively on how to manage a good home.

Coming into the second millennium, as noted when situating Julian of Norwich, some cloistered sisters managed to get a theological education. Most likely people like Julian came from a privileged background; learning reading, writing, arithmetic, and rhetoric, and Latin besides, was unheard of for the lower classes. Angela Merici and Mary Ward were pathfinders—even revolutionaries (and at great risk to themselves) in their insistence that (1) girls be *educated* in the liberal arts (that is, beyond domestic skills), even if they were not joining a religious order; and (2) women be their *educators* and this outside of convent cloister.

That women were forbidden to be educators in the public realm and to the general populace was long the official policy of the church. This prohibition was stated anew and officially by the Council of Trent (1545–63). To go against the directive of a General Council of the Church was hazardous, with the witch trials in full swing and the Inquisition ever vigilant for what it deemed heresy. Yet both Angela Merici and Mary Ward either ignored the prohibition of Trent or found ways around it. To appreciate their courage and the new day they launched in women's leadership through education, we need to have a sense of the dangers they faced. This may sound like an exaggerated claim, but they could literally have been burned at the stake.

THE HAMMER OF WITCHES

We already noted in Chapter 1 the inclusivity of Jesus's public ministry, highlighted by having women within his core group of disciples. All three synoptic Gospels record that the women at the foot of his cross "had followed Jesus from Galilee" (Matt 27:55), which, according to John's chronology, would mean they were with him and part of his inner circle for three years. Then the Risen Christ "appeared first to Mary Magdalene" (Mark 16:9) and made her the first witness of his resurrection to the other disciples (see John 20:17–18). In addition to Jesus's witness to equality and inclusion, the church's core beliefs included that women and men are both made in the divine image and likeness.

The early church soon failed to withstand the prejudice against women reflected in its cultural context. Pertaining to education, in particular, the church essentially embraced the position of Aristotle, repeated by Thomas Aquinas, that women have deficient reasoning and are incapable of being educated; at most, they can be prepared for the responsibilities of childrearing and homemaking.

Sadly, and surely an embarrassing memory now, the direst symbol of the church's chauvinism and misogyny throughout the Middle Ages and even into the modern era was its constant suspicion of women especially of witchcraft. Instead of an isolated example or a historical idiosyncrasy, historians agree that suspecting women of witchcraft was a constant attitude of the church of the time. It embraced without question and put widely to use the *Malleus Maleficarum*—literally "The Hammer of Witches." This was a totally prejudiced legal document used to try women for witchcraft; pretending jurisprudence, it argued that women can generally be presumed guilty of being witches.

The frequent trial of women suspected of being active witches ran from approximately 1450 to 1750—a three-hundred-year stretch. Historians estimate that some one hundred thousand innocent women were put to death (a conservative estimate, some say, and out of a far smaller population than today), following methods of investigation and trial as portrayed in the *Malleus*. From the time it was published in 1486, it functioned as the primary rationale and procedure used to try and convict suspects. Written by two Dominican friars in Northern Germany, Heinrich Kramer and James Sprenger, it was published in fourteen editions by 1520—amazing for the publishing world of the time and reflecting its widespread use. Some historians contend that it was the only document agreed upon and used by both Catholics and Protestants during the Reformation and its aftermath.

Taking as a decisive text, "You shall not permit a female sorcerer to live" (Exod 22:18), the *Malleus* constantly manipulated the scriptures to portray women as prone to witchcraft and to the darkest evils. Taken from "a bent rib of Adam," women are "of a different nature from men," intellectually far inferior and thus more likely to go astray. Ever since their creation, "the wickedness of women" knows no bounds; indeed, being "intellectually like children," they are "more prone [than men] to abjure the faith." Worse still, "since they are weak, they find an easy and secret manner to vindicate themselves by witchcraft." In an extraordinary instance of male projection, the text assures that "all witchcraft comes from carnal lust, which in women is insatiable." In sum, women "are prone to be witches" and are determined "to exterminate the faith" (*Malleus Maleficarum* I.6).

While today we find such a caricature horrendous, ludicrous if not so sad, the negativity toward women that the *Malleus* expressed resulted in the conviction and execution of countless innocent women—hung, beheaded, or more likely burned at the stake. This heightens our appreciation for the extraordinary courage of the women who stepped forward to found religious orders to educate and be the educators of women—against the law of the church. Indeed, it was precisely the execution of eight young women as witches in the Italian town of Brescia, where Angela Merici was living at the time, that prompted her to found the Ursulines, recognizing that what made the young women so vulnerable was their lack of education.

For Reflection and Conversation

- Perhaps your school was originally founded by a religious order of sisters, priests, or brothers. What do you know about them and their charism?
- How can that charism continue to inspire today, and who will carry it forward, especially as the numbers of vowed religious decline?
- What can we learn now from the role of the Christian churches in the witch trials? What legacy do we need to unlearn?

ANGELA MERICI (1475–1540)

Angela Merici was born in 1475 in Desenzano, a town in what was then known as the Republic of Venice. She came from a wealthy family and at sixteen, upon the death of both parents, found herself in charge of the family estate. In 1506, she had a spiritual experience or vision and felt called, as she later wrote, "to found a society of women in Brescia," a town about twenty miles away. Ten years later, she was invited to Brescia by a family friend. While staying there, she experienced a witch trial and, as noted above, witnessed eight young women being put to death. This was her catalyst; she became determined to begin a religious community to educate young women and to help prepare them for a better life.

Angela Merici the educator. In 1531, Angela gathered twelve women friends, many of whom she had come to know from her membership in the Third Order of Saint Francis (a non-vowed lay Christian community). They were to continue to live in their own homes and to enter into a spiritual bond, meet regularly for prayer and support, and begin to offer a holistic education—not one just for domesticity—to the girls and young women of Brescia. On November 25, 1535, Angela formally established the Company of Saint Ursula—the Ursulines. Their primary work was to be as educators—the first non-cloistered order of women to be so constituted—though they worked to care for the sick and needy as well. They were formally approved by Pope Pius III in 1544, a year before the Council of Trent opened.

Not unusual for the time, Angela left little formal writing. However, she did craft the founding documents of the Ursulines; we find these in her "Counsels to the Local Leaders" and a "Testament" that she wrote at the end of her life. Together they indicate her core values and philosophy of education. I draw out two that are of particular relevance to Catholic education and teachers in our time—and always: *promote social equality through education* and *love your students.*

Equality through education. Angela founded the Ursulines precisely to improve the quality of life for young women, convinced that they deserved an education on a par with that available to young men. Her writings encourage the Ursulines to lift up their students through holistic education and formation. To this end Angela was convinced that, within their own communities, the Ursulines should practice the kind of inclusion and respect for every member that they were to model to their students. She wanted her sisters to be consistent, putting their own communal spirituality and principles to work in how they were to educate young women.

To begin with, the order was to welcome members from all ranks of society, with all being treated as equals (many of the later orders

that emerged of both men and women had hierarchies of membership).
Then they were to function like a democracy, an amazing commitment for the time—long before democracy was the social pattern. In
spiritual terms she was convinced that the Holy Spirit works through
the discernment of the whole community and thus each member's
voice was to be heard and taken into account. "Consult together and
examine carefully what concerns the government of the Company . . .
according as the Holy Spirit inspires you" ("Testament," Legacy 7).
The sisters were to engage the active involvement and participation of
their students likewise!

Confident in the guidance of the Spirit, Angela had an amazing
openness to the future and to making changes as needed. She instructed the community: "If with change of times and circumstances
it becomes necessary to make fresh rules, or to alter anything, then
do so with prudence . . . as the Holy Spirit will direct you" ("Last
Legacy"). In her final counsel to her sisters, she urged them to "keep
your faith and hope alive" ("Last Counsel") —a courageous sentiment in their context.

For Catholic education. Lest we forget, Angela Merici reminds us that
the most eminent purpose of Catholic education is to form people in
life-giving ways, to enhance them as human beings, and thus to contribute to the common good of society as well. Rather than preparing
students simply to become producers and consumers, or to "fit in" to
the social structures, the ultimate political and spiritual goal of Catholic
education is humanization of students and reform of society—toward
inclusion, respect, and justice for all. Angela seemed to know this well
and can help us to remember it today.

The fact that she wanted education for girls in her time was nothing
short of prophetic. Our educating should likewise be prophetic, on the
cutting edge of social awareness, educating to enhance the well-being
of every person and the common good of all. To be faithful to Angela's
original charism in our time, Catholic education should be especially
opposed to all forms of sexism, chauvinism, and discrimination on the
basis of gender or sexual orientation.

Love of students. The discipline in the schools of Angela's time and for
long after was marked by cruel corporal punishment (sadly, often citing
the Bible for legitimation). The great philosopher of education John
Amos Comenius (1592–1670), writing a hundred years after Angela,
described the schools as "slaughterhouses"—so severe was the physical
discipline. It is amazing, then, that Angela strictly forbade all corporal

punishment in Ursuline schools and instead urged her sisters to shower their students with loving care. "Love all your daughters equally and do not show preferences for one more than another because they are all God's children" ("Eighth Counsel").

And she repeated this instruction often: "The more you love them, the greater care you will have for them" ("First Counsel"). She urged her sisters to "be kind and tender with your children" ("Second Counsel") and "surround them with real love" ("Second Legacy"). When discipline is needed, "correct them with love and charity" ("Eighth Counsel") and certainly never with corporal punishment.

For Catholic education. We can be inspired by Angela to love our students, all of them, not just our favorites. When we recall the great teacher(s) we have had, and hopefully all of us have had more than one, invariably we remember those who truly cared about us. It is not easy to "love them all," especially the challenging students, and yet this is the spiritual commitment asked of our vocation as educators. Certainly, there should never be corporal punishment in a Catholic school. When discipline needs to be administered, it should be done with kindness and with a sense of restorative justice—enabling the perpetrator to somehow "make up" for whatever the infringement of discipline might have been.

After Angela's time the Ursulines continued to grow and spread, first throughout Italy, then into other countries of Europe, and eventually to "the ends of the earth," providing education in the spirit of their founder. They came to Quebec from Paris in 1639 and were the first order of religious women dedicated to the education of girls in North America. The first Ursulines to arrive in the United States came to Mobile, Alabama, in 1719; again, they were the first order of vowed religious women to work in the country.

Interestingly, when the Council of Trent expressly forbade women religious to teach or have any such work outside of the cloister, it likely had the Ursulines in mind—they were the most obvious candidates for this prohibition. And yet they went on teaching, finding imaginative ways to circumvent Trent's mandate. Might the example of Angela's resistance back then be an inspiration regarding some church prohibitions in our own day?

For Reflection and Conversation

- What stands out for you from this brief introduction to Angela Merici?

- What would it take and what might it teach to have a "democratic spirit" in your classroom?

MARY WARD (1585–1645)

In the two-thousand-year history of Christian faith, there are few women more amazing than Mary Ward (other than the woman whose name she bears—Mary the mother who first taught Jesus). Simply stated, Mary Ward insisted on the full equality of women with men, and this against overwhelming sociocultural odds and at great risk to her own safety.

The Inquisition, stretching from the twelfth into the early nineteenth centuries, was designed to try for heresy people who appeared to deviate from official church teaching or practices, and if they were unrepentant, to imprison and even execute them as heretics. While the witch trials noted above were part of this cultural atmosphere, they were focused primarily on deterring magical practices. The Inquisition had a more doctrinal function—to stomp out anything contrary to official Catholic teaching and practice. (By the nineteenth century the Inquisition's function was renamed the Holy Office, and today it is the Congregation for the Doctrine of the Faith, and with a more positive than negative approach to its function.)

For her insistence on the equality of women, and in particular that girls receive an education comparable to boys, Mary was under suspicion and resistance from the church throughout her life—constantly threatened and eventually arrested for a time by the Inquisition. And though she died an apparent failure, with her community in ruins and officially suppressed by the church (1631), she kept hope alive to the very end of her life—and after it.

Her spirit and dream of a women's religious order serving outside the cloister to educate girls was revived some forty years after her death and lives on today in the Institute of the Blessed Virgin Mary (IBVMs or Loreto Sisters) and now reaching throughout the world. (This is a different order from the Sisters of Loretto—two "t"s—an American order founded in Kentucky in 1812). To appreciate this amazing woman and her early championing of what we know now as women's rights, we need to situate her in her historical context.

Elizabethan England. In 1527, King Henry VIII of England requested that Pope Clement VII annul Henry's marriage to Catherine of Aragon so that he could marry Anne Boleyn. The dispensation was refused repeatedly, and eventually Henry had himself declared head of the church in England (1534). Among other things, he claimed the right to grant such dispensations, which he did for himself, to name bishops, and to dissolve the monasteries (1535–40), commandeering their lands and properties for the Crown. Henry, however, and the church in England retained many of the features and practices of traditional Catholic faith.

Under Henry's son, Edward VI (1547–53), England moved further toward forging a national church, with no allegiance to Rome and more in line with the Protestant reforms. Edward issued a *Book of Common Prayer* and *Forty-Two Articles of Faith* that reflected the Reformation movement, ordering these to be embraced by all. He was succeeded, however, by Queen Mary I (1553–58), a devout and overly zealous Catholic (also known as Bloody Mary for her execution of Protestants), who ascended the throne and brought about a Catholic restoration.

This going back and forth ceased, at least for a while, with the ascension to the throne and long reign of the Protestant Queen Elizabeth I (1558–1603). Elizabeth favored the Anglican faith (by then the English version of Catholicism) and allowed practice of the more reformed Protestant faiths (Puritans, Calvinists) as well. In 1570, however, Pope Pius V excommunicated Queen Elizabeth "and all who obey her" and foolishly directed English Catholics to rebel against her. Elizabeth responded by making it treason to practice the Catholic faith or to obey the pope; the penalty for those convicted was to be hung, drawn, and quartered. There were innumerable Catholic martyrs at this time.

In sum, Mary Ward grew up in what was by then a predominantly Protestant country, at least in governance, and where, between 1534 and 1689, there was intermittent and often severe persecution of Catholics in England. This was all the more intense under the Puritan Oliver Cromwell, who ruled as Lord Protector from 1653 to 1658; at that time many Catholics were martyred for their faith. Under King Charles II the monarchy was restored in 1660, and in 1689 the British Parliament passed the Bill of Rights. This strongly favored Protestant Christians, but at least ended the active persecution of Catholics in England. (Persecution continued under English rule in Ireland until the Act of Catholic Emancipation of 1829.)

Mary Ward was born on January 23, 1585—during the most intense Elizabethan persecution of Catholics—at Mulwith near Ripon in Yorkshire, England. Her parents were Marmaduke and Ursula Ward. Mary decided to become a nun and at twenty-one went to Saint-Omer, then in the Netherlands, and entered a Poor Clare convent there. (The persecution in England had forced convents to close, go underground, or move overseas.) After three years Mary decided that she wanted a public apostolate rather than the contemplative life of the Poor Clares.

Mary felt called to fulfill what always guided her as the greatest commandment—to love God and neighbor as oneself by directly serving those most in need. Mary perceived the greatest social need of the time to be the education of girls and young women. In 1609, Mary gathered a group of women to join her in her new apostolate of giving a well-rounded education to young women; the community was first located in Saint-Omer. Mary wished to found a community that would work outside the cloister, not have the responsibility of reciting the daily Divine Office together, and be self-governing—independent of the local bishop and answering directly to the pope. Their apostolate would be to educate girls and young women, her lifelong passion; she would educate girls the way the Jesuits were educating boys, and in a similar holistic and formative pedagogy.

Originally known as the English Ladies (avoiding the term *sisters* for safety reasons), her community grew quickly, with many local groups and schools emerging, mostly outside England. Eventually, their schools stretched across Europe into cities like Brussels, Liege, Vienna, Munich, Prague, Venice, Bologna, Naples, Lyons, Paris, and the list goes on.

In 1615, Mary drew up a *Rule of Life* for her community, now officially named the Institute of the Blessed Virgin Mary. In 1616, Mary prepared and sent a petition to Pope Paul V, asking that her women's congregation for the education of girls be approved and placed "under his guardianship and protection" (that is, not under local bishops). Among other things, she assured him that the sisters would be well formed in the "examen of conscience" and "other spiritual exercises" (in Chambers, 378).

This was a bold petition in that it directly contravened what we noted already in the prohibition of the Council of Trent against women religious having a public apostolate and being independent of the local bishop. At least one of the council's reasons was that the church did not want women to be working in ministerial services *alongside priests*. Mary had no such hesitation!

Pope Paul V gave no clear response to Mary's petition, so in 1621, she decided to go to Rome to plead her cause in person before Pope Gregory XV. Mary, with some companions, walked to Rome from where she lived in Saint-Omer, a journey of some two thousand miles; it took two months.

Though Pope Gregory XV seemed open to her cause, his cardinals were opposed, and Mary's petition was denied. Mary decided to stay on in Rome and to open a school there in order to prove the value of her work. Her school had great success, but the cardinals closed it after four years and ordered her to cease her educational work. Contrary to their directive, Mary reached out to found communities and schools in other Italian and European cities. For this explicit disobedience, she was imprisoned for a time by the Inquisition, held in a Poor Clare convent in Munich. Upon release, Mary went on founding her IBVM schools undeterred, even while the church continued to ban them and condemn her personally.

Indeed, Mary would visit Rome at least three times across the years seeking official approval for her community; she was always declined. In many ways she was a permanent pilgrim, visiting the numerous European cities where her community was becoming established and founding schools, always traveling on foot. (She dressed as a pilgrim; apparently they were generally respected by the brigands and robbers.)

In 1628, Pope Urban VIII finally issued a clear edict of suppression of the IBVMs; sisters were turned out of their convents and their property given over to the local bishops. Undeterred, Mary returned to Rome to renew her request directly to Pope Urban VIII. Again approval was denied, and though Urban seemed somewhat appreciative of Mary's work, she was officially declared a heretic—for no reason other than her commitment to educate girls. Furthermore, her community was totally banned by papal edict in 1631. This took effect first in the Papal States and Naples—the pope's places of immediate civil power—and soon thereafter throughout Europe.

Amazingly, Mary never gave up the struggle. She returned to England in 1639, where she immediately opened a convent school in London—clearly contravening the church's prohibition. The outbreak of civil war (Cromwell against the Crown) forced her to flee to her native Yorkshire in 1642, where she lived with some of her original community in a village outside the city of York. Mary died there on January 30, 1645.

Some forty years after Mary's death, a small band of her original sisters, now very old, gathered with Frances Bedingfeld as their leader (as a young sister she had been present at Mary's deathbed). They met at the village of Micklegate Bar, near York, and founded what came to be known as the Bar Convent (now the oldest surviving Catholic convent in England). It became the motherhouse of a renewed IBVM community, following a modified version of Mary's Institute and continuing her educational charism. In 1877, Mary's Institute was finally approved by the church, some 268 years after its founding. It carries forward Mary's spirit and charism today.

Mary Ward the educator. Catholic educators today can be greatly inspired by Mary Ward. Her courage and determination alone make her an amazing inspiration, especially regarding difficult issues in the church. The enduring witness of her life to her deep conviction regarding the education of girls and young women is breathtaking. Here we raise up only two spiritual foundations she suggests for Catholic educators today: (1) Mary's convictions of the *innate goodness of the human person* (a soul-sister to Julian of Norwich) to be nurtured and grown by good education, and (2) the mandate to educate toward the *full equality* of women, in church and society.

Innate Goodness of the human person. Reflecting her admiration of Jesuit education, Mary insisted on a holistic curriculum in her schools. She saw to it that they taught the basics of math, reading, and writing—in people's native language, rather than Latin—and then pushed out into the humanities, having the girls read classic literature. Grounded in the liberal arts tradition, she was convinced that the classics are a key resource in moral formation, precisely because they reflect the great issues and questions of life and imagine how best to respond. She was enthused about the graphic and performing arts like drawing and painting, drama, and music. Mary strongly encouraged the art of rhetoric and active debates, believing that young women need to know how to take a position and present a strong argument in the public realm.

As she stated in her petition of 1616 to Pope Paul V, Mary intended her community "to instruct young girls from the earliest years in piety, Christian morals and the liberal arts, so that they may afterwards according to their respective vocations profitably embrace the secular or the religious state." She was convinced that "such education of girls" would be a "means of salvation" for both teachers and pupils (in Chambers, 376–77).

By way of moral formation Mary had an even more positive approach than Ignatius. Recall that the first week of the *Spiritual Exercises* begins with an emphasis on the fact that we are all sinners, albeit in the hands of a merciful God. By contrast, Mary's starting point was to emphasize the essential goodness of the person, because all are created and ever graced by God. This means that we have the potential, by nature and God's grace, to live a virtuous life. For Mary, even our emotions and affections can draw us toward doing good and becoming our best selves, as God desires; by contrast, the spirituality of the time portrayed human affections as likely to lead people astray and into sin.

Mary believed that our desire to be good "comes forth of love, and a desire that all should be good [rather] than to keep them [the students] from sinning." With positive formation, all can have "a ready mind and courageous heart" for doing good (in Cover, 161). Note here the contrast with the understanding of women proposed in the *Malleus Malifacarum*—as prone to evil and dominated by lust. Mary's proposed anthropology, and especially her understanding of the equal rights and dignity of women, was diametrically opposed to the dominant ethos of her time, which, sadly, is still true too often in our time in both church and state.

For Catholic education. Echoing again, a major component of Catholic education is the moral formation of its students. This commitment should run throughout the curriculum, with particular potential for ethical formation from reading good literature. Furthermore, the Catholic intellectual tradition insists that both faith and reason be called upon for moral discourse toward formation. Catholic educators should presume and draw upon the natural law within people's souls *and* likewise teach the moral norms—commandments, codes, and virtues—as reflected in Christian faith. With this combination of faith and reason, those norms can be made persuasive, not simply as mandates from "on high" but crafted to appeal to the innate goodness and spiritual hunger in people. Catholic education has the potential to make such dual appeal to people's heads and hearts, and what a missed opportunity if it does not.

The particular wisdom for us to learn from Mary Ward is that such formation needs the spiritual foundation of a positive anthropology. This means seeing the person as disposed more toward good than evil, and being convinced that our efforts to live rightly are encouraged and sustained by God's grace. Pedagogically, it seems far wiser and more productive to portray such a positive self-understanding to young people rather than a negative one. This wisdom reflects a common insight from the social sciences concerning moral formation; if we project onto young people an expectation to be and do what is good, they are more likely to so choose and grow in the disposition. Instead of emphasizing or harping upon their sinfulness, Catholic education should presume and explicitly encourage the potential goodness of its students.

Full equality of women. That Mary insisted on the ability of women to take on the same work men were doing—"education and other works of Christian charity" (in Chambers, 376)—reflects her sense of their total equality. She wanted women to forge a new way of doing good through education and in the midst of the world. In gist, she and her daughters wanted to "embrace the religious state and at the same time to devote ourselves to the performance of those works of Christian charity towards our neighbor that cannot be undertaken in convents" (in Chambers, 379).

Mary wanted "to follow a mixed kind of life" and this "as we hold Christ our Lord and Master to have taught his disciples" (in Chambers, 376). It is commonly agreed that the church's rejection of all such petitions at the time and its insistence that women religious remain cloistered were precisely out of fear of them working in functions of ministry alongside priests—and being perceived as on equal footing.

Mary, for her part, was totally committed to the equality of women with men—an amazing consciousness for a person of her time and culture. We hear this commitment explicitly in her famous exchange regarding "but women." Apparently, when Mary's first petition to the pope in Rome for approval was being discussed, "a Jesuit Father" present made the sexist comment, "when all is said and done, they are but women." Upon hearing of this putdown, Mary wrote: "I would [like to] know what you think he meant by this speech of his, 'but women.' There is no such difference between men and women that women may not do great things, as we have seen by the example of many saints. . . . Wherein are we so inferior to other creatures that they should term us 'but women.'? For what think you of the word 'but women'? as if we were in all things inferior to some other crea-ture which I suppose to be man! Which I dare to be bold to say is a lie, and, with respect to the good Father, may say it is an error" (in Littlehales, 79).

Mary makes clear that her deep conviction of her own equality and the equality of all women with men arose from her spirituality. She writes on another occasion: "There was a Father who came into England whom I heard say that he would not for a thousand of worlds be a woman, because he thought a woman could not apprehend God. I answered nothing, but only smiled, although I could have answered him, by the experience I have to the contrary. I could have been sorry for his want. . . . His want is in experience." (in Littlehales, 80). Mary knew God and God's love for her from her own spiritual experiences; she saw the "Jesuit Father" as simply lacking in such experience.

For Catholic education. We return often throughout to the responsibility of Catholic education to educate for justice. As an aspect of such justice here, and to honor the memory of Mary Ward, let us highlight the mandate to educate for total equality between women and men, in church as well as society. For the church, in particular, the struggle to have women work with full equality alongside priests, especially in holy orders, is still a vision to be realized. There is a growing conversation, however, even among church leaders like Pope Francis, about women being admitted to the diaconate. If admitted to one holy order by ordination, a logical question would be, why not to the other two—priesthood and episcopacy?

It is also commonly agreed among Catholic theologians that the Apostolic Letter of Pope John Paul II of 1994, *Ordinatio Sacerdotalis*, denying priesthood to women, does not meet the criteria in Catholic theology to be an infallible teaching of the universal church. In other words, even in official Catholic circles, the ordination of women can still be considered an open question. As appropriate to age level and context, Catholic education should encourage such conversation. Meanwhile, and as Mary Ward well recognized and witnessed, Catholic education can and should be a powerful instrument for raising up the full equality and dignity of women throughout church and society.

For Reflection and Conversation

- How can you be inspired by Mary Ward's courage and her commitment to equal human rights for all persons, both in church and society?
- What do you imagine kept Mary's hopes alive—against great odds? What sustains your hopes?
- How can you be a beacon of hope for your students?

A GREAT CLOUD OF WITNESSES

Since the embrace by the Jesuits and the Ursulines of an educational apostolate outside of the cloister, there have been myriad religious orders of priests, brothers, and sisters that have carried forward the mission of Catholic education. This vast system of schools, from kindergarten to research universities throughout the world, has been shaped by the Catholic intellectual tradition, combining those partnerships of reason and faith, science and revelation, instruction and formation, knowledge and values, and so on.

+ Cath Int Trad has been used to support chauvinism; must be resisted from the outside

The dominance of vowed religious faculty and administrators prevailed in Catholic schools until the Second Vatican Council. For example, in 1960 there were approximately 112,000 vowed religious working in US Catholic schools; today there are about 3,700, constituting less than 3 percent of the faculty and staff, the rest being laypeople. This lay faculty and staff must be as well prepared and committed as any of its religious order predecessors to continue this good work. Meanwhile, we can be well inspired by remembering those shoulders on which we stand!

To conclude Part II and its search for spiritual foundations in the history of Catholic education and its Catholic intellectual tradition, let's consider very briefly two more founders of religious orders that have served with great distinction across the years. First, representative of all the many orders of religious brothers that have emerged, we turn to the pioneer educator Jean-Baptiste de la Salle (1651–1719). Then, to represent all other orders of vowed religious women that were subsequently established after the Ursulines and with education as their primary apostolate, we consider the pathfinder Saint Elizabeth Ann Seton (1774–1821), founder of the American expression of the Sisters of Charity.

Note, however, that these are two of the literally thousands of religious orders that continue to work in Catholic education to this day. The vowed religious life dedicated to Catholic education that began originally in the Northern Hemisphere—and has waned there—is now flourishing in the Southern Hemisphere. There are, for example, over five hundred indigenous women's orders in Africa, almost all involved in the work of Catholic education. Even in a context like communist-ruled Vietnam, there are over three hundred indigenous orders of vowed religious women and men who work as much as permitted in Catholic education. And in all contexts and cultures, the vowed religious are being joined and typically far outnumbered by lay Catholic educators. Let de la Salle, originally a diocesan priest, and Elizabeth Ann Seton, originally a widowed mother, be representative of them all.

Jean-Baptiste de la Salle. Jean-Baptiste de la Salle founded the Institute of the Brothers of the Christian Schools, known now as the Christian Brothers, among other names; it was the first religious order to have only brothers and no priests. He began his first school in Rheims (ca. 1680), and Lasallian schools spread out from there, throughout France first and then the world. His defining passion was to rescue poor boys from exploitation, crime, and destruction by giving them a good education. Again, in a long line of Catholic educators, he saw education as the most effective and lasting means of social reform.

A central emphasis of Jean-Baptiste de la Salle was that the brothers were to love their students and develop a positive and life-giving relationship with them. To this end he urged the brothers to embrace a spirituality that would nurture their own path to holiness of life by shaping how they taught and were present to their students. In other words, brothers were to teach so that they educated the boys and deepened their own growth in holiness. For such spirituality Jean-Baptiste constantly pointed his brothers toward Jesus as their model of loving service. This is reflected well in a slogan attributed to de la Salle that students in Lasallian schools—and many others besides—recite aloud and often throughout the school day: "Live, Jesus, in our hearts, forever."

Elizabeth Ann Seton. Elizabeth Ann Seton, the first US-born person to be formally canonized a saint (1975), founded the first free Catholic girls' school in America at Emmitsburgh, Maryland, in 1810. Raised an Episcopalian in an elite New York family, Elizabeth was married at nineteen, had five children, was widowed at twenty-nine and became a convert to Catholicism. Throughout her life she was involved in caring for the poor, beginning as a young woman growing up in New York, where she often participated in direct service. After her conversion to Catholicism, Elizabeth came in contact with the Sisters of Charity, a French order that had been founded in 1633 by Saint Louise de Marillac in collaboration with Saint Vincent de Paul. Elizabeth went on to found an American expression of the Sisters of Charity.

The order's charism was to move beyond direct service by individual persons and to organize a response that would address the *causes* of poverty. Elizabeth discerned that the most effective organized response to dire poverty was to provide a good education, which is a long-term social strategy, but a lasting one. The Sisters of Charity, along with countless communities of vowed religious women, have carried forward the good work of Catholic education in the United States and beyond ever since.

RENEWING YOUR VOCATION AS CATHOLIC EDUCATOR

Again, we close with a more in-depth reflection on the educator's *soul*, teaching *style,* and educational *space*. The visionary witnesses of Angela Merici and Mary Ward offer a rich treasury to appropriate and make our own as Catholic educators, as do the examples of Jean-Baptiste de la Salle and Elizabeth Ann Seton. The more we take their legacies to heart, the more we will experience the rich potential of our vocation in students' lives.

For the educator's soul. One of the church's fears in trying to confine vowed religious women to the cloistered life was to keep them from working alongside priests, fearful, among other reasons, that they might ever be perceived as priestly. In a biblical sense, however, all educators, then and now, exercise a priestly function. The Bible portrays the priest's role in the faith community as both to instruct the people (Jer 18:18) and to offer praise and worship to God (Ezek 44:15–16). In this sense being a teacher is a profoundly priestly function; the more we instruct our students to become fully alive, the more they give glory to God (Saint Irenaeus).

- Reflect on what it means for your own sense of vocation to see your work of teaching as priestly.
- Angela Merici and Mary Ward became teachers against great opposition. Recall how you came into this vocation. Are you at peace with this calling? Whether you answer yes or no, what is your response and action?

For the teaching style. Both Angela Merici and Mary Ward, as well as those following their example, like Jean-Baptiste de la Salle and Elizabeth Ann Seton, encourage Catholic educators to embrace a deep commitment to the equality, dignity, and inclusion of every student. Yet, most likely, we have all experienced educational contexts where some seemed more welcome and included than others.

- How can you deepen a teaching style that makes all feel included as active participants?
- How might you "go the extra mile" to draw in and affirm your reluctant or insecure students?

For the educational space. Both Angela Merici and Mary Ward encourage us to show love and care for our students as persons, encouraging them to recognize and grow into their own innate goodness.

- How can you create an educational space where students feel loved and valued for themselves and encouraged to live into their own potential?
- How might you structure your educational environment to encourage students to affirm and encourage one another instead of being in competition?

Part III

SPIRITUAL FOUNDATIONS FOR POSTMODERN CATHOLIC EDUCATION

Part III draws upon contemporary theology as relevant to fundamental issues for Catholic education in our time. These issues include how we understand the *human person*, the *community of persons*, and our *lives in the world;* and then how to *know* and promote knowledge, how to live with *public faith*, how to craft *religious education* in a diverse Catholic school, and a *pedagogy* to employ throughout the whole curriculum. Although these questions are not exhaustive, our responses to them are foundational for the practice of Catholic education in our postmodern time. As we take our convictions in faith and implement them throughout the curriculum of a school, they are integral to the *spiritual foundations* of the entire mission.

To lay such spiritual foundations, we continue to draw upon the teaching praxis of Jesus and the hope for all inspired by the Risen Christ (Part I). We build upon the wisdom already gleaned from some great exponents of the Catholic intellectual tradition (Part II). Then, drawing upon a contemporary Catholic theology, we are well positioned in this final section to weave together a philosophy, or better still—being faith based—a spirituality to inspire and guide the practice of Catholic education in our postmodern age.

Coupling the foundational themes to be addressed in Part III, we reflect on the person as person and the person in community, encouraging educators to craft, in more formal terms, their own anthropology and sociology of human beings, so significant for how we educate (Chapter 7). Then we reflect on the outlook on life and way of being in the world that Catholic education should propose, and the ways of knowing likely to encourage such a posture and worldview; this is more formally known as our cosmology and epistemology (Chapter 8). Then we reflect explicitly on the *public* nature of the *living* faith that Catholic education is to foster and thus prepare citizens committed to compassion and justice for all in civil society (Chapter 9).

In Chapter 10 we imagine how to craft the religious education curriculum of a Catholic school so that all might *learn from* it and Catholic students *learn into* their identity in faith. Our postmodern context and the growing religious diversity of both students and staff present religious education in Catholic schools with new challenges and fresh opportunities.

The Postlude draws together wisdom and insights to propose what might be a *Catholic pedagogy*. It offers a general approach to teaching across the disciplines that reflect the deep values of Catholic education as suggested in the previous ten chapters.

Our further digging into scripture and tradition with these contemporary questions remains far from exhaustive. Note, however, that I also elaborated extensively on the theological foundations of Catholic education in *Educating for Life* (1998); that book may still be helpful. The statement, here, is more precise and intentionally crafted to our present situation, some twenty-five years later. Also, and unlike the previous volume, this book explicitly grounds responses to foundational questions for Catholic education in the teaching praxis of Jesus and the grace of the Risen Christ—an enrichment, surely. Furthermore, we continue to mine more spiritual wisdom for your own *soul* as educator, for your teaching *style*, and for the educational *space* you create for and with your students.

7

Persons in Community and a
Community of Persons

The chapter title signals that we address together the dual features of our human estate, proposing that we are ever both personal and social beings, with the two deeply intertwined. This reflects the classic Catholic proposal that we live life best as persons in community and as a community of persons. How we understand ourselves as persons shapes our understanding of society, which has the reciprocal function of enhancing the personhood of its members and the common good of all.

Such a sense of our communal personhood and its correlative understanding of society arises from some deep structures of Catholic Christian faith that we review in this chapter. Note first, however, that this position often swims against the contemporary tide. As Charles Taylor summarizes, modernity "gave an unprecedented primacy to the individual," making individuals and their "rights" the guiding purpose of society, with little to no responsibility for the common good of all. Catholic faith, by contrast, continues to see the person as an individual -cum-social being. It emphasizes the responsibility of society to promote the dignity and value of the person and likewise the responsibilities of the person to the common good of their society. In other words, our anthropology and sociology are two sides of the same coin. This calls for Catholic education that promotes both the personal good of students and the common good of society, with these commitments working hand in hand.

The human sciences have rich fields of scholarship in anthropology and sociology, one focusing on the human person per se and the other on their sociocultural context. When approached from a Catholic theological perspective, however, and in particular for the practice of education, the two perspectives, personal and social, are deeply intertwined. If at times we appear to separate them, this is only for the

119

sake of analysis; in practice, we are ever persons in community and are to function as a community of persons. Catholic education is to prepare students to live their lives into the full potential of their own communal personhood and in ways that enhance the common good of their society.

Of all the foundational issues for Catholic education, nothing is more significant than how we understand the human person and the kind of collaborative existence and social living for which God creates us. Indeed, all the themes that follow—our outlook on life, our ways of knowing, our hopes for life in the world, our politics, and so on—are all elaborations of ourselves as relational human beings to one another, to God, and to all of God's creation. Even a moment's reflection will attest that how we perceive who people are and can become should shape the education we offer—ever enhancing their humanization. Education is to enable students to live into the full potential of their shared human estate and ready each to make their own unique contribution to the well-being of their society. Nothing is more formative of this outcome than the quality of education we offer.

Perhaps a contextual note for the United States will highlight what is at stake here. Many commentators, echoing Taylor above, claim that America typically gives too much priority to individual rights. Historically, this reflects the influence of individualistic philosophers like John Locke (1632–1704) and David Hume (1711–1776), both much in vogue at the foundation of the "great American experiment." While their championing of individual rights was a positive step toward liberty and justice for all, their position was selective to favor white males, and overstated, as if individual rights always are paramount and have priority over the common good. It is as if we are first and foremost individuals who may choose to join a society rather than innately social beings who become our "selves" only in community and share responsibility for the welfare of all.

As a result of this undue American emphasis on individual rights, private citizens can own an AK-47 rifle that can shoot ten bullets per second and claim that this is their *right* as individuals. Significantly, for every one hundred guns owned by American citizens, the British have three; for every one hundred acts of gun violence against self or others in America, Britain has three. We pay a very high price for what we claim is our individual right. Or, again, any person in the United States can spew Nazi-like hatred and claim this as their right to free speech. In Britain or any other Western democracy, they would be arrested immediately.

✳ deficiency in the liberal
  individualist tradition

As to be expected, then, this emphasis on the individual pervades American public education. So much of it now is focused almost exclusively on "standards" and academic "accountability," but with all focused on flourishing the individual student. Thus, the intent of the Common Core State Standards (2009) was to provide an education in which "Every Student Succeeds" (2015) in the "Race to the Top Program" (2009). In other words, education's purpose is to prepare young people to have the knowledge and skills needed to succeed as individuals in the labor market within a competitive global economy. That they have communal and civic responsibilities is, at best, an afterthought. Even the token civics course—yes, one semester—in American high schools has been largely set aside to make way for more STEM (science, technology, engineering, and mathematics) classes. (In Chapter 8 we elaborate on how Catholic education must resist this narrowing of our ways of knowing—our underlying epistemology—to favor a more holistic one.)

Of course, being realistic, it is imperative that education provides students with what they require to get a job and earn a livelihood. But to embrace this as the total purpose of education reflects a very individualized horizon for the human person and falls far short of their full flourishing as social persons who contribute to the common good of all.

As usual, the Catholic intellectual tradition favors a "both/and" position, affirming the agency and rights of the person and also the need for a society in which all have social responsibilities to contribute to the shared welfare. Instead of individualism (as in unbridled capitalism) or social totalitarianism (as in communism), Catholic schools need an anthropology *and* sociology that can inspire education for both the personal and common good. I propose that we have such a model reflected in the teaching and praxis of Jesus.

For Reflection and Conversation

- Reflecting on your own sense of human personhood, what do you recognize as some dominant features and capacities? (Don't overlook the obvious; for example, we are embodied beings, we can think and reflect, and so on.)
- How do you understand the communal aspect of the human person and our responsibilities for one another? How might this shape what and how you teach?

JESUS'S ANTHROPOLOGY

To summarize Jesus's anthropology-cum-sociology approach at the outset: (1) he deeply affirmed human agency and its *potential* for great good—posing the highest ideals to disciples; (2) all four Gospels reflect that we are communal beings, responsible to care for one another and the *common good* of all, and needing a faith community to live as disciples; and (3) Jesus also recognized our proclivity for sin and the reality of human suffering, and yet emphasized God's mercy for sinners and the *hope for all* lent by God's grace.

Our personal potential for good. Note that Jesus was well grounded in his Jewish faith, which lent him an essentially positive view of humankind. This is epitomized in the foundational account that God created humankind in God's own image and likeness (Gen 1:26) to be responsible stewards of creation, and that humankind draws its life from the very life-breath of God (Gen 2:7). Being well versed in Torah, Jesus would also have been familiar with Genesis 3. Western Christians, especially, refer to this text as "the fall" of Adam and Eve by an "original sin," yet Jesus's Jewish tradition drew no such dire interpretation for humankind.

Regarding our personhood, note that Jesus had deep confidence in human *agency*, clearly convinced that we have the capacity to choose and do what is right—or wrong. Such agency, of course, was a precondition for the potential he saw in disciples to choose to live as good people, doing good things. Note, too, that the general culture of Jesus's time did not highlight human agency or choice; people's lives were considered to be determined by their status in society, by the gods, or simply by fate.

In this context imagine how amazed poor peasants must have been to hear these words from Jesus, "You are the salt of the earth. . . . You are the light of the world. . . . Let your light shine before others" (Matt 5:13–14). So confident was he of people's human capacities and agency that many times he affirmed not only their faith in him and in God but also their faith in themselves. Often after healing someone, Jesus would say, "Your faith has made you well" (Luke 8:48), or when assuring someone of God's mercy, "Your faith has saved you" (see, for example, Luke 7:50). What an amazing affirmation of people's own agency for good!

Such confidence in people's potential for good was a precondition for the high ideals Jesus posed for all. Otherwise, he could never have proposed the utopian ideal that they totally give over their lives to living for the reign of God—here and now, on earth as in heaven. How cynical it would have been for Jesus to so teach if people, by God's grace, are not so capable. We can say the same about his posing of the greatest commandment as loving God and neighbor as oneself with one's whole being, even to include enemies. It would be cynical to pose such a challenging commandment if people were incapable of at last approximating it. Note, too, that the greatest commandment includes authentic love of *self*—again an affirmation of individual personhood.

Perhaps the highest point in Jesus's estimation of our human nature and its capacity for good is when he invites us to love as God loves. This is the logic in his "new commandment." Jesus's rationale seems to be that "as the Father has loved me, so I have loved you" (John 15:9). In other words, Jesus loves the way that God loves. But this is a gloss or elaboration on what he had previously proclaimed: "I give you a new commandment, that you love one another. Just as I have loved you, you also should love one another" (John 13:34).

Following the logic here, Jesus loves us the way that God loves, and disciples have a new commandment to aspire to such loving—to reflect to others the divine love in the world. Of course, we always fall far short, but what an ideal to which to aspire—to love as God loves and to be agents of God's love in the world. The point to note well by way of Jesus's anthropology is that he posed for people this ultimate challenge because we are so capable.

Of course, the greatest affirmation of our human condition reflected in Jesus—so obvious that it can be missed—is the Christian claim that he was the divine Presence in human history, the very Son of God. We hear this emphasis especially in John's Gospel. For example, Jesus claims that "the Father and I are one" (John 10:30) and that "whoever has seen me has seen the Father" because "I am in the Father and the Father is in me" (John 14:9–10). Through his very humanity, Jesus was the unique divine Presence in human history. What an amazing affirmation of our human state.

As Saint Paul proposes, reflecting upon the amazing Christian claim for the divinity of Jesus and yet his becoming one of us:

> Christ Jesus . . .
>> did not regard equality with God
>> as something to be exploited
> but emptied himself . . .
>> being born in human likeness.
> And being found in human form,
>> he humbled himself

> and became obedient to the point of death—
> even death on a cross. (Phil 2:6–8)

This incarnation of God in Jesus surely reflects the ultimate affirmation and potential of our human condition. How could God take on our human state if it were, for example, inherently sinful? Again, to cite John, in Jesus, God's own "Word became flesh and lived among us, . . . full of grace and truth" (John 1:14). Jesus's solidarity with our human condition—in the flesh—reflects that we too have the potential to be full of goodness and to know and live the truth. Jesus not only reveals God to us but reveals us to ourselves; Jesus reflects through his humanity who *we* are called to be. For Christian faith and because of Jesus, all people now have divine potential—"to become children of God" (John 1:12). We could have no higher calling!

Throughout his entire public life and teaching Jesus showed amazing respect for all people, insisting on the God-given dignity of every person and affirming their potential goodness. In his teaching and in his own personhood as God incarnate, Jesus Christ is the ultimate affirmation of our human condition. Add to this that the dying and rising of Jesus released God's abundant grace into human history, empowering all people to live into their full potential as people made in the image and likeness of our God.

Communal beings for the common good. Being steeped in his Jewish faith, Jesus was keenly aware that God had entered into a covenantal bond with the Jewish people. This covenant demanded that they function as a community—as the people of God. They had heard God to say, "I will walk among you, and I will be your God, and you shall be my people" (Lev 26:12). This covenant made them not only responsible to God but to and for one another as well. No tradition has placed more emphasis on the importance of community and people's shared responsibilities—before God—than Jesus's own Jewish people.

Likewise, Jesus was well schooled in the social teachings of the Israelite prophets, Isaiah being his favorite. As noted earlier, in his home synagogue at Nazareth on a sabbath day, when invited to read, he searched for and proclaimed Isaiah 61:1 (incorporating Isaiah 58:6) that the promised Messiah would bring liberty to captives, good news to the poor, and let the oppressed go free. He then claimed to be the fulfillment of this promise, and his subsequent ministry reflected as much (Luke 4:16–21).

Again, to state the obvious, just about all of Jesus's miracles could be designated as social services, contributing to the common good of people in need and restoring them to their dignity in society (disease, poverty, and so on took away people's social standing). We can say that Jesus lived—and died—for the common good. He worked miracles to feed the hungry (thousands of them at a time), to heal the sick, to comfort the bereaved, to offset the powers of evil, and more, all of this a service to his community.

Apparently he warned disciples that we will be judged according to how we care for the common good, and especially for those most in need (Matt 25:31–46). Indeed, if we only take care of our own needs and refuse to "see" and respond to the needs of others—especially those in dire circumstances—we will be condemned to "eternal fire" (Matt 25:41); our social responsibilities for one another are not to be taken lightly! God's will of fullness of life for all (see John 10:10) is to begin to be realized now, both in people's own hearts and in their community.

We recognize Jesus's keen sense of persons as social beings in his commitment to build up a faith community to be a catalyst for God's reign. While this reflected his communal sense of *living* faith as people of God, such faith reflects and enhances our relationality as human beings.

This was epitomized in the inclusivity of Jesus's intentional outreach to win recruits for his community—reaching out to fishing folk and farmers, merchants and homemakers, rich and poor, taxpayers and tax collectors, the righteous and sinners—all were welcome into his community. Perhaps most radically, he reached out to women and children as having equal dignity and to be fully included within his gathered community of disciples. Note, too, that Jesus welcomed all to the table—an ultimate symbol of social inclusion—and this from the beginning of his public ministry (see Mark 2:15–17). Clearly Jesus had and projected a very welcoming, respectful, and inclusive attitude toward every person, inviting all into his community to share the values he taught and lived.

Furthermore, from the very beginning of his public ministry, Jesus began to call coworkers to function as an effective community for God's reign in the world. For Jesus, to be a disciple meant to bond into a community of disciples that would share in his teaching mission. Having chosen "the twelve" for communal leadership, he sent them out "in pairs" (Mark 6:7; that is, in partnership) to recruit and build up his community. Shortly after, he chose "seventy others" and likewise sent them out in companionship to carry on his communal ministry for God's reign (Luke 10:1). Not only were leaders to work collaboratively, but they were to be servant leaders within their community. Six times, in one way or another, Jesus warned community leaders not to "lord it over" (see, for example, Matt 20:25) their companions but to enable all to work well together—as a community of equal citizens.

Perhaps the clearest gospel call into community, reflecting the communal nature of persons as well as of Christian faith, is the account of the Risen Christ—as Christians believe—addressing disciples on a hillside in Galilee, a few days after his resurrection. There he commissioned them to go and evangelize people to become his disciples and precisely to take them into community by baptizing them into the inner and communal life of God—Father, Son, and Holy Spirit. That divine Life is as both one and triune, reflecting our own estate as both personal and communal beings, as imaging our personal and communal God. Whether baptized or not, all people are made in the divine image and likeness, which means that each of us is one and unique and yet all reflect God's triune likeness as communal beings.

In light of the gospel witness, then, it is no wonder that subsequent New Testament writings all portray Christian faith as being communal, and this because of our very nature as persons as well as the nature of Christian faith. All of the New Testament metaphors for the church are communal, none more vivid than Paul's imaging of it as the body of Christ in the world. Paul states, "For just as the body is one and has many members . . . so it is with Christ" (1 Cor 12:12). He goes on to reflect on how each of the different parts of the body has its own unique function, we might say *person*ality, and yet all are to work together in collaboration as one—their *communality*. He climaxes with, "Now you are the body of Christ" (12:27). To live human identity with Christian faith is a deeply personal and communal affair. Jesus's anthropology and sociology were clearly two sides of the same coin. That of Catholic educators should be likewise!

Jesus was a hopeful realist. In his understanding of the person and of society Jesus was keenly aware of our personal and social capacity for sin. He also knew that life inevitably brings its share of suffering; he was well aware from experience that it is never "a bed of roses." Even as we can choose the good, we are also eminently capable of choosing sin, both personally and socially. Likewise, all of life in the world brings its share of suffering, with some people carrying heavier crosses than others, often because of social structures of injustice or oppression.

First, it is clear that Jesus recognized the reality of both personal and social sin, and he condemned both when encountered. Indeed, his acts of resistance to social sin were likely what ultimately got him into trouble. Many scripture scholars point to his "cleansing" of the moneychangers from the Temple as a challenge to the economic structures of his cultural context. Indeed, and as noted many times before, his whole preaching of the reign (*basileia*) of God positioned it as a political alternative to the Roman Empire (also *basileia*). That they crucified him with the designation "king of the Jews" is reported in all four Gospels; for the Romans, at least, the charges against Jesus were political.

It would appear that Jesus reserved his most scathing condemnation for two particular sins, namely, religious hypocrisy and leading children astray. Regarding hypocrisy, he condemned religious leaders for placing demands upon people that they did not fulfill themselves. He charged: "They tie up heavy burdens, hard to bear, and lay them on the shoulders of others, but they themselves are unwilling to lift a finger to move them" (Matt 23:4). And regarding those who lead "the little ones" astray, they would be better to be "thrown into the sea" (Matt 9:42).

Furthermore, Jesus was always keen for people to live by the spirit rather than the letter of the law. He practiced this sentiment by often dispensing with the sabbath prohibition of work when there was a greater social need. Clearly, he was aware of a hierarchy of importance within the social requirements of his Jewish faith and that some good deeds—feeding the hungry or curing the sick—outranked keeping sabbath, even though the latter was also his "custom" (Luke 4:16).

Though Jesus was fully aware of sinners and their sins, much of his ministry was to call them to repentance; to so dispose them, he even welcomed them to the table, an extraordinary act of inclusion in his cultural context. He defended this radical move by explaining: "Those who are well have no need of a physician, but those who are sick; I have come to call not the righteous but sinners" (Mark 2:17). In the famous incident of the people who brought a paralytic to Jesus, lowering him through the roof because of the great crowd around him, Jesus first said, "Friend, your sins are forgiven you." When some leaders objected that God alone can forgive sins, Jesus cured the paralytic to show that he had such authority from God and was happy to exercise God's forgiveness as needed (see Luke 5:17–26).

That God forgives sinners and even searches them out for mercy is vividly reflected in Jesus's portrayal of God as the good shepherd who will leave ninety-nine other sheep to go after the one that gets lost (see Matt 18:10–14). And he adds that "there will be more joy in heaven over one sinner that repents than over ninety-nine righteous persons who have no need of repentance" (Luke 15:7). Indeed, Jesus declares, "I am the good shepherd" (John 10:11), embracing the divine commitment to care especially for the lame and stray ones.

Jesus's portrayal of God's mercy and forgiveness clearly reflects the conviction that people are not inherently or irrevocably sinners. There is always hope that even a sinful life can be turned around. This will be a significant point to bring with us into the debate later in this chapter as to whether or not our human condition is inherently and irrevocably sinful; it would seem that Jesus did not think so but held out hope that all can repent and change their ways. In a sense we are all like the "good thief" (Luke 23:29–43), capable of sinning but also disposed to repentance.

Perhaps the most vivid example of Jesus's commitment to forgiving sinners is his encounter with the woman caught committing adultery. A group of scribes and Pharisees bring the woman to Jesus, precisely to test his faithfulness to Torah. According to a common interpretation, the woman should be stoned to death (see John 8:1–6). But Jesus invites, "Let anyone among you who is without sin be the first to throw a stone at her" (8:7). At least her accusers had the integrity to recognize their own sins, and "beginning with the elders" (8:9), they all walked away, leaving the woman with Jesus.

Jesus asked her, "Woman, where are they? Is there anyone to condemn you?" She responded, "No one, sir." Jesus responded, "Then neither do I condemn you. Go your way, and from now on do not sin again" (John 8:10–11). Note that while Jesus forgives her, he also recognizes the reality of her sin and urges her to sin no more. In sum, an integral aspect of Jesus's public teaching was calling sinners to repent, be forgiven, and then to sin no more.

Jesus was equally realistic regarding the suffering that comes with the journey of life; it climaxed in his own crucifixion. As noted already, much of his public ministry and teaching were to alleviate human suffering of every kind. In Matthew, Jesus invites, "Come to me, all you that are weary and are carrying heavy burdens, and I will give you rest" (Matt 11:28). Often, too, the Gospels portray Jesus as being "full of compassion" for suffering people (for example, Matt 20:34; Luke 15:20). Coming from a poor Galilean village and having lived his life among the poor, Jesus knew human suffering and injustice firsthand, and he gave his life to resisting both.

Jesus's ultimate solidarity with human suffering was surely his maltreatment and crucifixion at the hands of Roman soldiers. Put to death on trumped-up political charges, Jesus suffered a horrible death by crucifixion. Given Jesus's divine powers—even to raise people from death back to life (three different instances in the Gospels)—we might presume that he could have avoided his own death. But uniting himself with the suffering of all humankind, Jesus was crucified. Somehow his crucifixion was an act of divine solidarity with all who suffer.

Add to all of this, then, the Christian conviction that "God raised up this Jesus" (Acts 2:32) who was crucified, and likewise "will also raise us by his power" (1 Cor 6:14). In other words, Jesus's dying and rising, his paschal mystery, denies ultimate victory to human suffering and can be a symbol of hope for all people in the face of our burdens—even death. No cross need be unbearable or finally triumph because of Jesus's dying and rising for all humankind and by the abundance of God's grace that this paschal mystery catalyzed into human history.

For Reflection and Conversation

- What do you find most inspiring about Jesus's understanding of our human condition—as essentially good, communal, and yet prone to sin and suffering?
- How might such a spiritual foundation shape your pedagogy?
- How does Jesus's anthropology-cum-sociology compare with your own? What might he encourage you to deepen or revise?

THE GOOD AND COMMUNAL PERSON

From early days to the Reformation. The Catholic understanding of our human condition would continue to be forged over the next two thousand years. Yet it has remained consistent with Jesus's portrayal of our essentially positive potential and dignity as persons, and likewise, to our understanding of ourselves as inherently relational beings who are responsible as a society for the well-being of all its members. And while we are prone to sin and suffering, by God's grace we are not held bound by either.

Thus, across the centuries, there has been a general sense that people are essentially good, or at least more good than evil. Among the great theologians of Christian faith, one could say that Aquinas was more firmly positive about us than Augustine, the latter being unduly focused on the effects of "original sin." Though the notion predated Augustine, he was the one who placed it center stage (more below) in Christian consciousness. Yet the overall understanding of the person was generally positive, and though not naive about our "proclivity for sin" (Council of Trent), Catholic faith and the Catholic intellectual tradition continued to see us as ever reflecting the image and likeness of our One and Triune God, and of living out our lives within a regimen of grace more than sin. This positive anthropology remained a core conviction across the first fifteen hundred years of Christian history.

Regarding our personal-cum-communal nature, it is fair to say that, like all ancient cultures, the dominant consciousness that Christians originally had of themselves was as communal beings—within a tribe, village, parish—with a responsibility to contribute to the common good of all. Indeed, until about the year 1600—the beginning of the modern era—people's self-understanding was as more communal beings with little awareness of their individual personhood.

Some scholars did write of the person as an individual. For example, Boethius (480–524), a great Roman philosopher and Christian scholar, trying to describe our human identity, wrote that "the person is an individual substance of rational nature." While that does not sound too exciting, Boethius's definition became a classic and was taken over by Thomas Aquinas, some seven hundred years later, to help develop the notion of the human person's individual rights (but not at the expense of society, as in Locke and others).

For Aquinas, our rational nature also reflects our spiritual core, making the person a union of "body and soul." The soul, then, is the basis of our dignity as persons and thus as having God-given human rights. This rich aspect of the Catholic intellectual tradition developed later into the human rights tradition, highlighted by Pope John XXIII in his encyclical *Pacem in Terris* (1963), such as the right to respect as persons, to pursue and know the truth, to worship freely, to be educated, to have good work and just wages, to have decent healthcare, to participate in public affairs, and so on.

Meanwhile, the Catholic intellectual tradition constantly reflected the conviction that our individuality and communality are symbiotic. Therefore, it is not that we become individuals first and then choose to join community (again, as Locke and others argued). Instead, we cannot become persons by ourselves alone; our personhood and communality are coterminus.

Note, too, that throughout the first millennium and a half, Christians would have been keenly aware of "person" language being ascribed primarily to God, and God as a profoundly relational Being. Over its first five centuries or so, and finalized at the Council of Chalcedon (451), the church came to image the One God as a Triune Community of Persons, traditionally named as Father, Son, and Holy Spirit.

This central Christian doctrine of the Blessed Trinity sees each divine Person as "distinct and equal," and yet bonded by infinite love into triune communion as One God. The logic then is to recognize that people made in the image and likeness of this three-in-one God of love have their own "distinct and equal" identity and yet are to function and realize themselves in loving communion with others. To reflect the One and Triune nature of our God calls all to be persons in community and a community of persons.

Reformation controversies and aftermath. This general understanding of our human condition—its greater disposition for goodness over sin by God's grace, and its communal nature—remained unchallenged until the Protestant Reformation. Thereafter it became intensely contested, with both positive and negative consequences—for church and society. Note that the Reformation conflict and controversies were not just an inner church dispute; the separation of church and state was yet to emerge. Instead, religious controversies had a profound impact on the public realm, shaping both the social and spiritual life of the Western world thereafter, with mixed results regarding the potential goodness and communality of the person.

For example, the Reformation helped to further the autonomy of the individual and individual rights. However, it also diminished the communal emphasis of personhood and our responsibility for one another, including for one another's salvation, with salvation becoming more an individualized than a communal quest. While the Reformers tended to emphasize human sinfulness, they helped to alleviate people's fears of damnation by assuring them of salvation by the gratuitousness of God's grace. Concomitantly, however, their position lessened the sense of our innate goodness and responsibility as human persons to do good works with the help of God's grace. So, from the Catholic perspective—our focus here—the Reformers tended to overemphasize human sinfulness and individuality while Catholicism remained convinced of our essential goodness and both our need for and responsibilities to community, spiritual and social.

Setting these controversies in their historical context, the Reformers had good reasons for their challenges, mostly in response to exaggerations in the classic Catholic position. For example, Catholicism at that time was emphasizing the challenges to being saved and the imperative for people to do good works, as though we must earn salvation by our own efforts and without any sense of God's supporting grace. The Reformers, to their credit, wanted to emphasize that we are saved by God's grace—the gracious gift of God's love at work in our lives—and that salvation is available to all by faith rather than being earned by our own good works.

They tended, however, to take a too extreme position—at least from a Catholic perspective—as if we have nothing to contribute to what Saint Paul called "the work of our salvation" (Phil 2:12). In their desire to highlight the gratuitousness of God's grace, the Reformers tended to overemphasize our human incapacity for good works and our innate disposition toward sin and evil—Calvin more so than Luther.

Likewise, the Catholic Church of the time had arrogated too much power to itself, even to the point of presuming to be in charge of people's eternal destiny. It emphasized that one could be saved only through the mediation of the church and its sacraments as "channels of grace." In this spirit, the church continued to emphasize, as it had long claimed, that "outside of the church there is no salvation." The Reformers wanted to correct this exaggerated role of the church in mediating salvation and encouraged people to develop their own direct relationship with God—without dependence on the church and its structures.

This tended to lead, however, to undue emphasis on individualism and to the neglect of our communalism in both the social and spiritual realms. Of course, we are to have our own personal relationship with God, and yet, echoing the communal emphasis in the ministry of Jesus, we are to go to God together—in communion and community with other Christians. Indeed, the heart of Christian discipleship can be described as living in right and loving relationship with God, oneself, others, and creation—a personal-cum-communal affair!

Catholic both/and at work. To jump to the end of this story, we can say that what emerged out of the Reformation controversies for Catholicism was some of its most classic both/and positions, so typical of the Catholic intellectual tradition. This prompts an emphasis on the person *and* on the community of faith; on the need for faith in God *and* for doing good works toward our salvation; and on the need for the collaboration of God's grace *and* human agency, with God helping our own efforts to do good toward personal and communal well-being.

The full background story of these Reformation-era disputes and their consequences in both church and society would take us too far afield to review in detail here. It might not be an exaggeration to say, however, that the defining issue was how to interpret the first three chapters of the first book of the Bible: Genesis 1, 2 and 3. We have referred many times already to Genesis 1:26–27 as proposing that God made humankind—both male and female—in God's own image and likeness, and that they are "very good" (1:31). The familiar Genesis 2:7, reflects the conviction that humankind is ensouled by the divine breath of life and is to be a responsible steward of God's creation

(2:15)—reflecting our covenant partnership with God (these texts are echoed throughout the Bible).

Also reflecting relationality, the text makes clear that God made the man and woman to be *partners* to one another (Gen 2:20). (The best translation of the Hebrew *ezer* is "partner," not the traditional "helper.") God intended them to form a bonded family/community (Gen 2:24). All of this sounds as if humankind is exalted to divine potential with a deeply relational personhood.

There follows, however, Genesis 3, and the story of what Western Christians in particular interpreted as "the fall" of Adam and Eve. (Like our Jewish brothers and sisters, Eastern Orthodox Catholic traditions never emphasized the notion of an original sin that set everything awry.) As the familiar story goes, our first parents were tempted by the snake, ate the forbidden fruit in the Garden of Eden, and as a result, passed on to humankind the dire consequences of sickness, sin, and death. Though most theologians no longer take this mythical story as causative of our human condition, it yet reflects our proclivity for sin and our need for God's grace to do good.

For the Reformers, encouraged by Augustine's interpretation over a thousand years prior, "the fall" was a total corruption of the human condition. Calvin, more so than Luther, declared that because of the sin of Adam and Eve, humankind is inherently a *massa peccati* (mass of sin) and incapable of contributing anything by our own efforts to our salvation and well-being. Being totally sinful, we depend entirely on God's saving grace, and this is accessed only by faith in Jesus Christ.

The Reformers could readily cite scripture texts to buttress their claims; for example, Paul writing to the Ephesians boldly declares: "For by grace you have been saved by faith, and this is not your own doing. It is the gift of God" (Eph 2:8). Luther's favorite text on being saved by faith alone begins, "Since we are justified by faith, we have peace with God through our Lord Jesus Christ, through whom we have gained access to this grace in which we stand" (Rom 5:1–2). Seems like all God's work!

For the Reformers, then, Jesus's death and resurrection has augmented God's grace, which is made accessible to us by faith. Such faith is a heartfelt *trust* in God to save us through Jesus Christ—rather than depending upon a *living* faith of good works. Furthermore, such a faith is more our individual choice and responsibility than being realized through a Christian community. Indeed, "the fall" of Adam and Eve and their "original sin" also diminished the possibility of life-giving community, with the man, Adam, now ruling over the woman, Eve (reflected in Gen 3:16) instead of continuing together as equal partners.

Catholicism, for its part, recognized humankind's proclivity for sin and yet maintained that God's original grace in creating humankind was never lost, that we continue in the divine image, have the potential to grow in the divine likeness, and are alive by the very life-breath of God within us. As the *Catechism of the Catholic Church* summarizes, though "human nature bears the wound of original sin" we more so "desire the good" than evil and ever "remain an image of our Creator" (§1707; §2566).

In the classic formulation of Thomas Aquinas, grace works through and enhances our human nature, meaning that God's effective love in our lives augments our capacity to do good works. By God's saving grace in Jesus Christ, then, we can and need to participate in doing good toward our salvation, and such *living* faith requires the support, symbols, and sacraments of a Christian faith community.

Just as the Reformers had their favorite proof texts, Catholics did too. While there are lots of "Catholic-like" statements in Paul, their clear preference was the letter of James. It declares boldly that "faith by itself, if it has no good works, is dead" (2:17) and insists that "a person is justified by works and not by faith alone" (2:24). To hammer home his point, James continues, "For just as the body without the spirit is dead, so faith without works is also dead" (2:26).

For our communality and solidarity as persons, and likewise in faith, another favorite Catholic proof text is Paul's declaration about the church in 1 Corinthians, "If one member suffers, all suffer together with it, if one member is honored, all rejoice together with it" (12:26). This is because we are members of the one body of Christ. Then, to emphasize both Christian communality and individuality in faith, Paul explicitly declares, "Now you are the body of Christ and individually members of it" (12:27). While we are called to our personal relationship with God, and God's grace can work apart from the church, we are to be church together and to bond like the body of Christ in the world, helping to save one another.

In sum, the classic Catholic understanding of our human condition is that we are both essentially good and yet in need of God's grace, both persons with individual rights and also communal beings with responsibilities to one another. The classic Protestant position, too, can be helpful in that it highlights our human potential for sin and evil and our unqualified need for God's help. It also recognizes the deeply personal choice that is faith, grounded first and foremost in our own relationship with God. This emphasis on personal spirituality can moderate any totalizing of the role of the institutional church—a proclivity of Catholicism. And it can also help offset disappointment when the institutional church falls egregiously short of living the faith it professes.

For Reflection and Conversation

- Imagine that from within their very being, all people have potential goodness. How might such a positive conviction shape the curriculum of a Catholic school? Your own pedagogy?
- Imagine the kind of Catholic education needed to nurture the relationality of students, fostering their duty as citizens and helping them to live in right and loving relationship with God, self, others, and creation?

For Catholic education. In reviewing some of the great historical exponents of the Catholic intellectual tradition, we have said much already by way of implications for education of Catholicism's positive understanding of the person and its emphasis on the communal nature of human existence. In sum, we are to put to work the spiritual foundations that, by God's design and grace, people have tremendous potential as human beings and all the more so as we collaborate in community. Indeed, we are capable of sin and evil, and yet we are not inevitably sinful, as if programmed to sin without the choice of our own conscience or moral agency. To live with such realistic optimism and into our potential for goodness is far more encouraging for human beings—and especially for young people in our schools—than presuming the worst about them and ourselves.

We can attempt to "go it alone" and to "take care of Number One"; indeed, some thought leaders say that to live as "buffered selves" is the dominant stance of our postmodern time—caring for and by the self alone. But living in a cocoon of self-centeredness and self-sufficiency is not nearly as humanizing as living in collaboration with our neighbor—which is all humankind. Catholic education has a key role in nurturing the personal potential of our students for goodness and for collaboration in community. Though always two sides of the same coin, let us imagine first some of the practical potential of Catholic education when it reflects a positive anthropology and then as it promotes the communal sociology outlined in this chapter.

Catholic education with a positive anthropology. Catholic education must hold out the vision and mediate to all students that they have great positive potential as human beings; with the enduring help of God's grace, they assuredly can live good lives as good people. This calls Catholic education to care for them as whole persons, encouraging their growth to the fullest and to excel according to their gifts—academic, interpersonal, artistic, and physical.

Instead of being overly directive or forcing students to "fit in," Catholic education should encourage and draw upon their youthful idealism, their fresh outlook and questioning, their restlessness and dreams, their curiosity and creativity, their complaints and critiques. Conveying to them a sense of their own dignity and agency, we must encourage them to speak their own word, to name and reflect crucially upon their own reality, personal and social, guiding them to make good judgments and decisions, ever fostering their own agency and choice. We are to pose questions that engage them as persons and likewise encourage them to uncover and pose their own questions. Essentially, the spiritual foundations of Catholic education call us to educate rather than domesticate. Like the little boy in the Gospel who gave Jesus his five loaves and two fish for their multiplying to feed thousands of hungry (John 6:9), we must encourage our students to imagine that they each have gifts to offer and that God can multiply these gifts to enhance the lives of countless people.

In particular, and given its spiritual foundations, Catholic education has great potential to foster the moral formation of its students, to appeal to their hearts and souls with a noble and empowering vision. Because of how crucial formation is for both the personal and the public realms, we return to it again in the next chapter (in light of a holistic epistemology). Here, from an anthropology perspective, there is growing sentiment that a spiritually grounded ethic is far more persuasive for people than one based purely on philosophical reasoning.

For example, while Immanuel Kant's categorical imperative—act only in ways that could become a universal law—can enable people to recognize right from wrong, it does not motivate them to choose what is right. Why should they? But a spiritually grounded ethic that lives into a gracious Transcendent Horizon is more likely to be lived. Because of its faith-grounding in God, whose effective love disposes us to choose and do good, coupled with the values modeled by Jesus, Catholic education has a rich spiritual foundation to inspire such moral formation.

For moral formation, too, Catholic education should represent to students that Christian faith offers wise guidelines and mandates to be followed in living life well and wisely—which is precisely what God wills for our own good. These guidelines and mandates begin with the Ten Commandments—well named—that we inherit from our Jewish forebears in faith. These are not whimsical requirements of a capricious god to test or inconvenience us; rather, each one guides us toward true freedom, beginning with the first. Only the one true God keeps us free; all false gods soon enslave.

Then, add the greatest commandment of Jesus, the spiritual and corporal works of mercy that *must* get done for eternal life, the listing of seven "deadly" sins to be avoided, and more. And while these are wise guidelines that work for our human happiness and fulfillment during life, Christians also believe in "the life of the world to come" (Nicene Creed), where we will be held accountable for how we lived. Anything less would not honor our human freedom and its responsibilities.

Regarding moral formation, there is a practical implication concerning discipline in a Catholic school. The key is to hold students responsible for their behavior and yet not to act as if infringements define who they are. Even when people do "bad" things, this does not make them inherently bad people—a crucial conviction of a Catholic anthropology. So, if a student is mean to others or is caught stealing, or lying, or cheating, and so on, how do you respond appropriately? Of course, they must be held accountable and corrected for their misdeeds. However, a Catholic rather than a negative sense of personhood invites the disciplinarian to say to the perpetrator, in some way, "You are *not* a thief (or liar, or cheat, or mean person), so why are you stealing (or lying, or cheating, or being mean)?" By contrast, to say to a student, "You *are* a thief (or liar, or cheat, or mean person)" is to encourage their self-image as if *inherently* so. The social sciences assure that what teachers (or parents) project onto students has a powerful influence on who they become; in other words, their self-understanding is greatly influenced by how their community perceives them. It is far wiser, then, to recognize and affirm people's potential goodness, even when they are falling short of it. And Catholic educators have the spiritual foundations to do so.

Catholic education with a communal sociology. There is significant research that Catholic schools generally have a deeper practice of community compared to corresponding schools in similar sociocultural contexts (see Bryk, Lee, and Holland, esp. chap. 5). This should not be surprising, given the communal emphasis and spiritual foundations of Catholic faith. The environment of Catholic schools should be that of a community, with their cohesion lent by their shared spiritual vision. The whole life of the school should implement the communal sociology of Catholic faith.

Practically, this means that Catholic schools and their environment are to reflect a deep respect for the dignity and rights of all participants—students, faculty, and staff. It should be an environment where all feel welcome and included; as noted before in the Catholic intellectual tradition, this is an essential aspect of being "catholic." Furthermore, a Catholic school is to have particular favor for the poor of any kind—the financially poor, and then those who suffer discrimination and injustice because of their race or ethnic background, their gender or sexual orientation, those who are academically challenged or differently abled, and so on. This is the faith that Catholic schools are to put to work, lending the spiritual foundation to follow in the footsteps of Jesus and make, as he did, an option for the poor—favoring the ones who need the favor most.

The whole environment of a Catholic school should *incarnate* the values of Christian faith, disposing students to do likewise. This means putting faith to work in every aspect of shared life. With the dominance now of technical reasoning, even Christian faith can become what some authors describe as "excarnated," as if it were only a system of ideas, whereas it must ever be "incarnated." A Catholic school needs to "make flesh" its faith throughout its entire enterprise. This calls for spiritual practices within the school (opportunities for prayer and worship, for spiritual mentoring, retreats, and so on) and for programs of engaged learning and service in the local community.

In sum, Catholic education has the spiritual foundation to encourage students to live in right and loving relationship with God, themselves, others, and all creation. It has the theological rationale to so convince because of its realistic optimism about the person, its confidence in God's abundant grace, and its sense of ourselves as communal beings. Catholic schools are ever to represent to young people that the most life-giving way to live is as *persons* in community and within a *community* of persons.

RENEWING YOUR VOCATION AS CATHOLIC EDUCATOR

Let us reflect now more specifically on what such a positive understanding of the person and their sociality might encourage as we put such spiritual foundations to work within our own *soul* as educators, through the teaching *style* we employ, and in the educational *space* we encourage.

For the educator's soul. The positive personal and communal sense of ourselves outlined above from the depths of the Catholic intellectual tradition and contemporary Catholic theology clearly calls us to trust in and encourage the potential goodness of our students. However, note also the challenge it can be at times to have confidence in *our own* worth and goodness as educators. Without self-confidence we are likely to foster negativity in our students. And often, affirmation and appreciation for teachers is in short supply.

- How might your faith in God's grace enable you to embrace your own potential goodness, and not be held bound by your faults and failings?
- How might confidence in God's mercy and forgiveness lend hope to your soul and sustain your journey in faith?

For the teaching style. We already highlighted the Catholic intellectual tradition's encouragement of a pedagogy that actively engages students in the teaching/learning dynamic, and this echoes again in the chapters ahead. Consider, here, how a positive personal and communal understanding of people fosters practices of collaborative learning, encouraging students to work together and to teach and learn from one another. There is significant research that *collaborative* approaches to teaching can be most effective to the learning outcomes.

- Have you used some collaborative approaches in your own teaching— inviting students to work together rather than being directly dependent on the teacher? What are your insights from that experience?
- What might be some advantages of collaborative learning? How could you encourage and practice it more deliberately?

For the educational space. Clearly, the *space* of Catholic education—the whole school community and each classroom, laboratory, or library— should be marked by a deep respect and affirmation of every participant, and likewise encourage collaboration to foster community. It should nurture the potential goodness and gifts of all and enable every member to contribute to the common good of the school community.

- On a scale of 1 (not at all) to 10 (very much) how would you score the level of affirmation for all participants in your school? How is this reflected in your own teaching space?
- What does your school already do well to foster a totally inclusive and welcoming community? How could it do better?

8

A Catholic Outlook on Life
and Ways of Knowing

A classic Catholic way of perceiving and embracing life in the world is to see it as sacramental. A sacramental consciousness invites us to be aware of the mystical in daily living as if everything can recall and mediate Mystery that is munificent toward us—God. (The early church used *mysterium* and *sacramentum* interchangeably). Grounded in everyday life, the sacramental/mystical invites us to experience and recognize the Ultimate in the ordinary, the eternal in the temporal, the transcendent in the immanent, the infinite in the finite, the Creator in creation, with every day as gift and God present in all things. In sum, sacramentality is how we encounter God's presence and grace—effective love—at work in our daily lives and world. And while Catholic faith sees this principle of sacramentality as most effective in seven sacraments, their core symbols are deeply reflective of the everyday (bread, wine, water, oil, lovemaking in marriage, and so on).

A key function of Catholic education is to encourage in students a sacramental consciousness in their daily lives. I write often throughout of encouraging students' *critical* consciousness, which is a discerning awareness that is alert for what may be awry in society and to imagine how to put it right working hand in hand with a critical one. A *sacramental* consciousness puts emphasis first on recognizing what is right in the world—the signs of God's grace at work—and inviting our collaboration. *Critical* and *sacramental* consciousness are two sides of the same coin. As with critical consciousness, a sacramental outlook can both confront and console, question and affirm, gift and ever demand our faithful response.

Imagination is key to a sacramental consciousness; perhaps that's why the poets are often its best exponents. A classic and oft-quoted summary of the sacramentality of life is from "God's Grandeur" by poet Gerard Manley Hopkins (1844–89):

141

The world is charged with the grandeur of God.
It will flame out, like shining from shook foil.

In a smilar vein the Irish poet Patrick Kavanagh (1904–67) writes in "The Great Hunger":

God is in the bits and pieces of Everyday—
A kiss here and a laugh again, and sometimes
    tears,
A pearl necklace round the neck of poverty.

And in her epic poem "Aurora Leigh," Elizabeth Barrett Browning (1806–61) writes:

Earth's crammed with heaven,
And every common bush afire with God;
But only he who sees takes off his shoes
The rest sit round it and pluck blackberries.

With a sacramental imagination, we might well go "shoeless" all the time. For we are ever before the burning bush—encountering the sacramentality of the ordinary, the divine Presence in the everyday.

With this sense of sacramentality as backdrop, this chapter takes up two more foundational issues from the Catholic intellectual tradition and thus for Catholic education, namely, the basic *outlook toward life* that it proposes and the *ways of knowing* it encourages. Both reflect the principle of sacramentality. These foundational themes might be more formally labeled as our cosmology and epistemology. Originally the study of cosmology referred to discovering the order, purpose, and design in the cosmos (the opposite of chaos); now it refers more to people's outlook in their daily life and how we make sense of it all—if we do. Epistemology, from the Greek *episteme*, meaning "knowledge," refers to what we can know and the ways of knowing, both from and for our lives in the world. Regarding each, Catholic faith suggests some deep convictions that can be put to work as spiritual foundations of Catholic education.

Cosmology and epistemology are deeply intertwined. Our outlook on life permeates what we know and how we know it, and our ways of knowing greatly shape our perspectives and how we make sense of life in the world. Echoing its positive anthropology and sociology, discussed in the previous chapter, the Catholic intellectual tradition's cosmology offers a life-affirming outlook, grounded in faith, that can encourage education that lends people a deep sense of meaning and purpose in life. Likewise, the Catholic intellectual tradition suggests an epistemology that mediates knowledge and ways of knowing which engage the whole person (not the mind alone) and are profoundly life-giving and humanizing for self, others, and creation. Catholicism's *cosmology* invites beyond the immanent into a Transcendent Horizon to make meaning out of life; its *epistemology* includes and reaches beyond knowledge toward wisdom for life.

Such a sacramental outlook on life and corresponding ways of knowing are much against the grain of our postmodern context and culture. To begin with, the dominant worldview more than ever can be summarized in sayings like "*this* is all there is" or "what you see is what you get." Put more formally, we have already noted Charles Taylor's portrayal of the dominant cosmology now as a totally immanent take on life, excluding all sense of a Transcendent Horizon. Our secular age encourages the person to embrace an "exclusive [of God] humanism" as if our meaning in life is entirely of our own making. It reflects the glib assumption that such a secular stance, if thought about at all, is more reasoned and scientific than a faith perspective—ignoring all the mysteries that are beyond the reach of reason or science alone.

Equally reasonable as any scientific claims, a Catholic cosmology offers spiritual foundations that can ground an education that well prepares people for an immanent stance toward the world—readies them to *make a living*. Concomitantly, it lends them the sense of a Transcendent Horizon that empowers their own transcendent reach to *have a life* that has ultimate meaning, purpose, and ethic. Such a gracious Horizon—God revealed in Jesus Christ—invites people beyond their own flourishing to care for the well-being of others as well. What a gift it is for people to live their lives as ultimately worthwhile, for themselves and others, and to be empowered by a sense of divine help from beyond their own resources—by grace.

Meanwhile, a transcendent faith stance toward life, though far more life-giving, is now also far more challenged; it is certainly not an inevitable choice in our postmodern world as it was for people in the premodern one. There was a time, not so long ago, when the cosmos was more imaginable, with God "looking down" from heaven (see Ps 14:2) upon us on earth, with a sun, moon, and stars in our firmament, and with people happily believing that God made the world in six days and on the seventh day, God rested. Creation was static, fixed, and in place, with a beginning, a present, and the promise of a definitive end time. There even were scripture scholars who claimed they could calculate the exact year that God created the world, and others who tried to calculate its end time—calling to repentance before it is too late.

By contrast, we now have to imagine our lives located within a *limitless* universe, with millions of galaxies, each with millions of stars and planets, some of them eons of light years away, and all beginning with a "big bang" some fourteen billion years ago (the scientists' present estimate). We cannot even begin to imagine such limitless space and time, and most people no longer try to—to avoid being overwhelmed. What a challenge it is to believe that "our God" is the God of it all, the Spirit/Energy of this whole universe and yet a personal God who is in partnership with "us"—on our little grain-of-sand planet. And while imaging the universe is a new challenge to faith in a personal God, we still have the old deterrents to belief—suffering, evil, and death. How can we possibly imagine an eternal home "up in heaven" now?

People of faith can well ask the "exclusive [of God] humanists" why there was a Big Bang in the first place rather than continuing silence. Or how do they explain the ever more amazing design and order of this universe. Or, closer to home, what of our human capacity for love or our ability for second-level reflection (to think, and then to think about our thinking). Or, why are there things of beauty that engage us, or people of great ethic and integrity? The "proofs" for God's existence go on and on.

It is also true that our reaching into a universe and its fathomless mystery can encourage a transcendent perspective on life, driven by our hunger (why do we have it?) to find meaning and purpose that seems nigh impossible within a purely immanent frame. It is like a necessary choice for each of us: either my life has meaning, or I am absurd. Personally, I know in my bones that my life is not absurd, so there must be meaning and purpose and an Ultimate Horizon that sustains as much—God.

Furthermore, as Taylor argues persuasively, a purely immanent perspective can lend a "deep malaise" and a "terrible flatness" to the everyday. Pragmatically, it is far more life-giving to believe that life is worthwhile than to live without meaning and purpose. More humanizing by far is to embrace an immanent *and* transcendent stance toward life in the world. As Blaise Pascal (1623–62) argued, faith is the wisest gamble we can make for life, albeit always a leap and never simply a pragmatic or rationally certain calculation. It was the same Pascal who proposed that there is ever "a God-shaped hollow in the human heart that nothing else can fill."

Likewise, by way of epistemology—our companion theme in this chapter—there is a rich but often forgotten heritage in Western culture of holistic ways of knowing that reach beyond rational knowledge toward wisdom for life. Both Plato and Aristotle were convinced that what we know should shape our very being—who we are—toward virtuous living. In the Hebrew scriptures the verb "to know" is *yada* and in the New Testament *ginosko*; both the Hebrew and Greek terms also mean "to make love." This surely suggests the full, relational, reflective, soul felt, and bodily process of human knowing.

Gradually, the practice of knowing and knowledge in the West became reduced to reasoning alone (the legacy of Descartes), typically about empirical data (the legacy of Francis Bacon), in the quest for the sole goal of rational certainty. And the epistemology of our postmodern times seems further reduced to a technical rationality, aimed at production and consumption, spurred on by technology of every kind and indifferent to human values or enhancing us as human beings. By contrast, the Catholic intellectual tradition never sold out to reason alone as our sole mode of knowing, among other things, maintaining its partnership with faith. As a result, it can still suggest ways of knowing that engage the affections and soul as well as the whole mind (reason, memory, and imagination) and that draw upon faith and holistic ways of knowing to reach beyond knowledge to values, virtues, and wisdom for life.

Clearly, two foundational issues for any system of education is the outlook on life and the "meaning making" it encourages, and the kinds of knowledge and ways of knowing that it engages. I have the impression that most schools make these choices by default, or habit, or allow the curriculum publishers (what power they have!) to decide for them, and never even think of their cosmology and epistemology as needing to be intentionally chosen. Catholic schools can access a rich resource from the Catholic intellectual tradition on both of these issues and put them to work as spiritual foundations throughout the whole school and curriculum.

Again, to propose such a positive outlook on life and a holistic way of knowing we turn to its original inspiration for Christians—Jesus of Nazareth.

For Reflection and Conversation

- Take a few moments to recognize and reflect upon your own dominant stance toward life in the world (cosmology). On a scale of 1 (negative) to 10 (positive and hopeful), how would you score it? Reflect on some of the "story" behind your cosmology. For example, how significant is your faith to your outlook on life?

- As you look at the typical teaching style in your school, how would you describe its dominant ways of knowing (epistemology). What do you most want people to *know* from your own teaching and how do you want them to know it—at what level of their *being*?

JESUS'S OUTLOOK AND WAYS OF KNOWING

As with us, Jesus's *outlook on life* and *ways of knowing* were deeply intertwined. However, to clarify each one, let us consider them separately.

Jesus's cosmology. The most foundational aspect of Jesus's stance toward life was his deep faith in God. His whole public life was marked by profound awareness of and commitment to God as his Transcendent Horizon, not just as a remote deity but as a personal God he could address directly in prayer and ask for help, as he might a loving parent. Jesus *knew* God in the very depths of his being as if God were fully present *to him* and present *through him* to the world. The scriptures witness to Jesus's symbiosis with God, highlighted in John's Gospel with such statements as: "The Father and I are one" (John 10:30), and again, "Whoever has seen me has seen the Father" (John 14:9). Everything about Jesus's life was permeated with constant awareness of God's presence.

Following on, Jesus's public ministry reflects the conviction that God reaches out with deep care, indeed with unconditional love, for the welfare of all humankind, inviting us to live in covenant partnership with God and one another. As Jesus would have learned from his Jewish faith, recounted in Exodus, God is willing to intervene in human history to set oppressed peoples free. Jesus personified that God who actively cares for all people, especially for the downtrodden, the enslaved, the excluded, the marginalized, the victims of poverty and injustice. He taught that when we help such people, we can encounter God through doing what God wills for them. And the more we reach out to people in need—as our God does—the more we enhance our own meaning and realize our purpose in life, which is to become ever more *godlike*.

Jesus's sense of God as the gracious Transcendent Horizon of life and what this means for humankind is epitomized in the central theme of his teaching—the reign of God. As outlined in Chapter 1, from the very beginning of his public ministry Jesus proclaimed that God's reign of fullness of life for all is to begin *now*, that people are to turn their lives toward God's reign and embrace living by its values—his gospel.

"The time is fulfilled, and the kingdom of God has come near; repent, and believe in the good news" (Mark 1:15). For Jesus, the supreme way to find purpose and make meaning in our life is to live for the reign of God.

Throughout his public ministry Jesus made clear that God's reign is open to all people. It is to be realized "on earth as in heaven" (Matt 6:10) the more we promote God's will of fullness of life for all—as Jesus himself modeled. In the "Our Father," Jesus emphasizes that people need enough bread for the day and to be relieved from burdening debt—two pressing social issues of his time and context. Furthermore, "Jesus went throughout Galilee, teaching in their synagogues and proclaiming the good news (*evangelion*, "gospel") of the kingdom and curing every disease and every sickness among the people" (Matt 4:23). Note that both his teaching and practice of care are constitutive of God's reign. In sum, and by God's power in him, Jesus worked miracles to feed the hungry, to cure the sick, and to raise up and restore marginalized people, all of whom were integral to realizing God's reign. Thus, living for the reign of God was Jesus's way of making meaning out of life; disciples are called to find meaning by living likewise.

Jesus saw God's invitation to find meaning in life by a stance of *living* faith as a free choice. His call to would-be disciples of "come, follow me" to work for the reign of God was more invitation than command. When some declined discipleship, as they did, Jesus respected their freedom of choice (see, for example, John 6:66–69; Mark 10:17–22). Clearly, Jesus was convinced that his own life, and all lives, have purpose and meaning because God is real and *invites* us to live as people of God. We become fully alive by choosing *living* faith in such a compassionate and loving God and by allowing this faith to sustain our hope, to prompt our love, and to shape our whole way of being in the world.

As noted in the previous chapter, Jesus's utopian view of life did not make him naive about the reality of human sinfulness. Yet his whole gospel, from the very beginning, was a call for all to repent (see Mark 1:15), for all are in need of repentance. The Greek term *metanoia* means "to redirect one's life," and for Jesus, this meant toward the reign of God. This was Jesus's perennial call—to keep on living into the realization of God's reign. He was confident that by God's grace people *can* reform their lives, and he made it clear that all people are in need of some reform. Indeed, the humble tax collector who admits his sins and asks mercy of God becomes more justified than the self-righteous Pharisee who boasts of his good deeds and feels no need of repentance (see Luke 18:9–14). Likewise, we can petition forgiveness to the measure that "we forgive those who trespass against us" (Matt 6:12).

* B.H never completed: no
utoPiA!

If Jesus's life had ended in his terrible passion and crucifixion, his outlook on life as most meaningful and worthwhile when lived for the reign of God would have been negated. But Christians have good cause to believe that "God raised up this Jesus" from the dead (Acts 2:32)—God's ultimate affirmation of his life of faith and good works. For Christian faith, then, Jesus is not simply a model to imitate, though he is surely this. But Christians claim as well that Jesus is God's ultimate sacrament to humankind, revealing God to us and becoming the primary mediator of God's grace for our lives.

As elaborated in Chapter 2, Christians believe that the life, death, and resurrection of Jesus released into human history what Saint Paul described repeatedly as "an abundance of grace" that now "overflows," not only for Christians but as "a free gift" that brings "justification" "for the many"—for all people (Rom 5:15–17). As a result, and by "the riches of God's grace" (Eph 1:7) it *is* possible for us to at least approximate and gradually live into the horizon of God's reign as Jesus did. There is no better way to find meaning and purpose in life than to follow in Jesus's footsteps and embrace his *living* faith as our own; it can enable us to live with life-giving purpose, deep responsibility, and great historical significance.

So, we look to Jesus for what lends meaning and purpose to our own lives as for his own—*living* faith for the reign of God. And like Jesus, having come forth from God, our life purpose is to journey home to God, with the help of God's grace along the way. There could be no greater source of meaning and worthwhileness for life than living this *way* modeled and made possible by Jesus, the Christ.

Jesus's epistemology. The *teaching* ministry of Jesus reflects a holistic sense of knowing and of knowledge. We can say that both the knowing process he employed and the knowledge outcome he promoted engaged all of people's "minds, hearts, and strength" (Mark 12:33)—their whole *being.* Some scripture scholars opine that a summary of the whole Gospel of John is the verse: "And this is eternal life, that they may know you, the only true God, and Jesus Christ whom you have sent" (John 17:3). So, to *know* God in Jesus is the ultimate knowledge to be *known,* and it can bring eternal life. Surely this entails much more than "knowing about" some teachings or "being objective" regarding data. Jesus modeled and taught by a way of knowing that was personally engaging, reflective, emotive, and relational—far beyond the narrow cognition that has come to dominate Western epistemology. Here again, recall the biblical symbiosis of knowing and loving.

We elaborate in Chapter 10 on Jesus's particular pedagogy. We review it briefly here insofar as his pedagogy reflected his epistemology and the ways of knowing that undergird it—as for all educators. Almost invariably, Jesus began his teaching events by turning people to look at and reflect upon their own lives in the world; this could be about fishing, farming, baking, hiring workers, raising children, borrowing money, and the list goes on. Or it could be as simple as to look at the birds of the air or the lilies of the field or a small seed growing or to the clouds to foretell the next day's weather. His overall pedagogy, then, was first to engage people's interests by turning them to the ordinary and everyday of their lives—their own experiences (as John Dewey might say) or to their life praxis (Paulo Freire) or sensory activities (Maria Montessori).

Furthermore, he encouraged people to reflect upon their lives, often critically—in other words, testing and questioning their own socioculturally shaped assumptions. So, the Samaritan becomes the neighbor, the prodigal son is welcomed home, Lazarus goes home to God and the rich man to hell—all contrary to what people would have assumed from their culture. Such examples were his way of inviting people to think critically for themselves about their own experiences and the assumptions of their historical context.

Then, having people look at and reflect on their lives in the world, Jesus taught his gospel "as one having authority" (Mark 1:22), in other words, with confidence. His gospel was faithful to his Jewish tradition and to the demands of Torah, yet he also felt free to reinterpret his tradition toward a new vision (for example, "You have heard it said, but I say . . . " (Matt 5:17–48)). And Jesus drew upon people's own experiences and accessed the broader story from their faith tradition and the vision of God's reign precisely to invite them to integrate these two sources and choose to become disciples of *living* faith.

The pedagogy of Jesus, then, reflects a way of knowing that deeply engages people's own lives in the world and their reflections upon them. And when we reflect upon our own journey, we cannot do so dispassionately; to recognize and share our own story always engages our hearts and souls as well as our heads. Jesus's holistic way of knowing was equally committed to accessing the wisdom of the ages handed down through tradition and leaning into the future and its horizon of God's reign. Then, throughout all his teaching, Jesus respected the agency of the learners, drawing upon what they could learn from their own lives, from accessing traditions and horizons of faith, and all toward the learning outcome of coming to see for themselves and decide how best to live their lives. We can say, then, that Jesus's epistemology was to lead participants beyond knowledge toward spiritual wisdom for life.

Indeed, many contemporary New Testament scholars now locate Jesus within the wisdom tradition of Jewish faith as a way to identify the content and mode of his teaching. In both Luke and Matthew, Jesus says of himself that "one greater than Solomon is here" (Luke 11:31), Solomon being the epitome of wisdom in the Hebrew tradition. Saint Paul explicitly names Jesus as "the wisdom of God" (1 Cor 1:24). We do well to take him as our model and promote ways of knowing for our students that include but reach beyond knowledge toward wisdom for life.

For Reflection and Conversation

- If you were to state briefly your own cosmology—sense of purpose and meaning in life—what would you be sure to say? How might Jesus's outlook on life enrich your own?
- How would you describe the dominant way of knowing that shapes your way of teaching? What can you learn from the epistemology of Jesus (for example, by connecting with your students' real lives in the world)?

LIFE AND KNOWING IN THE CATHOLIC INTELLECTUAL TRADITION

Though the Catholic intellectual tradition's epistemology flows on from its cosmology, again it will be more clarifying to set them out separately at first and then review how together they might shape Catholic education.

A Catholic cosmology. First, a Catholic perspective on life in the world resembles its positive understanding of the person as we outlined in the previous chapter. Just as the person is inherently good and capable of contributing to the common good of all, so a Catholic outlook sees the world that God created and the cultures that humans create within it as essentially good. Nothing that God has made or humans make is inherently evil. Certainly we can ill use or destroy God's creation and our own creativity, but this is by our free choice rather than being predetermined or inevitable. On the contrary, given the positive potential of the world we live in and our own graced agency for good within it, we can invest our lives in ways that make them meaningful and worthwhile for ourselves and also enhance the well-being of all. This is the core of a Catholic outlook on life—its cosmology.

While there is an innate goodness and meaningfulness to our *being* in the world, much depends on our perspective and the agency that we take on; in one sense, life in the world depends on what we make of it. The most life-giving sense of meaning is to live into that Transcendent Horizon of life—God—who lends purpose to it all. Thus, our life has meaning because it is grounded in Ultimate Meaning—God. Then, we can go further.

God is not simply a highest *idea* (as Plato might argue) or an indifferent *deity* (as Enlightenment Deism contended), inspiring us but leaving us to depend entirely on our own efforts. Rather, as we outlined in the previous chapter, in a Catholic theology of nature and grace God is an active partner with us and acts through us within the world. We are in covenant with God, who is constantly mediating the grace to empower our own best efforts to live well for ourselves and for the common good of all. This constant availability of God's grace, through the ordinary and everyday of life, brings us back to the classic Catholic outlook of the sacramentality of life in the world.

As noted earlier, sacramentality reflects the core Catholic conviction that life is the theater of God's grace, empowering our human efforts, mediated to and through the ordinary and everyday. *This* is where and how God is at work through us now and throughout human history to advance us toward the fullness of God's reign. As Saint Paul summarizes, "We are God's servants, working together" in "God's field," which is the world (see 1 Cor 3:9).

As we also noted earlier, Catholic Christians celebrate seven official sacraments that we believe are effective in mediating God's particular graces. And yet, the seven sacraments are each climatic celebrations of the graced nature of all of creation and of life within it.

That God's grace is at work through the ordinary and everyday of life means that all good work done well gives glory to God; every vocation well lived is a priestly life of worship of God. Likewise, every academic subject and aspect of life that we study can be a reach into the ultimate mystery of God's creation, an uncovering of the meaning, design, and purpose that is there, and yet never exhausting its mystery.

With such a cosmology, our daily lives take on ultimate meaning and purpose, making them eminently worthwhile when lived into the horizon of God's reign. As noted earlier, we can well think of our lives as a *journey*, coming forth from God, alive by sharing in the very life of God, in order to return home to God as our eternal destiny. Along the way we are sustained by God's grace, which is mediated for all—not just Christians—through the everyday of life. Like the wind, God's Spirit, and thus grace, "blows where it chooses" (John 3:8). As an old

Celtic wisdom saying proposes, "There is an ebb to every tide, except the tide of God's grace." While every tide rises and falls, God's grace is always at high tide toward us—empowering us to live our lives well and with great meaning and purpose in the world.

Such a positive understanding and sacramental outlook on life are obviously challenged by the reality of human suffering and sinfulness. Regarding suffering, the consistent Catholic intellectual tradition position is that God never causes it, for example, as punishment for human wrongdoing. Our sins can have dire consequences, but in the normal sequence of cause and effect. Jesus's care for human suffering makes vividly evident that it is not God's intent for anyone to suffer; rather, suffering is the result of the precariousness within nature and the freedom within people.

Apparently we are entitled to cry out to God in protest of human suffering; over one-third of the 150 psalms in the Bible are laments to God regarding this mystery of our human condition. And while faith does not protect us from suffering, it can lend us hope in the midst of it, if only in knowing that Jesus walks with us, lightening our burden by pulling his side of that double yoke (see Matt 11:28–30) and somehow raising us up toward the hope of new life.

Regarding evil and the reality of it in the world, we face another great mystery, and one that ever challenges the positive cosmology just outlined. There are times when life and the world seem full of sin and destruction caused by evil human choices. Here we encounter the mystery of the freedom that God grants to humankind. We always have a choice between sin and goodness; we are never required to sin. Indeed, God ever graces us to choose the good, but without suspending our freedom or agency. We must *choose* to do what is right, yet we are terrifyingly capable of choosing the opposite. Instead of suspending our choice, God respects our freedom. This being said, there is a strong sentiment in Christian scriptures and tradition that we will be finally held to account for the choices we make in life; we live with a fundamental option for choosing the good—and God. The choice is ours!

This is the *optimistic* yet *realistic* outlook on life that Catholic education is to represent persuasively and consistently to its students. Its cosmology can serve as a spiritual foundation that can be implemented throughout the curriculum, with the whole school environment reflecting a positive outlook on life and all the disciplines of learning encouraging likewise. In one way or another, all of them—math, science, social studies, literature, and so on—can enable students to reach into the Transcendent Horizon of life with the confidence that their lives have great meaning and purpose.

A Catholic epistemology. As indicated throughout Part II, one of the richest aspects of the Catholic intellectual tradition is its epistemology. Essentially, its way of knowing is *holistic* in that it aims to educate the whole person as a responsible human being in the world. Its intended learning outcome is *humanization* for a student's own good and for the common good of all. This intellectual tradition was inspired by Jesus, the teacher, and also by the early Christian encounter with Greek and Roman cultures, which saw the humanization of citizens as the primary aim of all education.

To ground such education, the Catholic intellectual tradition embraced the both/and partnerships that came to identify it. As noted earlier, such partnerships are between faith and reason, science and revelation, ideas and virtues, knowledge and wisdom, information and formation, instruction and experience, and so on. These partnerships largely dissolved throughout Western education, triggered by the emergence of public schools and the Enlightenment movement, which favored reason alone, science alone, ideas alone, knowledge alone, and so forth. This eventually led to the triumph in education of a technical rationality that prepares people to "fit in" and to succeed in a market economy. Devoid of ethics or values, such epistemology has brought us to the brink of nuclear and environmental destruction.

The great contemporary scholar Jean-Luc Marion has posed *epistemology* as the crisis issue of our time. That may seem far-fetched, given the myriad problems of our age. However, unless a more humanizing way of knowing is put to work throughout all education, we will never really *know* what needs to be done and how to do it so that all people can have the horizon of living into fullness of life. I make a small contribution here by proposing the kind of humanizing knowledge to be taught by Catholic education.

We review the holistic and humanizing nature of a Catholic epistemology—thus pointing toward the education that it must encourage—under three cumulative headings: (1) the *sources* of our knowing, summarizing that we know from both *experience* and *tradition*; (2) our *ways* of knowing that will engage our heads, hearts, and hands (wills); and (3) the *dynamics* of cognition, which refer to the cumulative sequence of *attending, understanding, judging,* and *deciding* that enable us truly to know in ways that reach toward values and wisdom for life.

Sources of knowing. When we stop and consider our process of learning and knowing, we realize that we learn and come to know all the time, *constantly*. Anticipating what we outline below as the dynamics of cognition, in the wink of an eye we can pay *attention* to the data of experience (for example, I look out my window); try to

✗ Perfect equilibrium?

understand it (I see someone across the road); make *judgments* about it (recognize it is my neighbor); and *decide* (he's working from home today); which starts a whole new cycle. The key is that most often this dynamic originates by our own agency and human capacity for knowing (attending, understanding, judging, and deciding) without anyone teaching or instructing us. It is innate to the capacity of our minds, a gift of our divine creation—from God!

Over time, from our own encounters with life and by these cognitive capacities to learn from them, we come to vast reservoirs of self-initiated knowledge. We are natural "knowers" simply as human beings in residence and with consciousness in the midst of life. The philosopher Jacques Maritain proposed that we have an "inner vitality for knowing," and Maria Montessori suggested that our will to know is prompted by "the personal and universal force of life within the soul." In other words, our ability to know is from God and through the spark of divine life within us.

When we bring our disposition and capacity to be knowers into formal education, we must surely conclude that a primary source of knowledge remains students' own lives in the world. There is an enduring and regrettable stereotype that teaching is simply a didactic process, with those who know something telling those who don't know. Yet, the better philosophers of education have recognized this as deeply false and misleading; in all formal education people's own learning from life must be integral to the curriculum. Dewey designated this source of knowing as people's own *experience*; Freire named it our *historical praxis* (reflection upon what we're doing or what is going on around us); and Montessori referred it as our *sensory activities*.

All three of these more contemporary authors and the better philosophers of education across history would add that we learn from our experience the more we reflect on it, think about it, probe it, and reach beyond what is obvious and immediate. Dewey would say that we need to "reconstruct" our experience—asking the whys and the wherefores of it, its sources and likely consequences. Freire said that we need to reflect critically on our praxis, recognizing how our interpretation and what we know is shaped by our social context. We can summarize this self-evident truth by saying that a primary source of knowing is our own *life in the world* and our reflection on it—the more in-depth the better.

Then, just as we learn from our experience, we recognize that this has been true for people from the beginning of time. And what *they* have learned over time has accumulated and congealed together into disciplines of learning, a legacy that all are entitled to inherit. So, to study engineering, we don't need to "reinvent the wheel" from our own experience; we can inherit the most sophisticated of technologies (how amazing is GPS!).

This legacy from the ages—let us call it *tradition*—has been assembled into various disciplines of study. We have the liberal arts, like philosophy and history that help us to understand our heritage and responsibilities as human beings; the sciences, both natural (like biology and physics) and social (like psychology and anthropology); the studio and performing arts (like painting and dance); and the often overlooked trades and occupations (like carpentry and farming). Patently, these traditions are primary sources of knowing for us, and education should give people ready access to the knowledge, competencies, and wisdom that they represent, and do so in ways that they can make them their own.

In sum, and echoing the epistemology of Jesus, we can name our primary ways of knowing as *experience* and *tradition*—another classic Catholic intellectual tradition "both/and." A persistent challenge for educators is to craft a pedagogy that honors both and enables people to integrate them into holistic knowledge, so that what students learn from life enhances what they can learn from traditions of learning and what they learn from tradition can enhance what they learn from life. This requires imagination and creativity on the part of teachers. Whatever they are teaching, they must constantly ask: How can I engage and connect with students' own lives, drawing upon what they already know from life in the world, *and* give them ready access to traditions of learning, to then encourage their integration of the two sources into their own knowing?

Ways of knowing. Ways here refers to the human faculties we draw upon to come to knowledge and wisdom; as such, it points to the kind of pedagogy needed to honor all the students' cognitional capacities. Let us first make a parenthetical note here advised by developmental psychologists like Jean Piaget. Our ability for cognition develops from the concrete thinking of childhood to the formal operational reflection of adulthood. However, as the tree is in the seed, even younger children can be encouraged to think for themselves, albeit about very concrete issues. This being said, the full ways of human knowing engage our *minds*, our *hearts*, and our *hands* (wills).

Obviously, we begin our knowing with the *mind* and add immediately to include all three of its capacities—reason, memory, and imagination. In the Enlightenment triumph of reason alone, the memory and imagination were often forgotten or even deliberately set aside.

Descartes, for example, cautioned that the imagination is likely to lead reason into fantasy and stray from the truth. As counterpoint from the Catholic intellectual tradition, recall Augustine's insistence that reason, memory, and imagination are to function with a unity akin to the Blessed Trinity.

Our faculty of reasoning must be engaged to think about the data that we receive from the senses—as we noted in Aquinas—in order to begin to craft and test ideas. The testing calls for a critical or discerning reflection whereby we, as knowers, not only think, but we think about our thinking. In this second level of reflection we are able to discern the sources of our knowledge, and the sociocultural influences that shape how and what we come to know.

Likewise, our faculty of memory needs to be engaged to remind us of what we know from past experiences and from encounters with traditions. Memory can access what we "know already" but can readily forget unless deliberately "re-membered." Memory, also, should be engaged to recognize the biographical influences on and sources of what we know—our own story. Such remembering alerts us to how our membership in various contexts across time are shaping what we know now. As feminist epistemologist Sandra Harding summarizes, "There is no view from nowhere." In other words, our thinking is ever shaped by where we come from and the social contexts of which we are a part. Consciously remembering our background makes our knowing all the more reliable.

Then, *imagination*, likely our most under used faculty and the least trusted by the rationalists, must be engaged to look to the consequences, possibilities, and responsibilities of what we know, and to imagine new horizons for our lives in the world. Envisioning is particularly the work of imagination; without it, we can lose hope and "perish" as people (see Prov 29:18). Encouraging people to envision who they want to become and what they want to do with their lives has tremendous potential for humanizing education.

I use *heart* as a symbol of our emotions and our affective capacities, or we can well say, the soul. Again, the cognitivists have a bias against the role of affections and desires in the process of knowing. The poet William Butler Yeats writes wisely in "Poem for Old Age":

> God guard me from those thoughts men think,
> In the mind alone;
> He that sings a lasting song
> Thinks in the marrow bone.

Yeats's "marrow bone" is another name for the soul, the deep-down sentiments and desires that arise from our own spiritual center and that prompt all our knowing in the first place. Indeed, we are wise to use our reasoning to monitor the heart's hungers, but likewise the desires of the heart can be a counter source to the undue rationality of what Yeats calls "the mind alone."

Interestingly, as we noted in Chapter 4, the heart was the principal agent of knowing in the first thousand years of the Catholic intellectual tradition, whereas the head has been far more favored in the second millennium, with the emergence of the universities and theology as queen of the sciences. The truth is that we need both—the monastic and Scholastic, the soul and mind—if our efforts to know are to enable us to live humanly for ourself and for others.

In using the metaphor of *hands*, I highlight the role of our wills as integral to the knowing process. Hands can also remind us of the role of bodily knowing and the wisdom that can arise from our own corpo-reality. It is significant surely that our term *biography* comes from the Greek *bios graphia*, which literally means what is "written on/in our bodies." Sometimes, the body can remember what the mind forgets. We need to listen to our embodied wisdom (what an old friend calls her "tummy talk"), especially in our quest for self-knowledge.

More formally, people's *will* must be engaged, especially to attract toward virtue and right living. The entire curriculum of Catholic education must raise up value issues and proposals for how to live rightly; otherwise, we neglect the formative aspect of education, particularly of educating *from* and *for* faith. As noted earlier, the liberal arts are particularly effective, especially in the potential of historical and classic literature to focus on the great issues of life and offer proposals for how to live well and wisely. But all the disciplines of learning have the potential to be formative, teaching values like honesty, truthfulness, integrity, and care for self and others. I have known a college math teacher who constantly raised issues of social justice in the mathematical problems she posed for her students, prompting them to learn math *and* heightening their social consciousness.

Though it is vital to enlighten students in good norms and values, hoping to shape their *being*, formative education is not limited to a theory-to-practice sequence. In fact, the *doing* of good things can be the starting point of formation in values. The service programs—now well renamed as participatory or engaged learning—that are integral to the curriculum of many Catholic schools are a good example of *doing* that leads to *knowing* and on into formation in virtues and ethical living. The "action" should be reflected upon to heighten its formative potential, but the "knowing" can begin from the praxis of the good being done. Indeed, Aristotle gave priority to such a sequence—praxis to theory to renewed praxis, rather than theory to praxis—for values formation.

Dynamics of cognition. One of the greatest contributions of the renowned Catholic philosopher and theologian Bernard Lonergan (1904–84) is his description of "the dynamic structure of people's cognitional and moral being"—note the cognitive *and* moral. Indeed, we have referred to these dynamics many times already. Lonergan crafted his insight by drawing heavily upon the Catholic intellectual tradition, especially the epistemology of Thomas Aquinas, around the fourfold dynamic activities of *attending* to data, then *understanding*, *judging*, and *deciding* about it. The faithful performance of these four cumulative cognitive activities leads not only to reliable knowledge but can also encourage moral formation and reach on into wisdom for life.

So, the cognitive-moral process begins by *paying attention* to data; this can be one's own sense data from life in the world or data encountered in the disciplines of learning—traditions. Such attention has the natural impulse then to progress to *understanding*, trying to understand for oneself the particular data of attention. Note that much teaching tends to stop there, satisfied if students reach *understanding*. For authentic cognition, however, we must push on to what Lonergan calls *judgment*; by this he means discerning whether something is true or false, right or wrong, beautiful or ugly, and so on. In my own pedagogy, which we review in Chapter 10, I expand the judgment dynamic as participants making the knowledge their own, appropriating and subsuming it into what they already know, and coming to see for themselves its potential meaning and consequences. Then Lonergan names the fourth activity *deciding*—making decisions regarding what one knows. The decisions can be cognitive, affective, or behavioral—deciding what to believe, trust, or do. It is by the latter two dynamics—*judging* (or appropriating) and *deciding*—that learners can reach beyond knowledge and appropriate wisdom for life.

Lonergan attests that we can discern this fourfold dynamic within our own consciousness if we stop and reflect upon how our knowing unfolds. He also counsels that these activities are implemented most reliably when done with "conscious intentionality." In other words, we are to self-consciously evaluate our performance of each function by reviewing them through all four functions. For example, the process is most reliable when we not only pay attention to data but pay attention, understand, judge, and decide how well we are attending to data—and so on in evaluating and testing our performance of all four functions.

For pedagogy, a key to students performing these dynamics of cognition and testing their validity is that teachers pose the kinds of questions and reflective activities that encourage their progress through the entire dynamic, rather than stopping, as is so typical of teaching, with understanding. Lonergan contends that when performed consistently, this dynamic of cognition encourages our authenticity as persons and what he calls "conversion"; he describes the latter as being intellectual, moral, and spiritual. In sum, education that intentionally facilitates the full dynamics of cognition is a powerful source for people to live as authentic human beings. Catholic education should surely encourage no less.

We are ready now to discern more explicitly what a Catholic outlook on life and sources of knowledge, ways of knowing, and cognitive dynamics might mean for Catholic education.

For Reflection and Conversation

- To find meaning and purpose by living into a gracious Transcendent Horizon as a journey home to our loving God; imagine how this spiritual foundation for Catholic education might encourage its students in such a positive outlook on life.
- How might you implement the epistemology suggested by the Catholic intellectual tradition: (1) drawing upon and engaging people's own lives in the world as well as accessing traditions; (2) broadening the ways of knowing to head, heart, hands; and (3) encouraging the full dynamics of cognition? Imagine the kinds of questions and questioning activities that encourage such an approach.

FOR CATHOLIC EDUCATION

The faith-filled outlook on life in the world as eminently meaningful and worthwhile and the holistic epistemology suggested by the Catholic intellectual tradition have huge implications for Catholic education. Many have been suggested already simply in describing such a cosmology and epistemology; here we become more specific.

First, the Catholic intellectual tradition cosmology calls for an education that is tremendously life affirming for students and through them for others. It encourages Catholic educators to nurture in students a sacramental consciousness, a way of looking *at* life that sees *through* it to recognize the more in the ordinary, the ultimate in the immediate, the Creator in creation, and God in the everyday. A sacramental consciousness enables people to recognize God's presence and grace at work in the immediacy of their lives and to respond as agents of God's grace. Likewise, it lends a sense of Transcendent Horizon to all of life that can encourage great meaning and purpose along the way.

All the disciplines—whatever is being taught—can encourage such a sacramental outlook in students. A personal recollection here is that my high school science teacher was the one who most nurtured my sacramental consciousness; his whole approach to studying science was to uncover the marvels of God's creation, though seldom using God-language. (Ironically, he was also my "religion" teacher, and a poor one!)

Regarding epistemology, and we have noted this legacy repeatedly throughout the Catholic intellectual tradition (Aquinas, Julian of Norwich, Ignatius, Mary Ward, and others), the ways of knowing of Catholic education call for a pedagogy in which students are active participants rather than passive recipients. This suggests that the overall teaching paradigm be one of *conversation* more than *didaction*, encouraging students to reflect on and share about their own lives as sources of knowing as well as having ready access to traditions of learning and wisdom. The intent always is to lead students to their own knowledge and wisdom, enabling them to "see for themselves" and "make their own" what they come to know in ways that humanize and enhance their agency for life in the world.

This is in contrast to education dominated by the exclusively rationalist approach to knowing that now dominates Western education, epitomized in the intense focus on science, technology, engineering, and math (STEM) courses. Much of this education simply intends for students to learn the "right answers"—whatever the subject may be—or even to *tell* them what those answers are. Teaching as telling is still rampant. A Catholic education should reflect ways of knowing that invite students into an open horizon, encouraging them to come to know for themselves and to appropriate their own knowledge in ways that shape their very *being* as life-giving for self and others.

In Chapter 7 we began reflection on the imperative for Catholic education to be formative of the person's moral identity. We return to formation here in light of the epistemology we've outlined for Catholic education, especially as informed by Lonergan's foundational cognition of attending, understanding, judging, and deciding. While more reflection on the need for Catholic education to be formative may seem excessive, it is likely the greatest challenge now facing all education.

As lamented repeatedly throughout this work, what has been lost—to the detriment of public education in the Western world—is commitment to moral and values formation. There is some strange assumption abroad that to engage students in ethical reflection would, somehow, be an invasion of their privacy. Why does it seem fine to shape people's ideas but not their values, to prepare them to "fit in" to society but not to change it as needed? To be faithful to its spiritual foundations, Catholic education must be totally committed to the moral formation of its students. To imagine a pedagogy that encourages both knowledge and wisdom, ideas and values (the Catholic both/and), Lonergan's schema can be most helpful.

Note that in Lonergan's outlining of "the dynamic structures of cognitive and moral being," he was reflecting the Catholic intellectual tradition's perception of the cognitive and moral as deeply intertwined. For moral formation we constantly need to pay attention to the data of the ethical issues involved, come to understand them and their social context, and then make moral judgments and wise decisions—that we then act upon. For Catholic education intentionally to encourage this moral formation dynamic, let me suggest a threefold pedagogy of *questioning, proposing,* and *inviting.* Note again that each dynamic is to be primarily conversational, inviting students to share their opinions, to raise their questions, to listen to and hear each other with respect, even when they disagree on contested ethical issues.

Questioning. All teachers, no matter their context or academic disciplines, are in a position to raise ethical and value-laden questions that engage students' discernment about life and their own lives in the world. It can be as simple as inviting, "So what do *you* think about (some ethical issue)?" or, "From your experience, what might be the fairest way to address (whatever)?" or "What values, in your opinion, are at stake here (regarding some current issue)?" The key is to pose questions that prompt students to recognize and name their own ethical positions and attitudes—what they already know and value (or not) from reflecting on their lives. And even as you pose such questions, encourage them to ask their own as well.

Then, according to grade level, teachers can pose a second level of reflective-type questions, inviting students to go deeper, to "think about their thinking." This can be as simple as, "So why do you think you say that?" or "Who or what has influenced your thinking on this issue?" Enabling students to recognize how their cultural context is shaping their values and positions (Lonergan's judgment) is key to developing their own social consciousness that not only makes them aware of injustices but disposes them to act for social change.

Proposing. In a Catholic school, ethical formation does not need to be an open-ended discovery of ethical guidelines and moral values, with a kind of false liberalism that neglects to make proposals out of fear of imposition. This is what seems to be paralyzing the formative potential of public school education, at least in the United States, as if proposing any moral code or system of values would be an imposition on students. Schools are *so* reluctant that they offer no moral guidelines at all. (It seems unfair, really, to put people in jail for stealing, for example, if we have never taught them that stealing is wrong.) This certainly should not be the stance of Catholic schools.

Being education *from* faith, Catholic ethics can be inspired by deep and common values reflected in all the great religious traditions—compassion and care for those who suffer, truthfulness, honesty, mercy, promoting justice for all, and so on. Then, moral formation in a Catholic school needs to draw upon the ethical mandates of the faith itself—modeled in Jesus—from its traditions of values and virtues, of commandments and beatitudes, and of its ethical wisdom for life.

We can persuade to such moral commitments, not as fiats from on high or out of fear of punishment, by enabling students to see for themselves that being ethical and virtuous is the most life-giving way to live for one's own good and the common good of all. Ethical living is its own reward. To stop short of such proposing—lest we impose— would be a profound failure to our identity as Catholic educators, with potentially dire consequences for our students and society.

Inviting. The final pedagogical move toward formation is to invite students to recognize—and it is more recognition than cognition—what are the best morals and values by which to live, and to decide how to respond in the everyday (here again honoring Lonergan's dynamics of *judgement* and *decision*). Rather than stopping short at *learning about* ethical norms, we must invite students to at least *learn from* them and dispose them to *learn into* them in order to shape their own moral being. The decisions can include what to believe and what to hope for. Yet, for ethical formation toward practice, it is imperative to invite students to decide what *to do* in response to their reflections and what they discern to be the ethical way to live—for themselves and for the common good.

The added benefit of working through such a dynamic in conversation and community—the classroom or the whole school at times—is that students will be encouraged by the emerging wisdom of the group and can be an inspiration to one another as they raise their own questions and responses. Note, too, that such a dynamic of *questioning, proposing*, and *inviting* can be done in a five-minute, one-on-one exchange with a student or with a whole group over an extended period of class time.

RENEWING YOUR VOCATION AS CATHOLIC EDUCATOR

Cosmology and epistemology are not easy topics for consideration, and yet they are foundational to effective education. In some ways they are analogous to inviting fish to become aware of the water they swim in; and, as the saying goes, the fish are the last to discover the water. Perhaps it will help make them more concrete by reflecting on what a Catholic cosmology and epistemology might suggest for the educator's *soul*, for their teaching *style*, and for the educational *space*.

For the educator's soul. Our efforts to encourage a sacramental consciousness in our students, to encourage them to "see God in all things," surely expects as much of ourselves. To this end, it becomes imperative that we develop our own antennae for God's presence and grace at work in our lives.

- Recall some of the most sacramental moments in your own life, times when you were keenly aware of God's presence and grace at work. What can you learn as you recall and dwell on such memories?
- Imagine ways that you might encourage a sacramental consciousness in your students. For example, what kinds of questions could you raise? How might you get them to really *look* at life; to really *see*; to really *listen*?

For the teaching style. Likely one of the greatest challenges for teachers is how to help students to integrate what they can learn from their own lives *and* from the disciplines and traditions of knowledge. For example, John Dewey championed learning from experience *and* from what he called "the funded capital of civilization"—dubbing these *progressive* and *traditional* education, respectively. However, he struggled with how to honor both and prompt students to integrate them as their own knowing.

- In your pedagogy, how do you draw upon students' lives in the world as a source of knowing and wisdom? How might you do this more effectively?
- How can you give your students ready access to disciplines of learning and traditions of wisdom in ways that are not simply "banking" education—a transfer of data—but encourages their personal appropriation

of these disciplines and traditions into their own knowing and wisdom for life?

For the educational space. Every school environment reflects a shared outlook on life that it proposes to students and likewise a dominant epistemology that reflects how it understands both teaching and learning.

- How do you describe the outlook on life that your school generally proposes to its students—especially regarding what will make for success?
- How might your school renew its ways of knowing to be more holistic and humanizing for all?

9

Forming Citizens in a Public Faith

As echoed throughout, this book proposes that Catholic education is to educate *from* and *for* faith—lending its spiritual foundations. Likewise, a constant theme is that we are to educate for *living* faith, reaching beyond *belief* to right *relationships*—with God and others—and *doing* the works of faith. Here we make explicit that such faith is to be lived as *public*, with its educating deliberately crafted to enhance the public realm of civil society. Catholic education is to advance the common good through the formation of students to be *good citizens*, with particular commitment to compassion and justice for all.

Such civic responsibility deserves particular emphasis in Catholic education, not only to serve the needs of society, as should all education, but also to honor the deeply public faith that lends its spiritual foundations. Catholic faith demands that we educate citizens who don't simply "fit in" to their sociocultural context but are committed to reforming it as needed to promote human dignity and quality of life for all.

In our own time the great liberationist educator Paulo Freire retrieved for us the conviction of Plato and Aristotle that all education is inherently political in that it is to shape the lives of citizens for society. Surely education grounded in Catholic faith has serious social responsibilities to educate citizens who promote the common welfare. To this end, Catholic educating draws upon the spiritual foundation of its very public faith to educate for the values of God's reign throughout civil society.

Social commentators consider *civil society* to be made up of three overlapping but distinguishable components, namely, the *government*, the *economy*, and then the *public realm*—the world at large. With its emphasis on *living* faith, and highlighting, in this chapter, works of justice and compassion as integral to such faith, Catholic education must embrace its possibility and responsibility to make a *faith-based* contribution to civil society and, in particular, to the public realm. It does so most immediately through educating its students to become good citizens.

Here we highlight dual themes that are often overlooked, even denied, namely, the *public* nature of Christian faith, and then the *sociopolitical* nature of education. In this light I can imagine resistance to my proposal on two grounds: (1) that religious faith should be a private matter that is wisely excluded from the public realm; and (2) that education likewise should be apolitical, teaching "objective" or disengaged knowledge and avoiding social agency or advocacy. Before proceeding, we need to debunk both common but false perspectives.

Regarding the privatizing of Christian faith, the great contra sign is the very *public* nature of the faith taught and lived by Jesus. If we could reduce Jesus's greatest commandment to love of *God and oneself*, we might be able to keep Christian faith a private matter. But combining Deuteronomy 6:5 with Leviticus 19:33, Jesus taught to love God by loving *neighbor* as oneself—and even added enemies (see Matt 5:24). We cannot limit such radical love to the strictly private realm; indeed, we can say the same for all the values of God's reign that Jesus modeled and taught, so many of them demanding public and civic expression. Many scripture scholars now propose that, historically speaking, Jesus was put to death because of political charges stemming from the very public faith that he taught and lived. How then did such faith as modeled by Jesus become confined to people's private lives—and increasingly so?

One reason is that the whole modernist process of secularization is determined to exclude all religious influence and spiritual values from the public square. The dominant Western mentality now is to view religious faith and civil society as two different spheres of life: one private and personal; the other public and social. This traces back to the French philosopher Jean-Jacques Rousseau (1712–78), who separated "the individual" from "the citizen," proposing that the former belongs to the church and the latter to the state. This led to the crafting of civil constitutions that strictly separate between church and state—as in the First Amendment to the US Constitution.

At least in Western cultures, after many eras of undue meddling by the church in political matters, the separating of church and state came as a wise and welcome constitutional arrangement. However, it also encouraged the false separation of faith from public life, which for Christians should be impossible. Indeed, anyone who denies the sociopolitical import of religion(s) is not reading the pages of history or the morning news feed. Furthermore, Rousseau's formulation forgot that the *individual* and the *citizen* are one and the same person—not two different beings. To fulfill his proposal requires a kind of personal schizophrenia. Holding both together, a Catholic education should educate for faith in ways that encourage people to become good citizens as well.

Regarding the role of all education to form good citizens, the Enlightenment era's claim for the "objectivity" of knowledge encouraged teaching with neutrality, particularly on socio-ethical matters. Some of this was due to Immanuel Kant's separating of theoretical from practical reasoning—the former to be concerned with scientific knowledge and the latter with matters like religion and politics. Such separation, however, allowed the modern sciences to develop without a sense of ethical responsibility to the common good. No wonder we have come to the brink of destroying our environment!

Add to this that *knowing* was further reduced to the technical rationality favored by the modern era—as reviewed in previous chapters. Such a non-personally engaging epistemology encouraged the notion that schools could and should teach only rational knowledge and objective data without any attention to formation in social values or tending to the political responsibilities of education. One symptom of this state of affairs is the wholesale abandoning of the traditional civics curriculum in American public schools.

Education that overlooks its social responsibilities and claims to be apolitical is betraying its ancient role—consistent across the centuries until quite recently—to form citizens who serve the common good of all. Aristotle, for example, recognized that people have a natural instinct to bond into community and then form a city state. For the state to function effectively, however, its citizens—*polites*—must be formed in civic virtues, with each citizen contributing to the common good, and the social unit serving the personal good of all its members. For Aristotle, such formation was grounded in reflection upon the actual practice of civic virtues, considered the ultimate purpose of education. Plato favored beginning with ideas instead of practices, but likewise argued that education's ultimate purpose is to form people in civic virtues to serve the common good of their society. Because of their convictions, Plato and Aristotle always wrote of education within their treatises on *politics*.

And think about it, what shapes the life of a society and the people within it more pervasively than the education it offers its citizens? Just to take one example, a strong education, especially in a STEM curriculum, has huge social advantages for its graduates now, almost assuring their "success" in life, at least financially, and in climbing the social ladder while blindly embracing the political status quo. But note, then, the correlation in American society between education and incarceration—with poverty and racism mixed in. People with a poor education—because their schools are in poor neighborhoods and depend on local taxation—are 300 percent more likely to end up in jail than those with a good education. Education always has social consequences, positive or negative; it is never politically "innocent."

Thomas Jefferson recognized this well, arguing that a successful democracy would require people well schooled in democratic values. John Dewey contended that education is the most effective means of social reconstruction and reform. As noted earlier, people like Paulo Freire, bell hooks, and Nel Noddings have revived our consciousness that education is an eminently political activity. It has the potential to fit people in as functionaries in society to maintain and succeed within its status quo or it can prepare them to be agents of its reconstruction and reform, as needed, toward equality and justice for all. As in the time of Plato and Aristotle and always, nothing is more influential to the well-being of society than the education it offers its citizens. Catholic education has a crucial sociopolitical role; it must educate its students to become citizens who bring their faith into the public square and put it to work toward the common good of all.

Certainly, this proposal does not threaten the positive ground gained by the separating of church and state. The last thing we need is to return the church to meddling in party politics, to favoring a particular political party, or even to sponsoring its own—as it has done at times. Clearly, individual Christians should bring their faith-based values and put them to work in all three forums—the *government*, the *economy*, and the *public realm*. Both the economy and government are badly in need of Christian social consciousness and values.

Meanwhile, the church as a public institution is *not* to engage in civil government or to interfere in party politics, nor is it to define its identity as a trader on Wall Street—the economy. However, it is perfectly entitled as a public institution, nay demanded by the public nature of its faith, to participate in the public realm, shaping the lives of citizens and thus of society as well as providing social services for the benefit of all.

Indeed, the Catholic Church, in particular, participates already and in extraordinarily significant ways in the public realm of civil society. The network of Catholic social services and hospitals throughout the world is likely the largest single provider of compassion and healthcare. The same can be said of the worldwide network of Catholic schools, likely the largest of any educational system, and having the potential of great positive influence on the common good of so many societies.

* most Congressmen are christian!

This is belied in our common language of referring to such schools as private. They are eminently public—an asset to civil society through the citizens they prepare for the public realm. Catholic schools *must* prepare good citizens because of the very public faith that began with the teaching and practice of Jesus.

For Reflection and Conversation

- Recognize some of the ways that your own faith has an impact on your life as a citizen in the public realm. How do you bring your faith and put it to work in society at large?
- Reflect on the political power of education, particularly faith-based education. What should be some of its commitments in civil society (for example, compassion for all in need, opposing racism and promoting racial justice, working for the human rights of all, to care for the environment, to raise people out of poverty)? How would you name and rank its public faith priorities?

JESUS'S PUBLIC FAITH OF COMPASSION AND JUSTICE

Scripture scholars agree that compassion was the hallmark of the public ministry of Jesus; and with a contemporary consciousness we can recognize that this included a deep commitment to justice. For Jesus, compassion and justice were two sides of the same coin. First, we do well to situate his practice and teaching of compassion and justice within his holistic understanding of faith, how his *living* faith was expressly social and public—anything but a private affair.

Jesus's public faith. To recap, Chapter 1 outlined the *living* faith of Jesus for the reign of God that he modeled and taught; this echoes loudly here with emphasis now on its *public* nature, more precisely as grounding responsible citizenship for Christians. Chapter 2 described *living* Christian faith as a holistic way of life that engages people's heads, hearts, and hands. As such, it is to shape their beliefs and convictions, their relationships and spiritualities, their values and commitments. Furthermore, we proposed that *living* Christian faith according to the way of Jesus is to be *alive, lived,* and *life-giving*—for all.

Here we highlight that Jesus's own *living* faith was enacted in the public arena of his sociopolitical context. He modeled that every aspect of *living* faith be brought to public expression; no aspect can be simply a private matter. Even the prayer he taught us should prompt our commitment toward God's reign to be realized on earth as in heaven. Likewise, for disciples and the education they might sponsor; *living* faith as Jesus did requires "going public" with it. Let us briefly review how for him all three aspects of *living* faith were to be realized in the *public* realm.

Alive faith as public. That faith be *alive* means that it be fresh and vibrant, ever renewing and deepening, and reaching into new horizons of faithfulness. *Alive* faith continues to grow and develop across a lifelong journey until we finally rest in God. In his conversation with a Samaritan woman at a well (John 4), Jesus promised her that his gospel would always be like "living water," similar to "a spring . . . gushing up to eternal life" (John 4:10, 14). We need to return often to the fresh waters of Jesus's gospel to prevent Christian faith from becoming stagnant.

The fresh waters of the gospel of Jesus make clear that an *alive* faith must be constantly conscious of people in need; unless alert, we can miss out on seeing and responding to them. Take a look again at Jesus's portrayal of our final judgment (Matt 25:31–46). Notice that neither the sheep nor the goats actually saw God in the needy; both ask with great surprise, "When was it that we saw you"? So the only difference between the sheep and goats is that the sheep *saw* the people with various social needs and responded to them, whereas the goats did not even see them. A faith *alive* is one that grows into ever keener consciousness to see what should be seen by disciples and that they respond to it in their sociopolitical context.

Similarly, Jesus often blessed people for having "eyes that can see" and "ears that can hear" (for example, Matt 13:16). Clearly, he meant more than physical sight and hearing. Often the poor and those in need are hidden from us by the culture, or we just prefer not to see their needs or to hear their cry.

Note, too, that new issues can emerge for recognition in our public faith—injustices that we did not see before, for whatever reason. For example, given our relatively newfound ability to destroy the environment, we are recently more aware of our mandate to be good stewards of creation and to redress climate change. Likewise, Christians are gradually becoming aware of how we have discriminated against people who are LGBTQ, based on false science, medical and social; Christian faith demands we cease and desist from such social injustice. An *alive* faith must be a growing and public one, ever calling us to deepen and widen our awareness of its social responsibilities.

Lived faith as public. From the beginning of his public ministry Jesus invited disciples to follow his way, to walk in his footsteps. Echoing this invitation Jesus proclaimed himself "the way, the truth and the life" (John 14:6), and his first disciples were nicknamed "followers of the way" (Acts 9:2). Jesus repeatedly prioritized *lived* faith as the measure of discipleship, and here we could pile on the quotations. One example: "Not everyone who says to me, 'Lord, Lord,' will enter the kingdom of heaven, but only the one who does the will of my Father in heaven" (Matt 7:21). So, not the *confessing* but the *doing* is what makes for lived faith.

For Jesus, then, faith must get done, and he did it himself most often in the public realm—for all to see and notice. In the Gospels he is constantly being surrounded by crowds as he worked miracles of healing, feeding, restoring, and so on. When John the Baptist sent messengers to ask Jesus, "Are you the one who is to come, or are we to wait for another?"—that is, are you the Messiah?—Jesus responds by pointing to what he is *doing*, demonstrably in the public realm. He sent the messengers back to the Baptist to relate "what you hear and see: the blind receive their sight, the lame walk, the lepers are cleansed, the deaf hear, the dead are raised, and the poor have good news brought to them" (Matt 11:2–5). It would seem that Jesus intended his publicly lived faith to identify him as the Messiah. Indeed, it was such public faith that got him crucified.

Life-giving faith as public. It is amply clear that Jesus lived and taught a life-giving faith that is to be salvific for oneself, for others, and for the public realm. Such public faith, of course, was best symbolized in his teaching and praxis for the reign of God, itself a social and political symbol. It is not possible to love the neighbor as oneself—including enemies—and keep it a totally private affair; it must be lived in all arenas of life—personal, communal, and sociopolitical.

Importantly, many of Jesus's miracles had social and cultural implications, especially his works of healing. While these might seem purely personal to the recipient, they also had public implications of restoring people's dignity in society and returning them to their sociocultural status. Likewise, his table fellowship was not simply a kind gesture of offering food; it challenged the culture of exclusion so common in his context. To welcome women and children, tax collectors, and public sinners to the table was a powerful act of public faith.

Jesus's faith was surely a public *way of life*. That this meant being committed to compassion and social justice in the public realm is already evident in what we have noted above; here we can be brief. For clarity, we can recognize first Jesus's commitment to compassion and then to justice—though always two sides of the same coin.

Jesus's public faith in works of compassion. It is clear from the Gospels that Jesus practiced his faith in all the ways typical of an observant Jew. He prayed regularly to God (the Gospels note this over thirty times), he participated in his faith community and kept sabbath (see Luke 4:16), he was honest and truthful in all his dealings, he did not swear falsely, he celebrated the holy days, he forgave even those who wronged him, and so on; this was all included in his *living* and public faith. However, the epitome was his works of compassion for all in need.

The roots of the word *compassion* suggest a felt sense of "suffering with" others (the Latin is *com passio*). The Greek term in the Synoptic Gospels, often attributed to how Jesus felt for people in need, literally means to have a "gut feeling of empathy." With the parable of the Prodigal Son, Jesus attributed the same disposition to God (see Luke 15:20).

Let us briefly recall some of Jesus's most obvious works of compassion, typically done in the public realm. Taken together they represent what later scholars came to call Jesus's option for the poor—a very public stance in faith. Such an option cannot be fulfilled simply in private. It meant that in every social circumstance Jesus favored those who needed the favor most—the "poor" of whatever kind.

We recognize the deep compassion of Jesus in his feeding the hungry. There are only two miracles retold six times in the Gospels—the resurrection, and then Jesus's multiplying of loaves and fish to feed hungry people (in all four Gospels, twice in Matthew and Mark). Being repeated so often, feeding hungry people must have been a central aspect of Jesus's public ministry. Feeding as many as five thousand at one time ("not counting women and children," Matt 14:21) was surely an act of public faith. And beyond the service of alleviating their hunger, Jesus *empowered* the poor by preaching his "good news to them" (Matt 11:5). The compassion of Jesus was to feed their souls as well as their bodies.

Jesus's compassion is evident in his curing people of various illnesses—physical, spiritual, and emotional. It would seem that Jesus worked hundreds of miracles of healing throughout his very public ministry. We often find a summary statement like, "And he cured many who were sick with various diseases and cast out many demons" (Mark 1:34). While scholars now think of his driving out demons as responding to emotional illness or addictions, Jesus clearly intended such miracles to free people from the grips of evil—of whatever kind—and to empower them to resist every addictive lure.

Furthermore, in many of his healings Jesus reached out to touch the sick, including lepers (see Matt 8:2–3), or was touched by them, like a woman with a hemorrhage (see Luke 8:43–48). That kind of touching would have made Jesus ritually unclean in his cultural context. He clearly rejected such shaming, socially liberating as well as healing those he touched—again, what great and public compassion!

Jesus's compassion is also evident in his healing people spiritually by saying—even publicly before a crowd of people—"your sins are forgiven you" (Luke 5:20). He portrayed God's mercy for the repentant sinner as reflecting a good shepherd who leaves the ninety-nine to go search for one lost sheep. Finding it, the shepherd (God) throws a party, rejoicing, "for I have found my sheep that was lost" (Luke 15:8–10). Jesus embodied God's boundless mercy, even "eating with tax collectors and sinners" (Luke 5:30)—again, an act of courageous compassion and of public faith.

We see the compassion of Jesus, too, in his sympathy for the bereaved. Three times, moved with compassion, Jesus restored people from death to life. He did so for the poor widow of Nain, who had lost her only son and thus her sole means of support (see Luke 7:11–16). He did so for the synagogue official Jairus, who had lost his only daughter (see Luke 8:40–56). Jesus himself experienced the pain of loss of a loved one with the death of his friend Lazarus (see John 11:1–44). We read first that "Jesus wept"—the shortest verse in the whole Bible (John 11:35). Then, in front of "the crowd" (John 11:42) that had gathered (that is, very publicly) Jesus raised Lazarus from the dead and gave him back to his sisters, Martha and Mary (see John 11:34–44).

Being compassionate toward people was such a priority in his ministry that Jesus even placed it ahead of keeping the Sabbath, the latter a socio-religious norm of highest rank. There are at least seven accounts in the Gospels of acts of compassion that Jesus publicly worked on the Sabbath, often despite criticism from literalists of the Law. Certainly, Jesus was not abolishing the Sabbath. By his actions, he was simply saying that there is a hierarchy of values in God's reign, and some good deeds are more important than others—like healing the sick or feeding the hungry over strict sabbath observance. Again, note the public faith nature of such a move, often to the strong objection of religious leaders. We could go on but the point is that Jesus's whole life was suffused with compassion and enacted consistently in the public realm of his life. Then, the sociopolitical nature of his *living* faith was also writ large in his concomitant commitment to *justice*.

Jesus's public faith and the work of justice. Jesus was deeply grounded in his Jewish tradition, being particularly familiar with Psalms and the prophetic literature; for example, he cited Isaiah at least eight times from memory. So, he was raised with a deep faith that God "is a God of justice" (Isa 30:18), who "secures justice and the rights of all the oppressed" (Ps 103:6). Jesus knew well that God delights in works of justice (see Jer 9:24), is a "lover of justice" (Ps 99:4), and hates injustice (see Isa 61:8). Jesus would have known deeply the repeated theme of the prophetic literature that the true worship that God desires is for people to do the works of justice (see Isa 58:6–12, for example).

As already noted, when invited to read on a sabbath day in his home synagogue of Nazareth, Jesus chose one of the strongest justice texts in the Hebrew scriptures, Isaiah 61:1–2a, and wove in Isaiah 58:6. He proclaimed the ancient promise that the Anointed One—the Messiah—would bring good news to the poor, liberty to captives, sight to the blind, freedom for the oppressed (58:6), and proclaim God's jubilee year of complete justice. Then Jesus boldly claimed, "Today this scripture has been fulfilled in your hearing" (Luke 4:21). Jesus went on to reflect this centrality of justice to his Jewish faith throughout his public ministry, epitomized, as so often noted, in his proclamation of the reign of God.

This central symbol of Jesus's life work and teaching was a deeply sociopolitical as well as a spiritual one. God's reign was to come, and God's will be "done on earth as in heaven" (Matt 6:10), thus shaping people's politics as well as their prayers. Jesus's perspective was shaped by how the symbol was emerging in the consciousness of his time. God's reign was to reflect shalom—the peace, justice, and well-being that God intends for all humankind and creation. Note, again, that the Greek word basileia—kingdom—also can be translated "empire." Jesus would have known well that he was proclaiming an alternative to the Roman Empire, and to all oppressive and unjust institutions, civil or religious. Surely he recognized the political risk he was taking in witnessing to such living public faith.

Recounted in all three Synoptic Gospels is a famous incident of Jewish leaders testing Jesus on whether to pay taxes to the Romans (see Matt 22:15–22). He asked them whose image was on their coin, and they responded, "The emperor's." Then he counseled, "Give therefore to the emperor the things that are the emperor's, and to God the things that are God's." This response has often been misinterpreted to justify not only a separation of church and state, but of faith from politics—to God what is God's and to Caesar what is Caesar's.

Contemporary scholars opine, however, that Jesus was contrasting the emperor's human image on coins with people's own personhood in the divine image and likeness. He was simply reminding them that the defining commitment for people of faith is always to the God they image rather than to whatever emperor they may have on their coins.

One's first commitment in faith is to God, not to Caesar; such faith cannot be confined to the private realm!

While all justice is to have social consequences, commentators recognize at least four varying kinds of justice: *commutative, distributive, social,* and *restorative.* Jesus practiced well and publicly all four. Catholic education must encourage its students to do the same, with each instance of justice being integral to their *living* faith and to their responsibilities as citizens.

Commutative justice demands honesty and truth telling in all personal relationships; without such basic justice, there can be no other kind. John describes Jesus as "full of grace and truth" (John 1:14), has Jesus assure disciples that living the truth as his disciples "will make you free" (John 8:32), and presents himself as "the way, the truth, and the life" (John 14:6). Jesus urges disciples to be people of their word, with their "no" being no and their "yes" being yes, making them trustworthy (see Matt 5:37). Given all the falsehoods and lies that are now "standard operation" in the public realm, even in the highest reaches of government, educating citizens for this commutative justice—even simple truth telling—seems all the more urgent in our time.

Distributive justice requires society to ensure that its common goods—cultural legacy, education, healthcare, political power—are fairly distributed so that all have sufficient for their needs as human beings. Thus, Jesus's miracles of feeding the hungry (thousands of them) can be seen as a work of distributive justice—meeting people's basic need for food. Indeed, we can say the same for all of Jesus's miracles of healing, that is, distributing healthcare to those who needed it most. His forgiving of sinners was his way of distributing God's mercy and assuring all of God's love. Indeed, his defining ministry of teaching was an expression of distributive justice, accessing the wisdom of God's reign into people's lives and welcoming all to become disciples. All of this and more reflected Jesus's commitment to distributive justice.

Social justice, strictly speaking, refers to the responsibility of society to honor and protect the dignity of all its citizens and to ensure that every person can participate fully in civil society. From the beginning Jesus was regularly charged with "eating with tax collectors and sinners" (Mark 2:15–17)—making the socially excluded feel included. Additionally, Jesus's amazing inclusivity of women, counting them among his core group of disciples (see Luke 8:1–3), contravened the patriarchy and social injustice of his culture (and ours) toward women. Likewise, at that time, children had no social status; they were considered simply as the property of their parents. Jesus counters by saying,

"Let the little children come to me; do not stop them; for it is to such as these that the kingdom of God belongs" (Mark 10:14). He intended even the children to feel fully included.

And, as noted already, in curing the sick, Jesus was reinstating them within their society, giving them back their honor and dignity. So, when he cured ten lepers of their leprosy, he tells them, "Go and show yourselves to the priests" (Luke 17:11–19); the priests had the social role of verifying such a cure and of reintegrating the person back into community. The lepers' cure was twofold—physical and social. At the core and throughout Jesus's public ministry, we see writ large his commitment to social justice.

Restorative justice is a biblically inspired approach that contrasts with punitive justice in that perpetrators may ameliorate their punishment by admitting their guilt and making amends, if possible, for their wrongdoing. A classic example of Jesus's practice of restorative justice was his acceptance of the repentance of the tax collector Zacchaeus (see Luke 19:1–10). The story is fascinating in that Jesus reaches out and forgives Zacchaeus even before Zacchaeus has explicitly repented. Moved by the generous mercy of Jesus, Zacchaeus gives half of his possession to the poor and restores fourfold what he has stolen from people. It was his newfound faith in Jesus that prompted Zacchaeus to practice restorative justice, and Jesus affirms his restoration into the community by staying at his house that night. In summary, then, Jesus practiced all the varied forms of justice. Catholic education must educate citizens convinced and well prepared to live all levels and forms of justice in both the personal and public realm.

Dire political consequences. Patently, Jesus practiced a public faith that ran afoul of the civil powers—political and religious. Gradually he came to be targeted by the authorities, and eventually he was tried and executed as a political threat to Roman rule in the Palestine of his day. The chief priests worried that if people keep gathering around Jesus, "the Romans will come and destroy both our holy place and our nation" (John 11:48). Regarding their "holy place," it seems likely that a major trigger to condemn Jesus was his cleansing of the Temple, an event recounted in all four Gospels. With this, Jesus was certainly "going public" with his faith, even interfering in the economy of his cultural context. People can become very angry when their purses are threatened. Consequently, "the chief priests and the scribes . . . kept looking for a way to kill him" (Mark 11:12–19).

With Jesus's entry into Jerusalem on the Sunday before his crucifixion—another event recounted in all four Gospels—the people came out and hailed Jesus as their new king in the line of their great King David (Luke 19:38), and as "the King of Israel" (John 12:13). The following Thursday evening Jesus was arrested and brought to trial before Pontius Pilate, the Roman governor of Judea at the time.

Again, in all four Gospel accounts, Pilate's concern is whether or not Jesus is aspiring to *be* a king—and thus a threat to Roman rule. He explicitly asks Jesus, "Are you the King of the Jews?" (Mark 15:2). During his passion the Roman soldiers put a crown of thorns upon Jesus's head and mocked him with "Hail, King of the Jews" (Mark 15:18–20). Finally, all four Gospels recount that the Romans affixed to Jesus's cross the charge against him—aspiring to be "the King of the Jews." They wrote this political charge in Hebrew, Latin, and Greek (John 19:20)— so the public would recognize what could happen to political opponents of Roman rule.

We can say, then, that Jesus died for the public faith that he lived for, in sum, the realizing of God's reign. His whole life served this sociopolitical symbol by a *living* faith that was both personal and public for all to see. To place Jesus at the *heart* of Catholic education demands that we also educate for such a public and *living* faith, informing and forming citizens to live with compassion and justice for all.

For Reflection and Conversation

- How do you respond to the public faith of Jesus, with its central commitments of compassion and justice? What can we learn from him for our own sociopolitical context and commitments?
- What are the challenges for Catholic educators today to educate good citizens who practice a public faith?

A PUBLIC FAITH OF COMPASSION AND JUSTICE IN CATHOLIC TRADITION

From the *living* faith of Jesus, the first Christians were fully convinced that they were to put their faith to work for the reign of God in the public realm, with a priority for those in immediate need and then for social reforms as well. While "the blood of martyrs"—those who died in witness to their faith—was a lure to attract newcomers to their *way*, also effective in winning new converts was the witness of Christians caring for *anyone* in need, never limited to their own community members.

An amazing aspect of the public faith of the young Christian community was that "they would sell their possessions and goods and distribute the proceeds to all, as any had need" (Acts 2:45). Indeed, "no one claimed private ownership of any possessions but everything they owned was held in common" (Acts 4:32–37). This is what allowed them the resources to help people "as any had need"—not just fellow Christians. Today, the social commitments of that first Christian community might sound like left-wing socialism!

The first Christians also were confident that the Holy Spirit was working through the Christian community to continue God's work of liberating salvation begun in Jesus. As elaborated in Chapter 3, it was such confidence, coupled with the mandate to put their faith to work in the public realm, that prompted the early church to embrace education as integral to its social ministry. Christians came to realize that the *political* work of education—contributing to the *polis* by educating its citizens—was integral to their mandate of *living* faith and a prime social strategy to advance God's work of liberating salvation. Thus began a two thousand year political and social service of Catholic education to the present day.

This commitment to socially responsible education, along with the church's many other social works of compassion and justice, was well symbolized across the centuries in what came to be known in Catholic practice as the corporal and spiritual works of mercy. Originally inspired by the texts in Matthew 25:34–40 (how we will be judged) and Isaiah 58:6–10 (the true worship of God), we list them here in their traditional rendering. Note that education, the first *spiritual* work listed, is "to instruct the ignorant"—language we might not use today! The ancient tradition is a sevenfold listing for both sets of works of mercy, pertaining to the body and the spirit. Pope Francis has added an eighth work to each category to encourage mercy *toward creation*—again reflecting a public faith.

The seven traditional corporal works of mercy are
- to feed the hungry,
- give drink to the thirsty,
- shelter the homeless,
- cloth the naked,
- care for the sick,
- visit (or ransom) the imprisoned, and
- bury the dead.

The eighth, added by Pope Francis, is
- care for creation.

The seven spiritual works of mercy are
- to instruct the ignorant,
- counsel the doubtful,
- admonish sinners,
- bear wrongs patiently,
- forgive offenders,
- comfort the afflicted, and
- pray for the living and the dead.

The eighth, added by Pope Francis, is
- contemplate God's creation.

Such works of mercy will always be central to the public nature of *living* Christian faith. Catholic education is required to form citizens committed to their practice in both the personal and public realms.

Over the past one hundred and thirty years, however, Christians have grown in consciousness that their faith requires them to go beyond (while still fulfilling) direct acts of compassionate service and to work more intentionally for justice throughout society and culture. In this expanded horizon for gospel social values, Catholic education must play a crucial role. This entails addressing the sociocultural causes of human suffering and working for political changes toward justice for all.

Beginning with *Rerum Novarum*, Pope Leo XIII's 1891 social encyclical, Christians' sense of political responsibility has expanded and deepened. It is no longer sufficient to show compassion to those who suffer injustice of whatever kind; we must also resist and try to change the social structures and cultural mores that cause the injustice in the first place.

As one might expect, the church's social *doctrine* (a term that places it in the top tier of Catholicism's hierarchy of truths) has evolved and developed with the times and circumstances, from Pope Leo XIII's concern that workers be paid a just wage (still an issue today) to Pope Francis's call to protect the environment (which also cares for the poor). One summary of this now well-established tradition is the 1971 statement of the International Synod of Bishops that "justice is a constitutive aspect of the Gospel" ("Justice in the World"). In other words, if Christian teaching and praxis do not include the works of justice, then they do not represent the gospel of Jesus Christ.

There were many contributing factors that expanded the social consciousness of Christians more explicitly toward justice. Modern biblical studies helped to deepen awareness of the Bible's constant call to justice, especially by the Hebrew prophets. For a long time justice in the Old Testament was understood simply as punitive, as

God punishing sinners for their wrongdoing. Biblical scholars came to recognize that this was a far too narrow understanding. Instead, the heart of biblical justice is to affirm the rights and dignity of every person, as well as to work toward reconciliation, healing, and peace. Justice is to bring about *shalom*, an extraordinarily rich biblical term with no English equivalent. It includes honoring the dignity of all persons, promoting their full inclusion in community, and building God's reign of true peace—not simply as the absence of war but with mutual respect and harmony.

Likewise, increased focus on the historical Jesus highlights, as already noted, his opposition to all forms of social oppression and cultural exclusion. Furthermore, the social sciences raised our consciousness about the nature of culture and society, with all political arrangements seen as the products of human history rather than "come down from heaven." If humans created their sociocultural reality, we can also act to change it—toward compassion and justice for all. Christians must embrace such a stance of historical agency as integral to the political and public nature of their *living* faith. The education we offer and the citizens it prepares are crucial to this service in the public realm.

In this light theologians began intentionally to address social and political concerns. Various liberation theologies have emerged from struggles against cultural and social oppression (like racism, sexism, homophobia, unbridled capitalism, environmental destruction, and so on). Such contemporary struggles prompt a rereading of the Bible and of Christian tradition, recognizing the "recessive genes" for justice that have been there all along but often overlooked or underdeveloped. Christian scripture and tradition are replete with what theologian Johann Baptist Metz (1928–2019) named "dangerous memories"; these are aspects of Christian faith that will always question the sociopolitical status quo and renew commitment to a public faith toward compassion and justice for all.

This call to justice as well as compassion demands that Christians develop antennae that are alert for all instances of injustice and oppression in church and society. Catholic schools must educate their students in a *critical social consciousness* that can recognize the sources of injustice in cultural mores and public structures, including that of the church. And *consciousness* is not sufficient; Christian social awareness must prompt us *to act* on behalf of justice as well. This surely lends a compelling spiritual foundation for the role of Catholic education in promoting a public faith of compassion and justice, and thus serving the public realm by preparing so committed citizens.

For Reflection and Conversation

- As you think about your own work as an educator, what do you recognize already as promoting the values of compassion and justice?
- How might educating for a *living* and *public* faith shape the curriculum of a Catholic school to prepare good citizens for their society? What are some implications for your own teaching toward such citizenship?

FOR CATHOLIC EDUCATION

I propose four functions that Catholic education can render to educate students in a public faith that encourages compassion and justice as central values in their lifestyle and shapes them as good citizens in the public realm: (1) educating the *heart*, (2) with actual *practices* of compassion and justice, (3) while encouraging *critical social and sacramental consciousness*, and (4) nurturing a *spirituality* to sustain such public and *living* faith.

Educating the heart. In Western culture the word *heart* usually symbolizes the emotive faculty, our capacity for empathy. To commit to compassion and the practice of justice surely calls upon our hearts. The very etymology of compassion, *compassio*, meaning "to suffer with," alerts us that this requires *feelings* of sympathy and solidarity. While this is a good start, the Bible broadens the meaning of *heart* beyond feelings and offers a wise caution.

There are few defining terms used more often in the Bible than *heart*; it appears about a thousand times. In Hebrew, the most frequent term is *Ieb* (or a variation of it) and the Greek is *kardia*. While both terms include emotions, biblically the heart is the sum of all that we are as human beings. So, heart is the physical organ that gives us life (Prov 4:23), the seat of our emotions (Ps 4:7), the source of our moral discernment (1 Sam 24:5), and the power of our intellect (Isa 6:10). For the Bible, then, *heart* is synonymous with what we might call *soul*—the defining core and capacity of our personhood.

The Bible also repeatedly makes clear—as we can attest from our own lives—that our heart can lead us aright or lead us astray, depending on how we respond to its promptings. In and of themselves, the desires of the heart are good, implanted in us by God. However, God also made us free agents who are capable of pursuing our heart's desires in ways that are life giving or life destroying—for ourselves and others. Spiritually, they can lead us to freedom by placing first in our lives the one, true, loving, and life-giving God, or our hearts can cause us to embrace idols—fame or fortune, power or pleasure, and so on. And, as noted before but worth repeating, all false gods enslave.

Jesus, too, cautioned wisely about the heart. On the one hand, those with "an honest and good heart" hear the word of God "and bear fruit with patient endurance" (Luke 8:15). On the other hand, "it is from within, from the human heart, that evil intentions come" and Jesus then listed some of our worst sins (Mark 7:21). In his Sermon on the Mount, Jesus recognized that "the pure in heart . . . will see God" (Matt 5:8) whereas our hearts can also dispose to lust and adultery (Matt 5:28). In a summary New Testament text, the letter of James recognizes that the heart can be the source of "gentleness born of wisdom," resulting in works of justice and peace, or it can be "unspiritual and devilish" (Jas 3:13–18).

The key is what we choose as the ultimate treasure of our hearts— the core of what we most cherish and desire. Again, Jesus advises that "where your treasure is, there your heart will be also" (Matt 6:21). Clearly, therefore, what we make the treasure of our hearts shapes everything about our lives in the world. Surely Catholic education has a crucial role to play in tutoring the hearts of its students.

Catholic education should constantly reflect to students the wiser and more human ways to live life, appealing to their feelings and desires as well as to their reasoning and judgments. We can pose models of compassion and justice to students and appeal to their souls to recognize that such is the most *reasonable* as well as the *wisest* way to live. We can raise questions and offer guidelines for their decision-making regarding sociocultural issues, inviting them to "see" for themselves. We can make both heartfelt appeal and well-reasoned motivation for living with such public values. In sum, we can and should encourage our students to choose wisely what will be the treasure of their hearts in order to embrace a *living* faith committed to compassion and justice.

Practices of compassion and justice. Consequent to the rationalist emphasis of modernity's epistemology is the assumption that the knowing sequence is always from theory to practice. This overlooks the ancient wisdom—both biblical and philosophical—that we often move and learn from practice to theory, with practice having its own wisdom that can enhance and clarify the theoretical. Aristotle gave priority to practice (*praxis*), and especially for the formation of virtue; he argued that "courage is found where courage is practiced." Likewise, Jesus counsels that those who *practice* what he preached are most likely to come to "know the truth," the kind of truth that "will make you free"—note the sequence (John 8:31–32). A Catholic school must be a place that practices and includes opportunities for students to practice the compassion and justice demanded by Christian faith within its curriculum.

To begin with, a Catholic school should be a place of kindness and respect for all students, faculty, and staff. Beyond this, it should reach out to those with particular needs within the school community, reflecting Jesus's option for the poor. Indeed, the "poor" students or the differently abled ones should be the most favored—because they need the favor most—receiving the extra encouragement or tutoring they may need to succeed.

Catholic schools, then, should be free of even the slightest trace of discrimination on any grounds—race, cultural background, gender, sexual orientation, economic status, and so on. Any semblance of social or cultural discrimination in a Catholic school betrays its identity and defeats its purpose—to educate for the reign of God through a public and *living* faith. On the one hand, if students graduate from our schools who are sexist, or racist, or homophobic, and so on, we have failed to give them a Catholic education. On the other hand, what a contribution it can make to society to educate citizens who refuse to practice and actively oppose such social sins.

Then, every Catholic school should encourage and provide opportunities for outreach into the local and broader community with acts of compassion and social justice; thankfully, such programs now seem to be a constitutive aspect of the curriculum of Catholic schools. Instead of an "us helping them" mentality, however, such outreach is now better understood as "engaged learning" in which students learn in partnership with a local community, to the benefit of each. The learning potential of such encounters is heightened when students are prompted to reflect upon their experiences, to probe the social causes of injustice, and to imagine how to work for change—which brings us to the third strategy.

Encouraging critical social and sacramental consciousness. For all the limitations of Enlightenment rationality, it has assets for developing in students a critical social consciousness. Summarizing what we've said before, and from lots of seeds in the Catholic intellectual tradition, Catholic education should encourage a *critical* social awareness in students, enabling them to analyze social conditions in order to "see" for themselves the reality and causes of social injustice. Note that the term *critical* here does not refer to negative criticism—though, depending on the circumstances, some critique may be appropriate. Instead, it refers to a posture of discernment (the Greek *krinein* is the root of both *critical* and *discern*), echoing what we saw in the Ignatian *Spiritual Exercises*. Critical reflection entails questioning the sociocultural structures and history that undergird present public practices and discerning what promotes or prevents compassion and justice.

For such critical reflection it is essential to prompt students, according to developmental readiness, to think historically about present social practices and cultural mores. This means to dig into their history, uncovering how such practices came about, to whose benefit, and to evaluate whether they promote or prevent compassion and justice now. While such sociocultural analysis can be challenging, some of its better exponents have boiled it down to asking of every social situation and cultural practice three simple questions: Who is making the decisions? Who is benefitting? Who is suffering? (see Holland and Henriot, *Social Analysis*). Promoting such social consciousness in students is constitutive to the kind of citizens we are educating.

Going further, and again according to developmental readiness, Catholic education is to encourage students to recognize how their own sociocultural context is shaping their convictions and commitments. Paulo Freire calls this the process of *conscientization,* which entails: (1) becoming aware of and naming oppressions and injustices; (2) uncovering their historical and sociocultural causes; (3) recognizing the contextual sources of one's own perspectives—in other words, to think contextually about one's own attitudes and values; and (4) being committed to working for change toward compassion and justice for all.

Even younger children can be encouraged to be kind, respectful, inclusive, and so on, *and* to reflect on why they should do so; this will sow the seeds for critical social consciousness and public faith commitment that can emerge at a more mature age. Again, and for all levels, educators can encourage such critical reflection in many ways, but surely the key mode is through the questions that they pose to students. Patently, the questions must move beyond simple recall of what the teacher or text has said and engage students in the kinds of critical reasoning, analytical remembering, and constructive imagining that we outlined in the previous chapter as integral to a Catholic epistemology.

Encouraging such *social* consciousness is integral to the work of Catholic education, especially to promote the works of justice. Note, too, the need to ever encourage its companion, namely, a *sacramental* consciousness. In order to keep hope alive, it is imperative that students be able to recognize the myriad instances of God's grace at work in their lives and social context, and to feel empowered to respond, always living out that partnership of nature and grace. Such a sacramental consciousness also enriches people's lives as citizens in their public realm.

Nurturing a spirituality to sustain public and living faith. Our first strategy listed above was about *engaging* the soul toward a public and *living* faith for compassion and justice; here we reflect on *sustaining* the soul in such commitments. For some, talk of a *public faith spirituality* may be heard as a contradiction in terms—an oxymoron. The "new age" image of spirituality is of something very private and deeply personal; it is not typically socially conscious or committed. Browse the spirituality section of a bookstore or online, and it becomes clear that the dominant postmodern version of spirituality is focused primarily on nurturing the buffered self (Taylor). This means providing by the self for the self and apart from any particular faith community, social context, or concern.

Now spirituality is variously understood, and we have summarized it throughout this text simply as putting faith to work. Here, we can add that spirituality entails a quest for holiness as wholeness or authenticity of life that reflects personal integrity and mutuality with others. This is very much in keeping with the biblical understanding of the spiritual quest for holiness. When Jesus said that he had come that people "may have life and have it to the full" (John 10:10), he was responding to our hunger for holiness as wholeness. This spiritual quest for holiness of life *and* living with compassion and justice go hand in hand; both are integral for citizens inspired by Christian faith.

Take a look at the great Holiness Code that is highlighted in Leviticus 17—26. The summary line in chapter 19 begins, "You shall be holy, for I the Lord your God am holy" (Lev 19:2). Note that in Matthew, Jesus paraphrases this text at the end of his instruction on loving enemies as "be perfect as you heavenly Father is perfect (Matt 5:48), whereas in Luke Jesus summarizes it as "be merciful just as your Father is merciful" (Luke 6:36). Returning to Leviticus, we see that of the some fifty directives for holiness that follow, at least half pertain to works of compassion and justice, including "love the alien as yourself" (Lev 19:34). Likewise, Christian holiness demands the works of compassion and justice and requires a socially aware spirituality to nurture and sustain it.

Having described spirituality holistically and as the quest for holiness of life, we need particular spiritual practices to nurture and sustain our journey—stories and symbols, prayers and practices, ways of worship and a faith community. Though not substituting for a parish, every Catholic school can and should provide opportunities for communal prayer and liturgy, for retreats and spiritual mentoring, and have recognizable symbols of Christian faith on display to remind one of the school's identity. The school must be careful not to proselytize or impose its faith on people from other or no faith tradition; and yet, it must be faithful as well to its own Catholic identity and spiritual foundations. We directly address this complex issue in our next and last chapter on religious education in a Catholic school.

RENEWING YOUR VOCATION AS CATHOLIC EDUCATOR

We conclude here with some brief reflections on what a public and *living* faith toward compassion and justice means for the educator's *soul*, the teaching *style*, and the educational *space* of a Catholic school.

For the educator's soul. When we are young in our vocation as educators, commitment to a public faith for compassion and justice seems to come more readily. However, as the fire and idealism of youth wane, it can be a struggle to keep on. We need to have our own spiritual practices that help to sustain and deepen the social commitments of our faith through the years. A helpful asset can be to recall the memory of a time when you suffered some injustice or lack of compassion yourself; this can become—as theologian Johann Metz names it—a "dangerous memory" for us. It can help to sustain commitment to a public faith, especially when enthusiasm wanes.

- Do you have a memory of suffering, cruelty, or discrimination that helps you renew your own "fire in the tummy" for *living* faith toward compassion and justice?
- What other spiritual practices have you found helpful to sustain your commitment to the works of compassion and justice, and to nurturing the same in your students?

For the teaching style. It is important not to make your students feel so overwhelmed by all the injustices in our world and society that they become paralyzed. Assure them that no one can commit to all the justice causes in contemporary society; there are far too many to take on. Wiser by far is to encourage students to select a favorite, perhaps one with personal appeal or resonant to a local context, and then to get involved, making a commitment to the cause.

- What are some pressing social issues in your context or neighborhood that might be of keen interest to your students?
- How can you guide their selection of some particular issue and enable them to get involved?

For the educational space. For the school to be effective in forming good citizens, its entire ethos needs to reflect a public faith that encourages such formation. Dewey argues wisely that if schools are to prepare citizens for a democratic society, then they need to function according to democratic principles; democracy must permeate the whole school environment. Surely we can say the same about compassion and justice.

- How might democratic values and formation for good citizenship permeate the ethos of your school? Imagine some practical and effective strategies.
- What are some core civic values that your educational space can intentionally encourage in students? Prioritize the three you consider most vital.

10

Religious Education
in the
Postmodern Catholic School

Frequently throughout this work we have drawn upon the writings of possibly the most renowned social philosopher of our time, Charles Taylor, who is professor emeritus at McGill University, Montreal, and a Templeton Prize winner. Much of his work focuses on understanding how Western cultures have shifted from an earlier age when everyone believed in God with a deeply enculturated faith (he selects 1500 as a likely date) to our own time, which he describes, as do many others, as a "secular age" that actively discourages faith. He claims that, functionally, the dominant paradigm now is to live as our own god, "buffered" in upon our*selves* instead of living "porous" (open) to others and the Transcendent.

Among the many social, political, and philosophical movements that have produced our secular age, Taylor names rationalism, atheism, humanism, immanentism, romanticism, scientism, undue materialism, communism and even deism as a reasoned belief in a god, but one totally removed from the world and unconcerned with us. Instead of expecting any kind of divine help or guidance in life, we simply have to "go it alone" now—and this is considered the more adult and *reasonable* thing to do!

None of these movements, however, explain the mystery of our universe with its design and order, or the mystery that *we* are, even to ourselves, with our own agency and sense of ethic and aesthetic, and likewise our disposition to raise ultimate questions of meaning, truth, and value. Nor can they satisfy the deepest longings of the human heart; they leave us with little sense of higher purpose or horizon. They encourage no sense of grace or community; everything depends on ourselves and is for ourselves. Instead of promoting human flourishing, this exclusively *immanent* frame renders what Taylor calls "a terrible flatness in the everyday."

Taylor argues, however—and he is not alone among contemporary thought leaders—that there is significant cultural and philosophical evidence now of a new day dawning for faith in what is often termed *postmodernity*. There are signs that we are turning the corner toward a more immanent *and* Transcendent approach to life, to embracing both horizontal *and* vertical perspectives and a more personally owned faith that is not dictated by the culture but chosen—often against the grain—with good critical reason. People are finding such a personally persuaded and owned faith, lived into a Transcendent Horizon of loving kindness toward us and encouraging as much toward one another, more life-giving by far than exclusive (of God) humanism or a totally secular imaginary.

While proponents of the secular pose themselves as being reasonable and scientific, dismissing faith as just wishful thinking, Taylor and postmodern scholars like him argue that a transcendent perspective is at least as well reasoned and credible as the exclusively immanent alternatives. Might this more favorable shift toward faith mark a new day for religious education in Catholic schools—to educate all students *for faith*, never by proselytizing but always by attraction to a more fulfilling, meaningful, and responsible way of life in the world?

A NEW CHALLENGE AND OPPORTUNITY

Catholic schools throughout the world are becoming increasingly diverse by way of the religious backgrounds of both their students and faculty. We cited the instance of Catholic schools in Hong Kong, most of which have some 90 percent non-Catholics in the student body and 75 percent in the faculty. This is a growing pattern in many other contexts. For example, as of 2020, in Korean Catholic schools, 83 percent of the students and 33 percent of the teachers are not Catholic. Many of Pakistan's Catholic schools (over five hundred) have had 90 percent Muslim students and faculty for much of their history (some for over two hundred years). Presently, 20 percent of students in Catholic high schools in the United States are of other or no faith traditions, and this number is growing rapidly. Add as well that a significant percentage of students from Catholic backgrounds are often more cultural than "practicing" Catholics.

There is no problem, of course, with a diversity of students from varied or no religious background participating in and benefiting from a

Catholic education—for all the reasons that we have given throughout this book. Though they arise from Catholic faith, the spiritual foundations of Catholic education can be appreciated and shared by persons of other or no faith tradition; they reflect universal values. We cited the statement by Pope Francis in the Preface that the increasing diversity in Catholic schools must be welcomed and seen as an opportunity to expand their contribution to the common good of their societies.

Clearly the values of Jesus were universal and humanizing; they can ground a life-giving education for any person or context. Interpreted with a contemporary consciousness, the same can be said of the Catholic intellectual tradition and its anthropology, sociology, cosmology, and so on, that have emerged over time. A Catholic education, grounded in such spiritual foundations and values, can be a powerful source of humanization for its students and a major contribution to the welfare of any society. In particular, it can be an antidote to the lack of moral formation and the neglect of spiritual nurture that mark the curricula of so many secular schools.

Regarding the religious education curriculum of Catholic schools, however, things become a little more challenging and demand particular sensitivity—though still very navigable. Such schools have always had the stated intent to educate their Catholic students—of whatever devotion or association—in their Catholic faith and in ways that form their identity as Catholic Christians. This has been integral to their purpose since the very first schools sponsored by the church in the early centuries and throughout the ages; it remains so today. This favored commitment for education in Catholic faith for Catholic students must never be compromised; it is essential to the identity and purpose of Catholic schools.

The challenge, therefore, is how to offer religious education in Catholic schools that encourages Catholic students to become Catholic Christians, and yet not in any way to proselytize the students of other or no religious tradition. To do the latter would be an egregious betrayal of trust—*and* of our faith. Indeed, even for Catholic students, the mode of religious education should never be "brain washing," or what the philosopher Michel Foucault called "knowledge control." Instead, the religious education curriculum, while disposing Catholic students toward embracing their Catholic identity, needs to be taught in ways that respect, enrich, and encourage the good discernment of all students in their choice of spiritual path. *The Directory for Catechesis* (2020) explicitly appreciates "the value that present-day culture attributes to *freedom* with respect to the selection of one's own faith" (*DFC*, no. 322).

Different contexts have made varied responses to the emerging challenge of a religiously diverse student body. Those Catholic schools in Pakistan, with a majority Muslim enrollment, hire Muslim teachers to teach the Muslim students their faith throughout grade school and high school. The late president of Pakistan, Benazir Bhutto (1953–2007), tragically assassinated, was educated in her Muslim faith at Jesus and Mary Convent School in Karachi. In some other contexts the non-Catholic students are dispensed from religious education classes and offered substitute courses instead, often called civics or character formation. This is an understandable strategy, especially for younger children.

According to 2018–19 statistics, 17 percent of those enrolled in American Catholic grade and middle schools are not Catholic. Many of those schools keep all the younger children together for religious education with the exception of second grade, when Catholic children are usually prepared for first holy communion; at that time the non-Catholic children have a different program or are simply sent to the library. This seems like an acceptable solution, at least for students from other Christian traditions, since there is not much that is uniquely "Catholic" in those early years; it is likely that 90 percent of the religion curriculum is generic Christian. However, with the *pedagogy* proposed in this chapter, I believe we can offer a religious education curriculum that does not proselytize students from other traditions to Catholic faith and yet can enrich their spiritual journey. To this end, the *pedagogy* will be key!

The phenomenon of non-Catholic students in Catholic schools is more common from the seventh grade upward. Thus, the most intense challenge for religious education pertains to Catholic high schools and colleges (in the latter religious education is often called theology or religious studies). For this level the general sentiment favors a more "objective" teaching of religion(s), with little attempt to shape the faith life and spiritual values of students; this is a lost opportunity to educate all *for* faith.

The alternative pedagogy proposed in this chapter can certainly be engaged in the upper grades and through college; it has already been widely used in a number of popular grade-school religion curricula as well (kindergarten to eighth grade). With good curriculum planning and sensitivity, we can lend access to the spiritual wisdom of Catholic faith specifically and to that of other faith traditions (world religions courses in the upper grades), and do so in ways that enhance the spiritual journey of all.

SO MUCH DEPENDS ON THE PEDAGOGY

Throughout the worldwide system of Catholic schools, it is possible and even *required* to offer a robust curriculum of religious education. It is required because Catholic schools present themselves to the world as educating *from* and *for* faith; surely the religious education curriculum is the flagship of their identity and of their promise to parents who choose it for their children. Catholic schools can offer a curriculum that educates *for* faith, fostering the religious identity of its non-Catholic students in their own traditions while nurturing the Catholic ones in theirs. Of course, much depends on the process of the pedagogy employed.

The traditional assumption regarding the purpose and pedagogy of school-based religious education was that there are only two options. The first is the "objective" teaching of religion(s), a learning about the data of a particular tradition or of varied traditions—much as in the academic discipline of religious studies. This, for example, was the favored option offered by the Religious Education Act of 1944 in England; it made the study of religion a compulsory subject in all state-funded schools but favored an "objective" teaching of varied traditions rather than formation in any particular religious identity, though there was some favor for the study of Christianity because of its cultural heritage to the country. This academic study of religion(s) approach is echoed in many European countries; it is at least an improvement over the context in the United States, where any semblance of teaching religion in public schools is simply taboo. When any religious tradition is included in a school's curriculum, the first responsibility is to teach well *about* it, so that students come to know and understand its core teachings.

The second option is what might be called a "confessional" or "catechetical" approach to religious education, where the intent from start to finish is to inform and form the particular faith identity of participants. Of course, this is the nature and purpose of a Catholic parish program, namely, *learning into* or *learning to become* good Catholic Christians. It is imperative for a Catholic family and parish community to provide education in faith that intends to form the identity of its participants as Catholic Christians. Catholics favor the term *catechesis* for such educating in faith; its etymology refers to "echoing onward" the faith tradition. It reflects the commission that comes with baptism for Christians—to hand on our faith, especially to our children. Effective parish catechetical programs are essential to augment the primary catechesis of the home and family, helping to nurture all—across the life span—in *living* Catholic Christian faith.

Therefore, there has long been a general assumption that religious education has only two options by way of intended learning outcome: one is to be "objective" in teaching religious data so that people *learn about* religion but with no intent to form their identity in faith; the other is to be overtly "confessional" or "catechetical" in the sense of persuading and forming people in a particular faith identity—for example, as Catholic Christians. So, the options seem to be either to *learn about* or to *learn into* a faith tradition.

Over the years I have joined with other religious educators (such as Michael Grimmit and Dermot Lane) to include these two options within a Catholic school and then to pose the possibility of a middle ground between them—the latter out of particular concern for non-Catholic students. Thus, the religious education curriculum would include, for all students, *learning about* particular tradition(s); it is always imperative to know and understand the content of the tradition(s) being studied. Then, this approach can also dispose participants from a distinctive tradition to *learn into* or to embrace their particular faith as their own, for example, to become Catholic Christians. The middle-ground possibility is that every participating student move beyond *learning about* at least to *learn from* the tradition under study, and in ways that enhance and enrich their own identity in faith and spiritual journey, regardless of their tradition (or none).

For example, this would call for teaching Catholic faith so that all students not only *learn about* it but also *learn from* it, and that Catholic students are disposed to *learn into* their tradition and embrace it as their identity in faith. Likewise, in a high school or college curriculum that is teaching other religious traditions, for example, Islam, it can be taught in a way that all participants can *learn about* it and also *learn from* it for their life in faith, and so that Muslim students be disposed to *learn into* their tradition as shaping their faith identity. The same can be said for studying Judaism and all the great religious traditions.

So, Jewish students in a course on Catholicism should be exposed to the rich spirituality of Catholic tradition so that it echoes and enriches their own Jewish faith, encouraging them to more deeply embrace their Jewish identity. I taught such an undergraduate course at Boston College—simply entitled "Catholicism"—for over thirty years. I stated my intent and crafted the pedagogy to enrich and deepen the faith of my many Jewish, Muslim, and other students, inviting them to become more convicted and practicing Jews and Muslims by their exposure to the Catholic tradition, while, hopefully, disposing the Catholic students to embrace their own Catholic identity in faith.

Again, my proposal is set within the understanding of a Catholic school as educating *from* and *for* faith, proposing to all its students a Transcendent Horizon—God—who reaches out to us with loving kindness and grace for the everyday, and invites us to live lives of purpose, meaning, and ethic as a people of God. My proposal also presumes upon the *soul* of students, that they are animated by God's own life within them and are ever recipients of God's grace. It is their souls that make all students capable of being educated *for faith* and to be spiritually enriched by exposure to any of the great religious traditions.

As suggested above and elaborated below, much depends on the pedagogy employed. It should be one that makes it possible for all to *learn about* and *learn from* the religious education curriculum of a Catholic school, and to dispose Catholic students to *learn into* the tradition and embrace it as their own. This requires a pedagogy that (1) personally engages students and their lives in the word; (2) gives them access, in persuasive ways, to the spiritual wisdom of faith tradition(s); and (3) encourages them to come to their own judgments and decisions—interpreting and deciding for themselves—regarding the tradition under study and how it might be a resource for their own faith and spiritual journey. For such a pedagogy we have something to learn from that of Jesus.

For Reflection and Conversation

- What are your own reflections and insights regarding the emerging complexity of religious education in Catholic schools?
- Given the challenges of offering effective religious education in today's Catholic schools, what kind of preparation and formation is needed for its religion/theology teachers?

JESUS'S PEDAGOGY: LIFE TO FAITH TO LIFE *IN* FAITH

Chapter 1 proposed that Jesus can be well identified as a *teacher*. Thereafter, we have drawn repeatedly on what and how he taught and to what end. Here, we distill the core of Jesus's pedagogy, not his general style and overall proposals—already noted—but the fairly precise pedagogical moves he typically made to teach disciples for *living* faith toward the reign of God.

We might summarize the overall dynamic of Jesus's pedagogy as inviting people "from *life to Faith to life* (in faith)." Note that he typically began by inviting people to turn to their own lives/experiences in the world and to reflect on them. Then, into their lives and historical reality, he taught his gospel. His constant intent was to invite disciples to integrate their lives and the faith he proposed as their own *living* faith—*alive, lived,* and *life-giving*—for themselves and "for the life of the world" (John 6:51).

In Chapter 8, we hinted at Jesus's pedagogy as a way to detect his operative epistemology; here we reverse and look at it more as his way of knowing put to work as his pedagogy. We can elaborate Jesus's typical pedagogy as unfolding in five distinguishable movements. Though often subtle, we can detect an overall pattern or approach. I call them movements because they are fluid; in Jesus's teaching praxis, they can occur, recur, and flow in different sequences. For clarity, I lay them out here sequentially; however, as a good teacher, Jesus knew that there is no "lockstep" method.

Movement 1: Beginning with life. Jesus often got people engaged and interested in what he had to teach by turning them to look at some experience, practice, issue, or concern in their daily lives. This could be about catching and sorting fish, sowing seed, baking bread, digging in a field, searching for fine pearls, hiring workers, going down from Jerusalem to Jericho, searching for stray sheep, losing a coin, a wedding celebration, building a house on secure foundations, observing the birds of the air or the lilies of the field or the buds on a tree, and the list goes on.

His favorite way of turning people to their own lives was through parables, allegories (for example, the Good Shepherd), or signs (for example, the wedding at Cana). By engaging people's everyday lives, he was tapping into their souls and inviting their active participation— what we've referred to before as "learning from life." Jesus typically initiated his pedagogy by turning people to the praxis of their real-life themes and issues of concern.

Movement 2: Reflecting on life. While Jesus began with people's own lives, he invited them to think more deeply about them—to recognize that great things like the reign of God and their own eternal destiny were being negotiated in the everyday. He also regularly encouraged them to question their attitudes and taken-for-granted assumptions, often to "see" in a whole new way: the Samaritan becomes the neighbor; the prodigal is welcomed home; Lazarus goes "to be with Abraham" while the rich man goes to "Hades"; the prostitutes and tax collectors are entering into the reign of God before the religious leaders. Such reversals were Jesus's way of getting people to reflect critically, to question the influences of their sociocultural context, and perhaps to change their minds and hearts to see their lives in a whole new way.

Movement 3: Teaching his gospel with authority. Then, into the midst of people's own reality, Jesus proclaimed his gospel and the in-breaking of God's reign *now*. From the beginning of his public ministry people recognized that he taught "with authority" (Mark 1:22). Given that he had no official capacity (he was not a trained rabbi or a member of the Sanhedrin) his authority must have been the integrity and witness of his own life. Furthermore, Jesus presented his gospel with great persuasion, intent that people come to see for themselves the blessings of living for the reign of God—such living being its own reward. It can bring real happiness (blessedness—Matt 5:1–11) or, as Jesus stated to the disciples on the night before he died, all his teaching was that "my joy may be in you, and that your joy may be complete" (John 15:11).

It is clear, too, that Jesus drew heavily upon his traditional Jewish faith, its great *story* across the centuries. And yet, he was also proposing a renewed *vision*, a new moment and possibility for the reign of God—like "now." So, on the one hand, he clearly cherished the Jewish faith of his people, obeyed its precepts, quoted its scriptures, and said that he had come not to abolish the Law and the Prophets but "to make their teaching come true" (Matt 5:17).

On the other hand, he claimed authority to reinterpret the tradition, to point to how people were missing out on the spirit of the Law, and to propose a renewed vision for living as a people of God. "You have heard it said . . . but I say . . ." (Matt 5:21–22). Furthermore, Jesus summarizes this faithfulness and openness regarding tradition when he says, "Every scribe who has been trained for the kingdom of heaven is like the master of a household who brings out of his treasure [storeroom] what is new and what is old" (Matt 13:52). The faith that Jesus taught always reflected both *story* and *vision*.

Movement 4: Inviting people to see for themselves. Pedagogically, Jesus's clear intent was that would-be disciples come to see for themselves and embrace with conviction the *way* and wisdom of his gospel. He wished them to take it to heart and personally to embrace what he was teaching—out of discernment and conviction. As noted earlier, he often blessed those with the eyes to see and the ears to hear. More than physical seeing and hearing, he wanted people to be open and to see and hear and embrace with conviction—of both mind and heart—what he was teaching. Yet his call to discipleship was always by invitation, leaving people free to discern and decide for themselves.

Movement 5: Decision for living faith. Throughout his public teaching it is clear that Jesus's intended "learning outcome" was that people personally make the decision for *living* faith and embrace his *way* as their own, implementing it in their daily lives. Always implied, he often made this call to decision explicit. At the end of the great parable of the Good Samaritan, after inviting the lawyer's discernment as to who was the neighbor (movement 4), Jesus tells him, "Go and do likewise" (Luke 10:37; movement 5). After washing the disciples' feet, Jesus told them, "I have set you an example, that you also should do as I have done to you" (John 13:15). His ultimate invitation to all was "Come follow me"—decide to live as disciples for God's reign. Many so chose, but many did not (see John 6:66).

Not in lockstep, yet consistently, we can recognize these five pedagogical moves in the overall teaching style of Jesus. In summary, he was always inviting people to bring their lives to their faith and their faith to their lives. Sometimes Jesus would appear to have done all the movements in just a one-verse parable. For example: "Look at the birds of the air (movement 1); they neither sow nor reap nor gather into barns (movement 2), and yet your heavenly Father feeds them (movement 3). Are you not of more value than they?" (Matt 6:26; movements 4 and 5).

ON THE ROAD WITH THE RISEN CHRIST

The pedagogical moves outlined above are evident in Jesus's approach to teaching throughout his public ministry. Nowhere, however, are they as vividly represented as in the story of the Risen Christ accompanying two disciples on the road to Emmaus (Luke 24:13–35).

The story begins with two bewildered disciples stumbling out of Jerusalem on Easter Sunday morning and making their way "to a village named Emmaus," about seven miles away. They are surely brokenhearted at the crucifixion of their beloved Jesus and the shattering of the hopes that they had placed in him. The Risen Christ joins "their company" as if a fellow traveler, but they are too traumatized to recognize him. Instead of intruding or imposing himself, however, the Stranger is content to "join their company and walk along with them." What a wise proposal for a teacher's mode of presence to students' lives. Pope Francis, for whom this is a favorite pedagogical passage, describes the Stranger's style as "accompaniment" of the two disciples; this highlights his willingness to *walk along with* them in their sadness, to draw them out with *good questions*, and to *listen* intently to their pain.

This accompanying Stranger inquires what they are talking about in such a lively fashion. When they hesitate, incredulous that anyone would not know of the tragic events that had just taken place in Jerusalem, he asks, "What things?" What an amazing pedagogical move—surely no one knew better than he what had happened in Jerusalem. His clear intent was to have them look at, name, and reflect upon their own painful reality. They proceed to tell him their *story* of "all the things about Jesus of Nazareth," how he was crucified, and to share their shattered *vision*: "we had hoped that he was the one to set Israel free." They add an "astounding" story that "some women of our group" had come back from Jesus's tomb with a report from "angels" that Jesus was alive, but who could believe such a fantasy (movements 1 and 2; note, perhaps, a cultural bias in their incredulity toward the women witnesses).

Only then does the Risen One share with them what we can call the *story* and *vision* of their faith community (movement 3). "Beginning with Moses and all the prophets, he interpreted for them all the passages of scripture that referred to himself" and "explained that the messiah had to so suffer so as to enter into his glory." Perhaps this is why they still don't recognize him; they were hoping for a great political messiah who "would set Israel free" from the Romans, whereas he came as a suffering servant. He has set up a dialectic between their hopes for the messianic promise and how it was actually fulfilled in Jesus.

At this point in what proves to be a day-long conversation, their own painful story and shattered vision and the *story* and *vision* of their faith community are on the table. Even so, the two disciples still do not "see," and the Stranger continues to resist telling them. In fact, he never *tells* them what to see but waits for them to come to see for themselves—as if this is essential to renewing their battered faith and lost hope. Coming near to Emmaus and their destiny, he appeared ready to travel onward. The Stranger intrigues them enough, though, that they press him, "Stay with us, because it is almost evening and the day is now nearly over." This offer of hospitality entices him to continue the conversation, so "he went in to stay with them." And as reflected throughout Jesus's ministry, his best teaching was often around a meal table.

As the three are seated at table, the Stranger *takes, blesses, breaks,* and *gives* the bread to them (the same four verbs as at the Last Supper). With that, their eyes are opened, and they recognize the Risen One in their midst. In a sense, the Stranger had now become doubly present—in the shared bread and as their conversation partner—enabling the two disciples to finally *see* him for themselves. It would appear that they had integrated their own learning from life experience (their own *story* and *vision*) with the tradition of their faith community (its *Story* and *Vision*) to come to a deep level of personal *recognition* (the Greek, *epiginosko*, reflects the recognition as between friends; movement 4). They were bonded with the Risen Christ, whereupon he vanishes from their sight, leaving them to decide what to do in response. Now that they have come to see for themselves, perhaps his pedagogical work was done.

Amazed at how he had set their "hearts burning" during his "opening the scriptures" to them upon the road, they make a major turnaround—literally—a life-changing decision. They get up immediately and return to a renewed life of faith in the Jerusalem Christian community. This would have been a hazardous journey at night; such recognition, however, simply "cannot wait" but must be shared and lived (movement 5). The Stranger had accompanied them *from life to Faith,* and now they recommit to a *life in faith*.

In Jerusalem, they join the community of disciples, reassembling after their trauma and trying to get their heads and hearts around what is nigh unbelievable: that God had raised Jesus from the dead. The two are greeted with, "The Lord has risen indeed, and he has appeared to Simon." So, a new Story of faith is gathering, the Christian Story and its Vision of a Risen Savior. While receiving this amazing *good news* from the community, the two from the road have their own story and vision to share: "Then they told what had happened on the road, and how he had been made known to them in the breaking of the bread" (Matt 24:35).

A few further notes. First, the conversation and presentation on the road were important, and yet recognition happened in "the breaking of the bread." Likewise, while our pedagogy is significant, far more effective is our relationship of love and care for our students—the many ways that we "break bread" with them. Second, the new *Directory for Catechesis* encourages what I'm calling here a "life to Faith to life" pedagogy. It recommends that educating in faith begin with "human experience" and "concrete life situations" that are then interpreted "in the light of the Gospel," with the intent to integrate these two sources into "life lived in openness and in harmony with the work of God" (*DFC,* nos. 197–98).

And while there are many expressions of Christian faith (scriptures and traditions, dogmas and doctrines, symbols and sacraments, and so on), the *DFC* notes the particular effectiveness of "narrative language" to access Christian faith because it engages the "affective, cognitive, [and] volitional" of people's lives (nos. 207–8).

For Reflection and Conversation

- When you think about the pedagogy of Jesus, what features most stand out for you?
- Reviewing Jesus's "life to Faith to life" teaching approach, what might be helpful to appropriate into your own pedagogy—regardless of what subject you are teaching?

GROUNDING A "LIFE TO FAITH TO LIFE" APPROACH FOR EDUCATING IN FAITH

For more than forty years I have been attempting to forge an approach to religious education that might be effective and adjustable for any context of Catholic parish or school, for any faith tradition, or for contexts with varied traditions. While my primary location and commitment is for my own Catholic Christian tradition and community of faith, I hoped it would be fitting and effective for religious education in other Christian traditions, certainly, and then with potential for educating in all the classic traditions of religious faith. (To date, it has been well received by Jewish and Muslim religious educators.)

My efforts in teaching with this approach at every grade level and then to articulate its scholarly foundations have resulted in writings that have spanned the spectrum, including grade and high school religion curricula, undergraduate theology texts, adult faith formation resources, and scholarly works intended for graduate seminars. (For in-depth review of the pedagogy, see *Sharing Faith*, 1991, or the more accessible, *Will There Be Faith?*, 2011.) The more scholarly writings explore the Western philosophical tradition, searching in particular for epistemological seeds—ways of knowing—that would contribute to a holistic kind of pedagogy, capable of informing minds, engaging hearts, and shaping values toward *living* faith. And there are lots of significant seeds to be uncovered again and replanted to bear the fruit of such a pedagogy. Let me give just two of the more notable examples.

Note, again, the biblical emphasis on spiritual wisdom as the pinnacle of knowledge and the Bible's deeply relational sense of knowing reflected in its verbs *yada* (Hebrew) and *ginosko* (Greek)—for love making. Clearly, a biblical mode of knowing is far more holistic, formative, and relational than our present favor for disengaged reasoning. Then, add Aristotle's insistence that a praxis way of knowing—reflection upon and learning from life—is most effective to educate in virtue and to form people's *being*—who they are and how they live. I found Aristotle's portrayal of praxis (and later Freire's) more agential than Dewey's notion of experience; the latter tends toward passivity (an experience is typically something we undergo), whereas praxis refers to what we initiate ourselves as well as what comes our way in our historical context. Nevertheless, *experience* is a more relatable term in English, and I often find myself using it as well, or subsuming both terms—praxis and experience—in the phrase *learning from life*.

As one might expect, I also drew heavily upon the Catholic intellectual tradition and its "both/and" commitments (to faith and reason, revelation and science, cognition and formation, and so on), and from the wisdom of its great exponents like Julian of Norwich and Ignatius of Loyola. Furthermore, I was informed by the theology that undergirds a Catholic anthropology, sociology, cosmology, epistemology, sense of public faith, and so on (see Chapters 7, 8 and 9). As a process emerged, I was most encouraged by coming to recognize a similar pattern in the pedagogy of Jesus, epitomized in the accompaniment by that Stranger on the road to Emmaus.

At first I was hesitant to make claims for Jesus's approach, not being a trained biblical scholar and having never found a New Testament expert who had focused explicitly on his pedagogical moves. (Pheme Perkins's *Jesus as Teacher* was helpful.) Eventually, I realized that, unlike myself, they were not bringing to the texts of the Gospels an interest in his pedagogy as I was. By not looking for the pattern of Jesus's teaching approaches, they were not alert to recognize them. All these scholarly sources, and there were many more, came together to form the approach to religious education that I propose here. And yet, if it is true that "all great ideas are simple" (attributed to Albert Einstein), then its essence can be summarized as "bringing life to Faith to life (in faith)."

When I write about it more technically, my proposal is called a shared Christian praxis approach to educating in faith. It is an overarching *approach* in that it can be implemented by many teaching styles and methods of instruction. *Praxis* signifies that it invites people to name, reflect upon, and learn from their own lives in the world. It is *Christian* (Jewish, or whatever tradition is being taught) in that it draws upon both the Story and Vision of Christian faith, meaning the whole faith tradition and what it asks of and promises to people's lives. And it is *shared* in that its overarching paradigm is *conversation*, conversation with and among participants, and conversation between their own praxis and the Christian Story and Vision. This exchange invites students to see and decide for themselves how to personally integrate the two sources into their own faith and spiritual wisdom. (This integrative process or *dialectical hermeneutics* (see below) is especially necessary to avoid proselytizing non-Catholic students.)

While a "life to Faith to life" approach entails many insights and commitments, there is none more foundational than its epistemology. This is to be expected; we need a way of knowing that can be readily implemented as a pedagogy and is likely to serve the desired learning outcomes of a *living* faith. Here, the aim is to encourage a *living* Christian faith; however, I will also suggest how the approach can promote *living* faith in other great religious traditions as well.

Drawing upon the Catholic intellectual tradition, we reviewed the aspects of such an epistemology in Chapter 8 as for all education; we assembled them under (1) the *sources* of knowledge as both *experience* and *tradition*; (2) *ways* of knowing that engage heads, hearts, and hands (will); and (3) the *dynamics* of cognition, which refers to the cumulative sequence of attending, understanding, judging, and deciding. To appropriate such an epistemology into religious education for *living* faith, we slightly alter the sequence here, beginning with (1) the *ways* of knowing; (2) the *dynamics* of cognition; and finally (3) the *sources* for knowing in faith. Having reviewed them more theoretically in Chapter 8, here we can be brief, appropriating them specifically for religious education.

Regarding the *ways* of knowing, religious education must engage the heads, hearts, and hands (will) of the knowers. Engaging students' heads entails drawing upon the capacities of their whole mind—reason, memory, and imagination. Reason will engage students to think, and according to developmental readiness, to think critically—with discernment. As noted earlier, such critical reflection encourages students to think and then to think about their thinking, recognizing their own sociocultural biases and the influence of their historical context on what they think. Likewise, critical reflection engages analytical memory and creative imagination to uncover often forgotten memories, what to learn from them, and to imagine consequences and new horizons.

Following on, religious education needs to engage the *emotive* capacities and affectivity of students, the hungers of their hearts and how best to meet them. It should be formative of students' ethic—their hands—offering them commandments, guidelines, norms, examples, reasons, questions, and practices that are likely to form them in good values and habits as integral to *living* Christian faith.

Regarding the *dynamics* of cognition, religious educators must surely prompt students to move beyond attending to data and understanding it to encourage making judgments and decisions as well, and doing so as deliberately and reflectively as possible (depending on age, ability, and so forth). Encouraging judgments and decisions is imperative because the religious educator's intent is that people at least *learn from* and make decisions regarding religious traditions and not just to *learn about* them, which stops at understanding. Furthermore, making judgments and decisions encourages students to reach beyond knowledge to embrace personally chosen truths, wisdom, and values and to appropriate their own spiritual wisdom for life. Note, too, that the *data* attended to and to be understood is that of students' own life in the world *and* the religious tradition(s) being accessed.

The dual *sources* of faith knowing are religious *tradition* and then what I have variously named as experience, praxis, or simply learning from life. The last term may be the most readily understood and comprehensive. It also signals that we can learn, literally, from every aspect and instance of our daily lives; we are always knowing and learning somehow from our life in the world. Then add, as noted earlier, that we must bring all our capacities for knowing—mind, emotions, and will—to reflect critically (discerningly) upon our lives in the world.

Also, though critical reflection on life in the world can sound aseptic and cognitivist, in fact, it inevitably also engages our emotions and values. We literally cannot think about our own experiences and lives dispassionately; such reflection always engages what we can know through our emotions and wills as well as our minds. This is why I often refer to students reflecting on their lives in the world as sharing their own stories and visions, in other words, what they know from where they are coming from, where they are, and where they anticipate or hope to go. Existentially, a favored way to share such knowing from life is through personal narrative in conversation—people's own stories—which inevitably engages people's hearts.

Then, turning to the second great source of our knowing, and as for general education, the pedagogy must also lend ready access to *tradition*. Here I represent *tradition* as the Story and Vision of Christian faith. Though often accessed in a narrative way, I use both terms metaphorically. Elaborating a little beyond what was outlined above, *Story* refers to the whole sweep of Christian faith over time (scriptures and creeds, symbols and sacraments, prayers and pieties, values and virtues, commandments and counsels, community structures and leadership, sacred times and holy places, and so on) and its spiritual wisdom for life now. Vision is a metaphor for all that the Christian Story offers to and asks of people's lives. Again, the ultimate Vision is for the reign of God that constantly invites people into *living* faith.

In the context of religious education, the accessing of *tradition* needs to be done in a persuasive way, one likely to encourage people to embrace as their own its truths and spiritual wisdom toward *living* faith. For Christian religious education, this requires presenting the Christian Story and Vision in ways that are credible and persuasive for people, not by dictate of authority but by representing its rich spiritual wisdom for the lives of all participants. Other traditions being taught within a curriculum of religious education should be presented as offering tried-and-tested spiritual wisdom for life that good and intelligent people have found believable and enriching across thousands of years.

So, the twin sources of *knowing* in Christian religious education are people's own reflection upon and learning from life—their own story/ vision—and then having persuasive access to the *tradition* of Christian faith, to its Story/Vision. The perennial challenge for its pedagogy is to enable people to integrate these two sources. To bring *life to Faith* in order to bring *Faith to life* requires integration by participants, not only in their minds but also in their hearts and lives.

Unless the Story/Vision connects with people's real lives, with what Freire described (and Jesus practiced well) as their generative themes— what really matters to them—they are likely, at most, to *learn about* the faith tradition but not to *learn from* or *learn into* it. Nor can it be a matter of having people reflect on their lives and then "answering" their needs by simply "applying" Christian (or whatever) faith. There must be what the Second Vatican Council called "a living exchange" between Christian faith and the diverse life situations of people in real life (*Church in Modern World*, no. 44). This process of living exchange is well named a *dialectical hermeneutics*.

Hermeneutics is the general process of interpretation. Religious educators need to constantly function as "hermeneutes," ever enabling participants to interpret the data from their own lives in the world and from the texts and traditions of learning that we are teaching. In religious education the subjects for interpretation are people's own praxis, their own story and vision, and then the Story and Vision of Christian faith (or of whatever tradition is being taught). *Dialectical* reflects a real give and take between the two sources—people's own story/vision and the Christian Story/Vision—a back and forth, much like a good *conversation* (Plato's understanding of dialectics). As with any good and honest conversation, there will be agreements and disagreements, old insights and wisdom remembered and new ones discovered. Such dialectical hermeneutics amounts to people interpreting—coming to see for themselves—and personally embracing what to take to heart from the faith tradition for their *living* faith in the midst of the world.

As we set out the pedagogical movements below, movements 1 and 2 reflect the hermeneutics of our own praxis, movement 3 is a hermeneutic of the Christian Story/Vision. Then the *dialectical* hermeneutics is especially present in movements 4 and 5, which interpret the interchange between the two sources and what they mean for each other. This is precisely what allows students to reach beyond *learning about* to choose to *learn from* a tradition that is not their own or to *learn into* a tradition that they embrace as their personal faith.

Instead of passively accepting what was taught by the teacher (and repeating it back), participants in movements 4 and 5 need to discern what they affirm, question, and imagine onward from the Story/Vision for their own lives in faith. In summary, dialectical hermeneutics means inviting students to claim their own insights and make their own decisions rather than simply having them repeat what the teacher just taught. Such dialectical hermeneutics encourages a deep freedom for students; it enables them to come to and embrace their own perspectives and decisions by their informed choosing.

The dynamic in movements 4 and 5, then, is similar to Lonergan's notions of judgment and decision, though instead of "judgment," I prefer "seeing for oneself" and "making one's own" regarding the spiritual wisdom of a faith tradition. The pedagogy employed should prompt and encourage such a dialectical hermeneutic rather than, as so often, telling students what to think and then having them repeat it back.

All of the above *sources* of knowledge, *ways* of knowing, and *dynamics* of cognition, along with the dialectical hermeneutics that mediate between people's own stories/visions and the Christian Story/ Vision, point to this approach as having the overarching paradigm of *conversation* within a *community* of co-learners. A purely didactic mode might be effective in *learning about* a tradition, but it is unlikely to encourage people to *learn from* or *learn into* its spiritual wisdom.

Of course, there is room for presentation within the conversation, and there is need for diverse ways of lending ready access to the resources of faith traditions. Yet the overall paradigm should be one of conversation rather than didaction that receives and repeats what the teacher teaches. Christian religious education should stimulate conversation within participants themselves, with one another, then with the Story/Vision of Christian faith and perhaps even with God, in order to place those two sources—life in the world and Christian tradition—in conversation toward their own discerning and potential embrace of *living* faith. Conversation also signals the communal and egalitarian nature of the process. Even the etymology of conversation, the Latin *con versatio*, means to "turn toward" another. A conversational approach encourages a *community of co-learners*, albeit most often with a teacher as the *leading learner*. This co-learning community should encourage each participant to speak their own word, to reflect upon and share their own reality and wisdom—to tell their own story and to hear the stories of others. Because it encourages such communality, *conversation* is a more appropriate description of the dynamic than discussion or dialogue.

For Reflection and Conversation

- When you look closely at your own pedagogy, what do you recognize as its epistemology—the ways of knowing that undergird it?
- How might the building blocks of a religious education pedagogy outlined above be suggestive for your own approach to teaching?

A SHARED CHRISTIAN PRAXIS APPROACH
(AKA LIFE TO FAITH TO LIFE)

For religious educators to implement the epistemology outlined above clearly requires a corresponding pedagogical approach, a consistent way of teaching that engages and implements the appropriate *sources*, *ways*, and *dynamics* of cognition. In sum, this pedagogy needs to engage actively the interests of participants by connecting with generative themes reflected in their day-to-day lives; invite their own naming and reflecting critically upon those themes; give them persuasive access to the Christian Story and Vision (or whatever religion is being taught); and then encourage participants to integrate their life in the world and this faith tradition into their own *living* faith. Such integration honors and encourages students' own personal discernment and decision-making—dialectical hermeneutics—whether to *learn from* the spiritual wisdom of the Christian Story/Vision or to *learn into* it as one's own identity.

In an actual teaching-learning event, a *shared Christian praxis approach* can be enacted around a focusing activity and five pedagogical movements. These are similar to the movements we recognized in the pedagogy of Jesus. Though they can occur, reoccur, combine, overlap, and vary in sequence (as movements in a symphony), for clarity I present them sequentially here.

To illuminate this necessarily brief description, I propose a possible outline of a theology class in a Catholic high school with juniors around the daunting theme of the Blessed Trinity in Christian faith. Later, I outline a class with a group of ten-to-twelve-year-olds in a parish catechesis program, around the generative theme "Jesus Is Our Friend." This will be a sample of the pedagogy with that age level and also for a catechetical context with a confessional language pattern. More briefly, I offer the outline of a college-level theology class on the Muslim tradition of zakat. All the examples arise from my own teaching over the years; they are offered here with an invitation for readers to imagine how they might craft and facilitate such a conversation.

Focusing activity: Establishing the curriculum around a life/faith theme. Here the intent is twofold: (1) to engage people as active participants in the teaching/learning dynamic, and (2) to focus and arouse their interest on a generative theme of life or of life in faith. This means to raise up a substantive issue that they can recognize as significant and of real import to their lives in the world.

Regarding our first example, it surely takes imagination to get adolescents interested in the Christian doctrine of the One and Triune nature of God and to make it seem relevant to their everyday lives. Many times I have begun by playing the Beatles' song "Love Is All You Need." In more recent years, of course, I've had to explain who the Beatles were. My hope is that the music and words will still engage their interest, if only for its surprise in a religion class. One might divide them into groups of three (of course) and give each group a copy of the words or display them on PowerPoint; then play the song, urging them to listen carefully and read along, taking note of what the words are proposing, what *they* are hearing, and their own personal responses. If nothing else, this has usually gotten them engaged.

Movement 1: Naming the theme as reflected in present praxis. Here the educator encourages participants to express themselves around the generative theme as reflected in their present lives and situations. They can name what they themselves do or see others doing, their own feelings, thoughts, or interpretations, and their perception of what is going on around them in their sociocultural context—apropos the theme of the curriculum. Their expressions here can be mediated through any means of communication—spoken words, art, writing, movement, construction, technology, and so on.

After listening to the Beatles' song and carefully reviewing the words, one might pose the following questions to students: What are the Beatles proposing here as the love that the world most needs? Does it ring true to your own lives, experiences, and practices of love—with family, friends, neighbors, in school, and so on? After some small-group conversation, bring all together for general sharing around those questions, inviting them to speak boldly from their own lives and convictions—agree, disagree, or add.

Movement 2: Reflecting critically on the theme of life/faith. The intent here is to encourage participants to reflect critically—historically, contextually, socioculturally—on the praxis they named and expressed in movement 1. Critical reflection can engage reason, memory, imagination, or a combination of them, and, depending on developmental readiness, will be both personal and sociocultural. Cumulatively, movement 1 and movement 2 amount to an expression of participants' own stories and visions around the generative theme.

Regarding young people and the Trinity, invite them, perhaps in whole group conversation, to critique the understanding of love reflected in the Beatles' song, how it might ring true or false, how they understand love from their own lives in the world, and what is shaping their perspectives. Then invite them to reflect on why it may be true—or false—that all the *world* needs now is love, and to imagine what kind of love would so deliver. Invite them to reflect on the gift and challenge of real love, how to distinguish between true and false love, wise and unwise love, and how their own context and young-adult culture is shaping their opinions and positions.

Movement 3: Accessing the Christian Story and Vision. Here the pedagogical task is to teach persuasively the Christian Story around the theme of the occasion toward the students' way of life as living faith (the Vision). Participants should have ready access to the truths, values, practices, and spiritual wisdom of Christian faith (or whatever tradition is being taught) around the theme and how it might be relevant to their lives here and now. Every great faith Story has a Vision to it for people's lives.

Regarding our example, one might begin movement 3 with a summary proposal: that maybe the Christian understanding of God as one and triune Love could shed light on our knowledge of ourselves as lovers and how we're called to live—in love. One might place this alongside the teaching of the Judeo-Christian faith that we—all people—are made in the divine image and likeness, and thus made to be loved and to be lovers. Then offer a contemporary understanding of this traditional Christian doctrine of the Blessed Trinity, highlighting how God within

Godself and always toward us is as one and triune Love, inviting us to so live—in divine likeness. The key is to raise up the rich potential that this traditional Christian doctrine might offer for our personhood today and how we might responsibly reflect such divine love in our lives—the possibilities and responsibilities it offers us, and so on.

Movement 4: Appropriating Christian Faith to Life. Movement 4 begins the move back to life again, focusing precisely now on how students can learn from or learn into the Christian faith. The pedagogy of movement 4 is to encourage participants to discern for themselves what a particular aspect of the Christian Story/Vision might mean for their everyday lives and according to their own perspectives. This is where dialectical hermeneutics is particularly called for in order to prevent proselytizing. Thus, needed here are questions that encourage students to recognize their own insights and responses from *their* perspective, to discern what they are coming to see for themselves and might make their own. The key is to encourage all students to at least learn *from* the wisdom of Christian faith by their own discernment, and for students of Christian background to learn *into* and perhaps be disposed to choose the tradition as their identity in faith.

In response to the exposition of the Blessed Trinity, one might invite the young people to reflect on and share what rings true to their own lives in this core symbol of Christian faith and invite them to discern what of its spiritual wisdom they can take to heart. The key reflection is around what they are coming to "see for themselves" regarding this symbol. This would entail being clear about the Christian doctrine of God as triune Love both within Godself and toward us, and then how they might imagine living lives of real and true love themselves.

Movement 5: Making decisions in light of Christian faith. Here, participants are invited to discern and move to decision about the accessed truths, values, and spiritual wisdom of Christian faith (or whatever tradition is being taught). Depending on the generative theme, decisions here can be cognitive, affective, or behavioral, shaping what people now believe, how they might relate with God and other people, or the values they aspire to embrace and live by.

With young people on the Blessed Trinity, I have often begun movement 5 by playing the Beatles' song a second time, and asking again if the Beatles might have it right—with some nuance to their understanding of it—that love is all we need. Back in groups of three and then all together, invite them to pause, recognize, and then share any fresh insights or decisions emerging for them, both about the nature of God as triune Love and what this could mean for themselves. I have often assigned some homework, for example, to write a page (double spaced) on their *understanding* now of this Christian doctrine of the Blessed Trinity and what new *recognitions* or *invitations* they discerned for their own life in faith.

Before offering some more samples, let me highlight a few practical notes. In a student group that is religiously diverse, the educator needs to use a descriptive rather than prescriptive language pattern in representing a faith tradition. For example, instead of saying "*we* believe in Jesus Christ" or "*we* celebrate seven sacraments," teachers need to say that "Christians believe," or "Catholics celebrate," and so on—not presuming that all present share such identity in faith. In a catechetical context, however, such personal ownership language is entirely appropriate.

I am often asked by high school religion teachers or college-level theology teachers about how to "grade" students when using this approach; schools usually require such evaluation (not the parish). The key is in the three terms: *understanding, recognition,* and *invitation.* These echo Lonergan's dynamics of cognition: attend to data, understand it, and then make judgments and decisions about it. A teacher can certainly evaluate students on their *understanding* of what was taught, expressed in their own words—a key sign of comprehension. Then one can also evaluate their judgments and decisions, not for their content—they are truly entitled to their own opinions—but for how seriously they performed these functions.

For example, many times, having taught Thomas Aquinas's understanding of the human person to undergraduates, I would set an exam or essay question, asking them first to explain in their own words their understanding of Aquinas's theology of the person. This segment of the essay can certainly be graded. Then I would further pose whether they agree or disagree with Aquinas's position, and what they might learn from his anthropology for their own lives. The latter two aspects I can grade for how seriously they address the questions, not for the students' personal opinion.

Let me note, too, from my own experience and the reports of many others that the unfolding pedagogy is eminently logical and cumulative, and with a little imagination, is readily implemented. With practice, it can become a *habitus* (Aquinas), your typical though always reflective way of teaching. This being said, after trying to practice this approach for a lifetime now, it still brings surprises and never goes exactly according to plan—likely because it respects the participants as human beings.

Note, again, that the movements have great flexibility and their sequencing can readily vary. For example, I have often begun with something from movement 3 in order to engage students' interest in the curriculum theme, then go back to movement 1 and movement 2 before coming back to movement 3 for a more complete presentation. Likewise, one can pose movement 4 questions—checking in on what and how students are hearing—and then return to movement 3 for further elaboration. In facilitating movements 4 and 5, which often combine, one may recall what was said at movement 1 and 2, as well as at movement 3, and so on. Note, too, in an existential event the movements may often be combined and can also be realized over different time frames and number of meetings. I have spread the focusing act and five movements over a week of three seventy-five-minute undergraduate classes, and so on. And now for another sample!

A Parish Program Example

When I have volunteered in a parish catechetical program with ten-to-twelve-year-olds, one of my favorite classes to teach is titled "Jesus Is My Friend" (a theme in their published curriculum). Though a confessional and catechetical context, with the intent that participants *learn into* their Catholic identity, this still engages their own choice and discernment. Working with a co-teacher, I outline how we typically have proceeded.

Limited to a fifty-five minute Sunday-morning class, we focus the generative theme by displaying a large image of a very friendly looking Jesus surrounded by children, invite them to look closely at and enjoy the picture, and then say: "Today we will learn about the best friend you will ever have; someone who will always be your friend, no matter what. His name is Jesus." We seem to get most of their attention and interest.

Movement 1: Theme in present praxis. We ask the children, "But first, what does it really mean to be a friend?" We invite them to choose someone they consider to be a good friend and then, taking paper and markers, to draw or represent their good friend. We invite them to share their drawings and tell the story of their good friend if they wish. Many do.

Movement 2: Critical reflection on theme. We then invite the children to reflect with such questions as "What does it mean to be a friend?" "How do we know when someone is a good friend?" "Why do we need friends in life?" "What are the joys of having a good friend?" "What are the demands?" "What makes for a best friend?" As a transition to movement 3, we often ask, "Have you ever thought of Jesus as a friend?" and "What kind of friend would you imagine Jesus being for *you?*"

Movement 3: Christian Story and Vision. We gather the children in a circle and focus again on the friendly image of Jesus. Then we tell some stories of Jesus's special outreach and welcome for children. Found repeatedly in all three Synoptic Gospels, we paint a word picture and invite the children to imagine the scene: parents trying to push their kids through a huge crowd to get a blessing from Jesus; the disciples holding them back; Jesus objecting, "Let the children come to me." He explained that theirs is the kingdom of God and encouraged the adults to become more childlike if they are to belong as well. As a sign of his loving care for them, Jesus embraced and blessed the children. We reflect further on the kind of friend Jesus is to them now and what it means to be a friend of Jesus today (the Vision).

Movement 4: Appropriating Christian faith to life. With the children we engage conversation around, "So what do *you* think? Can Jesus really be your friend? What does that tell you about Jesus? About yourself? What kind of friend will he be? How might you be a friend to Jesus? Some of the challenges? How would people know that you're a friend of Jesus?"

Movement 5: Making faith decisions. With the children (and typically running out of time), we invite them to make a decision and to write it in their notebooks: "One thing I will try to do this week to show that I'm a friend of Jesus." We welcome them, if comfortable, to share their decisions. Many do.

A World Religious Example

More briefly, now, in a Catholic college world religions course, imagine a class on the Muslim tradition of zakat (care for those in need). Since most of the students in my context are not Muslim, the pedagogy might begin by borrowing a little from movement 3 to introduce the notion of zakat, one of the five pillars of Islam, giving a brief summary of how this rich teaching is practiced by Muslims throughout the world. (The key is to make the theme of interest for all.)

The pedagogy might then focus on the reality of poverty in our world, including local poverty (maybe some statistics or a brief documentary or some personal experiences of poverty, and so on). Movement 1 and movement 2 could invite students to name and reflect critically upon the poverties of their own lives, of their society and world, on the causes and consequences of such suffering and injustice, and perhaps begin to imagine what can be done about it and how.

Movement 3 would teach persuasively the Muslim tradition of zakat. This very rich spiritual practice encourages a spirit of dependence on God's providence, requiring as gratitude our generosity toward people most in need. To have faith in Allah demands the practice of zakat—the Vision.

Movements 4 and 5 could invite students to discern and make a decision about how zakat might inspire them to respond to the various poverties in their lives and world. Christian students might be invited to learn *from* this rich spiritual practice and to find resonance in their own tradition (for example, the Sermon on Mount, how we will be judged, the spiritual and corporal works of mercy). Muslim students can be invited to consider making a personal commitment to the practice of zakat in their lives going forward.

For Reflection and Conversation

- What is your immediate response to a "life to Faith to life" approach to religious education? Can you imagine using it or some elements of it in your own pedagogy?
- What are some of the challenges to effective religious education in your school or parish community? How might this approach help meet the challenges?

FOR CATHOLIC EDUCATION

The freedom and promise to offer religious education as an integral aspect of its curriculum is what particularly distinguishes a Catholic school. Even by calling a school Catholic we signal that it offers education both *from* and *for* faith, that it puts faith to work from its spiritual foundations. This reflects education that *arises out of* and is *shaped by* faith convictions, and likewise that intends to encourage students in a faith stance toward life in the world. As stated often throughout, at a minimum this means inviting students to live their lives toward a Transcendent Horizon, a God of loving kindness toward them whose effective love—grace—is ever at work in their lives.

Beyond academic excellence, which is the rightful expectation of every Catholic school, we promise a faith-based education with a spiritual grounding for moral formation and for living life with a deep sense of meaning and purpose—reaching beyond "self" advancement to serve the common good. With such rationale and purpose, its religious education curriculum should be the flagship of every Catholic school, the cornerstone of the faith-based education and spiritual foundations that distinguish the whole enterprise. And the religious education curriculum in a Catholic school should be as "academically rigorous and systematic as the other disciplines" (*DFC*, no. 315).

Yet, if truth be told, religious education is frequently not the centerpiece of Catholic schools for a variety of reasons. Often, there is insufficient preparation of teachers to take on effective responsibility for its curriculum. For example, in American Catholic schools, approximately 90 percent of math and social-studies teachers have a background in their disciplines, but only 10 percent of religious educators have as much. It often happens, too, that the religious-education curriculum is dispensed with when teachers are under pressure to meet learning deadlines for government-assigned standardized tests.

Furthermore, in Catholic schools with a religiously diverse student body—increasing throughout the world—the greatest challenge is how to offer a school-wide curriculum that educates Catholic students into their Catholic identity and yet respects religious diversity and does not proselytize the non-Catholic students. Though the complexity entailed and sensitivity required to offer such a religious education curriculum to a diverse student population are significant, I hope I have contributed to a way forward here in proposing a shared Christian (or Muslim, Jewish, and so on) praxis approach—or the more friendly term, "life to Faith to life."

For sure, the kind of Catholic education that reflects the pedagogy of Jesus—its process *and* content—and that is inspired by the Catholic intellectual tradition can be a huge asset to the personal lives of participants and to the public realm, serving well the common good of all. Catholic education with a strong curriculum of religious education was never more needed than in this secular age. I believe it is ready and can be crafted to flourish anew.

RENEWING YOUR VOCATION
AS CATHOLIC EDUCATOR

Not all teachers in Catholic schools are assigned to teach religious education, and yet all can contribute to the faith ethos of the school. Every Catholic educator, regardless of specialization or assignment in the curriculum, can ask the kinds of questions and offer the kinds of resources that will nurture the faith and spiritual life of students, engage their souls as well as minds, and foster their character formation.

For the teacher's soul. Regarding faith, the ancient wisdom of *nemo dat quod non habet*—no one can give what they haven't got—is eminently true. As educators, then, we must tend to our own faith, ever nurturing it along the journey of life. Without growing in our faith, we are not likely to sponsor others along the way. Such self-nurture in faith requires some spiritual practices to keep us keeping on.

- How would you describe the present location of your own faith journey? Are you comfortable with being engaged in faith-based and spiritually grounded education? What do you recognize as its blessings? What are its challenges for you?
- What are some practices that currently sustain your faith journey? How might you deepen them or initiate more effective ones?

For the teaching style. Though the shared praxis approach was originally crafted as a pedagogy to educate in Christian faith, its movements can be adapted to other disciplines. We elaborate further in the Postlude that follows, but for now, just imagine! Might one begin a history lesson by having students focus and reflect upon some contemporary life theme that is reflected in the historical period for review, then study and understand the historical data of the period, and then discern what they can learn for their lives and our society today? Might such a pedagogy enable students to *learn from* rather than just *learn about* history? What of your own discipline?

- Can you imagine employing some aspects of such a pedagogy in your teaching of topics other than religion? What would be required as preparation and lesson planning?
- What might be some of the advantages or disadvantages of such a pedagogy to your discipline?

For the educational space. We are so accustomed to think of teaching as telling that even those of us well trained otherwise can be tempted. It can be challenging to mediate teaching as primarily a conversation and then to craft the classroom—and school—as communities of conversation.

- How do you imagine deepening the practice and quality of conversation in your own educational space? in your school?
- What are some requirements for good conversation? Pick one to put into practice immediately (for example, asking engaging questions or offering good listening).

Postlude

Seeds of a Catholic Pedagogy

The intent of this Postlude—echoing notes from all that has preceded—is to sound out what might be identified as a *Catholic* pedagogy. It invites us to imagine a consistent Catholic practice of the *art* of teaching, and, parenthetically, good teaching is ever a high art, far beyond a skill.

Often throughout this text, beginning with the pedagogy of Jesus and drawing upon the legacy of the Catholic intellectual tradition, I have suggested implications for this fine art of teaching. In Chapter 10, I proposed a pedagogy for *religious* education, in particular. Now, might all those sources suggest the seeds of a distinctly Catholic *approach* to pedagogy throughout the whole curriculum—in every subject area? I emphasize *approach* because a pedagogy includes but is more than methods of teaching. Ultimately, it is a way of *being with* people to facilitate a participatory teaching/learning dynamic, what we have identified before as the *accompaniment* style of that Stranger on the road to Emmaus. As a mode of presence *with* students and an art, Catholic pedagogy can be enacted by many different models.

Here, we recall the classic text *Models of Teaching* by Bruce Joyce and Marsha Weil, first published in 1972; its ninth edition appeared in 2018. This enduring classic reviews more than twenty teaching methods, like the "Advance Organizer Model" for teaching academic disciplines (say what you're going to teach, teach it, and then review what you've taught), or an "Inquiry Model" for teaching social studies (having students formulate questions, collect data, and analyze social relations to reach their own conclusions). Whatever models or methods of teaching are employed in a Catholic school, they should be enacted within and be consistent with an overarching *approach*—an artful pedagogy that reflects the school's values and spiritual foundations.

Thus, a Catholic pedagogy is to reflect the core spiritual foundations that define Catholic education and then to implement consistent pedagogical *movements* to enact those *commitments* within teaching/

217

learning conversations. These *commitments* and *movements* I propose are culled from the Preface and ten chapters here but now are focused precisely on the pedagogy that should permeate Catholic education, shaping how its teachers teach and how its students learn—across the entire curriculum.

We need to be selective in what to draw out from the previous chapters to shape a Catholic pedagogy; as expected, many of the core characteristics we highlighted in some chapters were echoed in others. After reviewing the core *commitments* that might distinguish a Catholic pedagogy (approximately following the chapter sequence), I propose the pedagogical *movements* that these commitments recommend, ever favoring an overarching dynamic of conversation instead of didaction.

CORE COMMITMENTS
OF A CATHOLIC PEDAGOGY

Preface. A Catholic school needs to be truly committed to its spiritual foundations and to its public identity in offering faith-based education. Its witness to such an identity is integral to its pedagogy; it teaches much by simply being a good Catholic school. To this end it needs to have a clear mission statement that identifies it as arising *from* Catholic faith and educating *for* a faith perspective on life that offers all a gracious Transcendent Horizon for finding meaning and living well for self and others.

In this light a Catholic school needs its principal (however named) to be *a spiritual leader*, supported by a cadre of likewise committed faculty and staff who can articulate the school's spiritual foundations, motivate others to embrace them, and be the custodians of its Catholic identity. Its faith-based and spiritually grounded curriculum should come as no surprise to anyone; instead, it should be explicitly stated and embraced by all participants—supervisors and leadership, faculty and staff, students and parents.

Jesus, the Christ (Chapter 1). Regarding Jesus as the *heart* of Catholic education, I propose three core pedagogical commitments; many others have echoed through the ages—along with this book. First, Catholic pedagogy is to presume upon and nurture the personal *agency* of all learners, convinced that each has their own gifts and capacities to grow as human beings, to develop and flourish through their native abilities for learning, however abled. There is a popular saying that "education is not the filling of a pail, but the lighting of a fire." Having so affirmed people's personal agency for the reign of God, Jesus would surely say, "Amen."

Second, and again reflecting Jesus's pedagogy, Catholic education is to engage students actively in the teaching/learning dynamic, ever encouraging them to come to *see* and *hear* for themselves and to make good decisions. Jesus initiated such a pedagogy most often by engaging people's own lives in the world and inviting reflection on them. Then, in one way or another, he asked questions over three hundred times throughout the Gospels and welcomed people to ask their own questions—even ultimate ones like: "What must I do to inherit eternal life?" (Luke 10:25). As for Jesus, good questions that the teacher poses or encourages students to ask are a prime prompt of both knowledge and wisdom for life. They are essential for encouraging students to reach their own good recognitions and decisions.

Third, and from Jesus, Catholic pedagogy is to propose to students some great ideals and hopes for themselves and for the world. What and how it teaches should be a utopian resource for students, not just as naive or wishful thinking but as something that inspires their best hopes and to which they can contribute in bringing about. We should lend their young dreams a horizon to live into for their own good, for the good of others, and for all creation, with even sowing small seeds having huge potential. We are to teach in ways that encourage and form students toward *living* faith with hope and love, all toward realizing God's reign.

Jesus as the Risen Christ (Chapter 2). Jesus's resurrection calls for a pedagogy that encourages in students a deep confidence in "the help of God's grace" and especially toward their own agency for doing good. To this end, it is to nurture their sacramental consciousness, making them alert for God's grace at work in their lives and how they can best respond. Indeed, our teaching should reflect to them that everything of good that they attempt in life can be initiated and sustained by God's grace. This is not a "cheap" grace, however; rather, it empowers their personal participation in the Divine/human covenant. And as we imagine a pedagogy that encourages the potential and gifts of each student in doing good, we need confidence that our efforts to teach well are also enhanced by the workings of God's grace—in both our own and in our students' lives.

The Didache (Chapter 3a). The outcome of the debate in the early centuries whether the church should sponsor general education should inspire Catholic educators, now and always, to see their teaching as "a work of salvation"—for both their students and their society. This was the conviction that inspired the early church to sponsor general education as an aspect of God's liberating salvation through Jesus to the world. Furthermore, all Catholic education should reflect the partnerships that epitomize the Catholic intellectual tradition across the centuries—of faith and reason, of science and revelation, of scholarship and formation, of ideas and values, and so on.

The *Didache* specifically advises that the key to such liberating and salvific education is to craft our pedagogy to encourage people to embrace a *way of life* that is truly life-giving for oneself and others—as epitomized in the greatest commandment—rather than a *way of death*. And even as we propose the ideals of the *way of life*, we need to be realistic about human limitations, as the *Didache* advised, and ever encourage our students to "do the best you can."

Augustine (Chapter 3b) inspires us to teach in ways that engage and draw out students' inner potential for wisdom of life—as ensouled human beings. Our teaching should encourage people to listen to their own "wisdom within"; even a simple question like "what do you think yourself?" can trigger such listening. And Augustine advises that in having students pursue a listening to themselves, they are likely to come to realize that God loves them—the ultimate truth to *know* for their lives.

We can also be inspired by Augustine's good pedagogical practices, noting the imperative to provide a positive and welcoming environment for students—emotionally, physically, and aesthetically; to be clear in our presentations; to lend students ready access to the resources of tradition; to respect their needs and engage their gifts; to build upon what people already know; and so forth. Two fun recommendations from Augustine were not to attempt teaching anything new in the afternoon, and to always maintain *hilaritas* within ourselves as educators. By the latter, he probably meant *enthusiasm*—though I like *hilarity*—for what we are teaching; that will be infectious for our students.

Benedict (Chapter 3c) encourages a pedagogy that engages the very soul of students. In other words, appeal to and have them name their own emotions and feelings, inviting them to recognize and learn from their hopes and fears, joys and sorrows, and by listening to and testing the sentiments of their own hearts. So much of our potential for spiritual knowing is through our own story and vision, the biography we are living and our hopes and dreams for its future. While being respectful of students' privacy, teachers can invite them to tap into and share the wisdom from within that arises from their everyday lives and the promptings of their souls.

Following on, we need to teach in ways that invite students to holiness as a wholeness and authenticity of life, to encourage them to become their own best persons, and to contribute to the common good of all; this was the foundational spirituality of the Benedictine *Rule*. Actively opposing a narrow sectarianism, Catholic educators are to encourage in all students a deeply "catholic" sentiment, welcoming all and sundry, open to difference and diversity. The great contemporary Jewish philosopher, Emmanuel Levinas (1906–95) proposed that we are to see the face of the *Other* in the face of the *other*; Benedict, with his mandate of welcoming visitors as if Jesus, would certainly so advise.

The Celtic monks (Chapter 4a), who shared the early monastic stage with the Benedictines, would encourage us to teach in ways that conserve traditions as well as opening into new horizons. Rather than discarding our historical legacy—such a strong impulse in our postmodern society—we must conserve what is of value from our past. In this, Jesus can be our inspiration. As he once explained, "Every scribe who has been trained for the kingdom of heaven is like the master of a household who brings out of his treasure [storeroom] what is new and what is old" (Matt 13:52). Note that the storeroom of God's reign will always contain the new and old; a Catholic pedagogy draws upon both.

Thomas Aquinas (Chapter 4b) strongly encourages us in a pedagogy that invites people to reflect on the data of their own experience—their lives in the world—and continually to bring this data to understanding, judgment, and decision. Those latter dynamics encourage students to reach beyond knowledge to wisdom for life, beyond cognition of ideas to formation in values.

Aquinas especially advises that we craft good questions for students, the kind that can turn them to reflect on their experience and then to move onward in the dynamics of knowing to authentic cognition and wisdom for life. His whole teaching approach was defined by the *quaestio*—to begin with a question that actively engages students and then to lay out its many possibilities for consideration. And perhaps Aquinas deserves to be named the greatest champion of the "both/ and" that marks the Catholic intellectual tradition, especially that foundational partnership for Catholic education of faith and reason.

Julian of Norwich (Chapter 4c) invites us to teach in ways that encourage students to trust their own spiritual experiences, to listen to their own hearts as sources of wisdom for life. In theological terms we are to invite our students to recognize that God reveals Godself to each of us through the experiences and contexts of our lives in the world, and that such experienced revelation requires careful and prayerful discernment on our part and in dialogue with our faith community.

Julian also encourages us to invite students to be faithful to their own convictions, even when this means swimming against the socio-cultural tide—and though those in authority may not be pleased. She also challenges us as teachers, given that words are the "tools of our trade," to speak *expansively* of God and *inclusively* of humankind. It seems obvious, but we easily forget that as teachers, our language patterns are integral to how and what we teach—to our whole pedagogy.

Ignatius of Loyola (Chapter 5) encourages a pedagogy that sees everything we study as ultimately uncovering the gracious Mystery that is the Ultimate Horizon of life in the world. As such, every field of study/learning can be pursued *ad maiorem Dei gloriam*—to the greater glory of God. Echo here that we need to nurture in students a sacramental consciousness that encourages them to see God in all things and, with contemporary social consciousness, to live as people "for and with others."

Ignatius also encourages a pedagogy that challenges students to excel according to all their gifts—academic, artistic, personal, athletic, and so on. Our educating should reflect care for them as whole persons. Likewise, our pedagogy should invite students to probe and evaluate, to discern, what spirits are moving their own spirit—for good or ill—and to choose wisely those promptings that are life-giving because faithful to the reign of God.

Angela Merici (Chapter 6a) calls us to reflect great courage in our pedagogy, not to be deterred from stepping out of old molds and expectations. We need to model for our students how to take a prophetic stance as needed, to go against the grain of structures and traditions that are oppressive in any way and for any people.

Angela invites us, too, to engage pedagogies that make our teaching effective for social reform and especially for the full inclusion and dignity of all people—women equally with men—in the public realm. And she inspires ways of being present to our students that reflect love for them, a deep care for their well-being. Indeed, our love and care for students may be the pedagogy that teaches most effectively, especially toward their becoming fully alive to the glory of God.

Mary Ward (Chapter 6b) invites us to a pedagogy that reflects deep courage and faithfulness to core gospel commitments, even against all odds and powerful social structures. We need pedagogies that prompt students to analyze and recognize the causes and the evils reflected in any kind or social structure of human discrimination. We must inspire and encourage students to stand for the full equality of all people—and honoring Mary's memory—especially for the equality of women in both church and society.

Mary encourages, too, that we continue to cherish the value of a liberal arts curriculum—theology, philosophy, literature, history, languages, graphic arts, and so on. The liberal arts are still a rich resource for the human development of people, especially their moral formation. Mary Ward saw their potential as crucial for advancing the equality of women; those liberal arts are still needed to promote the humanization and dignity of students today. Without them, we are reduced to training more than educating.

A Great Cloud of Witnesses: We suggested Jean-Baptist de la Salle and Elizabeth Ann Seton as representative symbols of the almost countless number of religious orders of vowed sisters, brothers, and priests that have been particularly committed to Catholic education. Typically, each of these "great cloud of witnesses" (Hebrews 12:1) had a distinct charism or emphasis that they put to work throughout their schools. For example, de la Salle was driven by his passion to rescue boys in danger; Elizabeth Ann Seton emphasized education as a great work of charity that also addresses the causes of poverty. Perhaps your Catholic school was founded or sponsored by a vowed religious order, or by some particular church leader or movement. Might you reclaim its originating charism—the emphasis it had from the beginning—and renew your commitment to it, lending a distinctive spirit to your school today.

A Catholic anthropology (Chapter 7a), in a compelling way, grounds much of the pedagogy proposed above and that follows here. We must practice the art of teaching in ways that reflect the positive nature and potential of the person and encourage their capacity to be good and for doing good as human beings. Our ways of teaching students should reflect their own dignity and worth as persons and the contribution they can make for the common good of all.

Such anthropology calls for a pedagogy that fosters students' agency for knowing, engaging them as active participants—not passive recipients—in the teaching/learning conversation. We need to encourage their own questions and questioning of life, fostering their curiosity and their youthful enthusiasm, even their often rebellious spirit that challenges the status quo. We need a pedagogy that encourages students' own knowing for themselves so that they can recognize what they don't know and can craft their interests and questions to pursue it.

A *Catholic sociology* (Chapter 7b) calls for a pedagogy that encourages students to work collaboratively toward becoming responsible social agents for their own good and the common good of all. Following on, our pedagogy should encourage in students a critical social consciousness, a dialectical stance toward their context that disposes them to contribute to it, critique it as necessary, and never simply to "fit in" to any status quo.

The school itself should reflect the social values of a Christian community where all are welcome and included. Likewise, models of collaborative pedagogy are most appropriate in honoring a Catholic sociology of the person.

A *Catholic cosmology* (Chapter 8a) calls for a pedagogy that encourages people to embrace their life in the world with relish, confident that it has meaning, purpose, ethic, and is most worthwhile. Indeed, we can portray it as a journey forth from God and home to God, with God's grace at work along the way to empower our own best efforts at living well and wisely.

Our ways of teaching should nurture not only a critical but a sacramental consciousness in our students, encouraging them to look intently *at* life and then to look *through* it to see the more in the ordinary, the ultimate in the immediate, and the Creator in the created order. We are to encourage students to recognize God's presence and grace at work in their lives and world, and to respond—as in that constant partnership of nature and grace. Again, asking reflective questions that engage their hearts as well as their heads, especially their imaginations, is a primary way to encourage a sacramental outlook in students.

A *Catholic epistemology* (Chapter 8b) and the pedagogical dynamics it encourages is writ large in our closing section on teaching *movements* below. Let us simply note here that a Catholic pedagogy should engage both of the prime *sources of knowing*, which we named before as *life in the world* and *traditions* of learning. This means to have students draw upon their own experiences and initiatives, and likewise give them ready access to the legacies of learning that have emerged over the ages, encouraging them to integrate continually the two sources into their own knowing and wisdom for life.

Further, we need pedagogies that engage all of people's *ways* of knowing; their heads, and likewise their hearts—their emotive capacities—and their hands, particularly what they can learn through engaged scholarship. Our pedagogy is to prompt the full dynamic of authentic cognition, inviting people beyond paying attention to and understanding data—whether from life or traditions of learning—in order to make good judgments and decisions about them.

Catholic education toward a public faith (Chapter 9) calls for pedagogies that encourage moral formation with a deep *social* and *sacramental* consciousness, committing students for life to works of compassion and social justice in the public realm. We are to teach in ways that prepare people to take their faith and put it to work in their civil society, to live as responsible citizens for the common good of all.

This calls for pedagogies that engage and educate students hearts and souls, that offer opportunities for engaged learning through works of justice and compassion, and that encourage the kind of deep contextual reflection that encourages both social and sacramental consciousness. Note, too, the need to nurture students in spiritual practices that can help sustain them in such a public and *living* faith.

Religious education in the postmodern Catholic school (Chapter 10) offered a "shared Christian praxis" approach to education in faith, and with a thorough review. But might such a pedagogy also be possible as a "shared History praxis" or even a "shared Mathematics praxis," with people not just learning about history or math but learning from them for life and even becoming able to think historically or to "do" mathematics? What follows reflects on the potential of such pedagogy throughout the whole curriculum of a Catholic school.

MOVEMENTS OF A CATHOLIC PEDAGOGY

How might the focusing activity and five pedagogical movements of my favored way of educating in faith inform the pedagogy of other disciplines in a Catholic school. It certainly could be effective for teaching the humanities. In presenting the movements below I outline a unit of social science or it could be of history in a Catholic high school.

Beyond that, however, I face the limitations of my own teaching experience; though a teacher now for over forty years, I've never taught anything other than theology or religious education. Thus, I can be of little counsel to teachers in the "hard" sciences—physics, biology, chemistry, math, and so on. Perhaps those teachers can imagine for themselves how to employ such a pedagogy and how its distinctive movements might be effective for teaching their discipline.

My presentation here renames the pedagogical movements from Chapter 10 and designates them as distinctive teaching dynamics that they are to encourage, favoring an overall paradigm of conversation. Reflecting the focusing activity and five pedagogical movements, I list them here as *engaging* (focusing curriculum theme); *expressing* (movement 1); *reflecting* (movement 2); *accessing* (movement 3); *appropriating* (movement 4) and *deciding* (movement 5).

As emphasized already, the movements need not be followed in the sequence laid out here; they are pedagogical commitments to be honored rather than a lockstep process. For example, one can begin with something from the *accessing* (movement 3) to introduce and prompt *engagement* with the curriculum theme (*focusing*), and then pick up with *expressing* (movement 1) and *reflecting* (movement 2) to then return to a more complete *accessing* (movement 3), and so on. For now, let me lay out the moves in their somewhat logical sequence.

Move to engage. John Dewey wisely opined years ago that it is nigh impossible to teach anything of significance to anyone unless they are *interested*. The first move of a teacher, then, is to get students engaged with the topic/theme to be taught and learned. Most likely, the surest way to engage their interest is to present the curriculum for the occasion as having pressing relevance for their lives, as "connecting" with them and their interests. Freire calls this establishing a "generative theme," by which he means something that is likely to engage students personally and their interests in the theme of the pedagogy. The move to engage amounts to readying students to be active participants rather than passive spectators in the teaching/learning event.

The example I propose is for a high school social studies unit on racism in America with a particular focus on the Fourteenth Amendment to the Constitution. Recall that this amendment of 1868, ended slavery and granted "equal protection of the laws" to all citizens, at least legally. The opening and *engaging* move could be to give an example, or statistics, or show a video that portrays racist discrimination continuing in America today and then begin a conversation that personally engages the students with this generative theme.

Move to express. Paulo Freire proposed that the most liberating move by a teacher is to invite people to personal expression, inviting them to speak their own word, to name their own reality around the theme. I think of this movement as inviting people to express (and their media of expression can be much more than verbal) what they already know from their experiences (Dewey), or from their historical praxis (Freire), or from their own sensory activities (Montessori). This movement, then, invites students to pay attention to their own lives in the world and to recognize what they already know as they begin to name or express their own sentiments, feelings, thoughts, observations, opinions, and so forth, on the generative theme.

In the social studies example the pedagogical move could be to invite from students their personal and initial responses, for example, to a movie clip on racism, what they saw and what it reflects, to express their feelings about it, and how they personally perceive and describe the issue of racism in America today.

Move to reflect. Every pedagogy must prompt, require, encourage, and facilitate people to think for themselves, to reflect critically on what they learn from their own lives in the world around the generative theme of the occasion. As appropriate, this reflection could be both personal and social, engage students' reason, memory, and imagination—their whole capacity of mind—and likewise their hearts (emotions) and hands (present commitments).

Depending on the topic and the age level of participants, the critical reflection of this move can be both personal and social, contextual and historical. This means to recognize how the context and its history are producing the present social reality and likewise shaping people's opinions about it. This is what encourages, as appropriate to the generative theme and the developmental readiness of students, what we've referred to often in this book as critical *social consciousness*. Similarly, we have emphasized the importance of nurturing a *sacramental consciousness* in students, an outlook whereby people can recognize God's presence and the availability of God's grace to empower their own response toward the reign of God. It is God's grace that ever lends hope, even in the direst of circumstances.

(Metaphorically, the focusing act and the first two movements invite students to express and reflect upon their own story and vision around the generative theme in conversation.)

In our social studies example, the teacher could invite students to reflect critically on the ample evidence of continued racism in America, especially against black and brown people; why it continues to be practiced; and what might be done about it. Critical reflection could be stimulated by some social statistics (for example, the huge imbalance in the incarceration of black people; their filling a high percentage of low paying jobs; their high health risk because of lack of medical insurance; and so on), and by historical analysis—reviewing the story of racism that has continued long after passing the Fourteenth Amendment in 1868. As students express their reflections, the teacher might invite them to "go deeper" and to recognize what is influencing their own positions and attitudes (nurturing critical consciousness). They might invite students to recognize signs of hope for racial justice and imagine how they, by God's grace, can be agents of social change toward greater racial justice in their country (nurturing sacramental consciousness).

Move to access. Every teaching/learning situation has the responsibility to access the "funded capital of civilization," as Dewey named the arts, sciences, and trades. We need to lend students "ready access" to this legacy, facilitating their encounter with it in ways that make the tradition all the more easily learned and embraced as their own. Not only should this move access with persuasion the resources of whatever is to be taught but also to highlight for people what it means and the possibilities it holds for people's lives—again both Story and Vision. Like any of these moves, this one can be achieved in myriad ways—with lecturing now being all the less likely to be effective (social researchers estimate young people's attention span as about eight minutes, the usual length of time between TV ads.). So, let the accessing use a variety of media; it can also be done in partnerships or research groups, favoring collaborative approaches to learning.

In our social studies example, *accessing* here might involve sharing some of the history of the Fourteenth Amendment, how it was meant to grant full citizenship to all native-born or naturalized people in the United States, regardless of race, creed, or color, and that it promised to all citizens "equal protection of the laws." It could review how the amendment has been interpreted across the years (for example, as in *Brown v. Board of Education* of 1954); how it has been and has not been well implemented; and what needs to be done now to help end the racism that still besets American society, and which the Fourteenth Amendment was meant to offset.

Move to appropriate. A highlight of Lonergan's life work was his urging repeatedly that the dynamics of cognition require moving beyond understanding to make judgments and decisions, and to do so self-consciously. Somewhat similar to his notion of judgment, I propose *appropriation* as people making their own what is being taught, coming to see for themselves what it might mean for their lives and for their society, and forging their own informed and convicted perspective on the generative theme of the teaching/learning occasion. In effect, this begins the integrative moment when the pedagogy encourages participants to appropriate the learning/wisdom from their own experiences with what they have learned from a particular tradition or discipline of learning that has been presented to them. As noted in Chapter 10, such integration calls for a pedagogy that encourages a dialectic—a give-and-take conversation—between what the teacher and the tradition are teaching and people's own perceptions from their life in the world. In gist, instead of students repeating back to the teacher what the teacher has presented to them, they are to come to their own opinions and recognitions regarding what the teacher has taught or arranged to be taught (for example, through text book, digital media, etc.).

In the social studies example, the *appropriating* should encourage students to recognize what they can see for themselves and how they might make good and ethical decisions regarding the issue of racism in America. This might be as simple as the teacher asking, "In light of the story of the Fourteenth Amendment, what do you really think now about racism in America today?" or "What are you coming to see more clearly about this issue?" Or they could begin to imagine the changes to be made and how to make them—anticipating the next movement.

Move to decide. For authentic cognition, the kind that leads on to wisdom and formation of values—that prepares good citizens—the pedagogy must now invite students to recognize their new knowledge and to consider a decision that they can implement. The decisions here can be *cognitive*—what they now know with fresh conviction; *affective*—how they respond emotively to what they've come to see for themselves; or *behavioral*—what they will do with their new knowledge and the difference it might make for their lives and civil society.

In our social studies experiment, deciding here, as noted earlier, can be cognitive, affective, or behavioral. Given the topic of racism in America, the teacher can invite students (it must be their free choice) to decide about their own attitudes toward this issue now, their strongest feelings about it, and how they might work to eradicate racism from their own lives, from their school and neighborhood, and ultimately from American society and the world.

(*The above example around racism and the Fourteenth Amendment was suggested by the work of Dermot Groome, professor of law at Penn State's Dickinson Law School, who sponsors similar conversa-*

tions *with the law faculty and students there and into other faculties of law, now at a national level.*)

In closing, I reiterate that these pedagogical movements can be altered in sequence, combined, and greatly varied in their enactment. The key is to realize the pedagogical intent that undergirds each of the movements. Remember that our friend and teacher Jesus often rolled all the moves into one verse. For example: "Look at the birds of the air (*engaging* and *expressing*); they neither sow nor reap nor gather into barns (*reflecting*), and yet your heavenly Father feeds them (*accessing*). Are you not of more value than they" (*appropriating* and *deciding*) (Matt 6:26).

Selected Bibliography

Aquinas, Saint Thomas. *Summa Contra Gentiles.* 5 vols. Notre Dame, IN: University of Notre Dame Press, 1975.

———. *Summa Theologica.* New York: McGraw Hill, 1964–73.

———. *On the Teacher (De Magistro).* In *The Philosophy of Teaching of Saint Thomas Aquinas.* Translated by Mary Helen Mayer. New York: Bruce Publishing Co., 1929.

Augustine, Saint. *First Catechetical Instruction (De Catechizandis Rudibus).* Translated by Joseph P. Christopher. Volume 2 in *Ancient Christian Writers.* Mahwah, NJ: Paulist Press, 1978.

———. *The Teacher (De Magistro).* Translated by Joseph M. Colleran. Volume 9 in *Ancient Christian Writers.* Mahwah, NJ: Paulist Press, 1978.

Benedict. *Saint Benedict's Rule.* Translated by Patrick Barry, OSB, Ampleforth Abbey. Mahwah, NJ: Paulist Press, 2004.

Bryk, Anthony S., Valerie E. Lee, and Peter B. Holland. *Catholic Schools and the Common Good.* Revised edition. Cambridge, MA: Harvard University Press, 1993.

Cahill, Thomas. *How the Irish Saved Civilization: The Untold Story of Ireland's Heroic Role from the Fall of Rome to the Rise of Medieval Europe.* New York: Anchor Books, 1996.

Chambers, Mary Catherine Elizabeth. *Life of Mary Ward, 1585-1645.* United Kingdom: Wentworth Press, 2016.

Clement of Alexandria. *Christ the Educator.* Volume 23 in *Fathers of the Church: A New Translation.* Translated by Simon P. Wood. Washington, DC: Catholic University Press of America, 1954.

Cover, Jeanne. *Love the Driving Force: Mary Ward's Spirituality.* Milwaukee, WI: Marquette University Press, 1997.

Cully, Kendig Brubaker. *Basic Writings in Christian Education.* Philadelphia: Westminster Press, 1960.

Dewey, John. *Experience and Education.* New York: Touchstone, 1938/1997.

Didache. Translated by James A. Kleist, SJ. Volume 6 in *Ancient Christian Writers.* Mahwah, NJ: Paulist Press, 1948.

Directory for Catechesis. Document of the Pontifical Council for the Promotion of the New Evangelization. Washington, DC: USCCB, 2020.

Farrell, Allan P., translator. Ignatius Loyola, *The Jesuit Ratio Studiorum of 1599 [Ratio Studiorum, Plan of Studies]*. Washington, DC: The Jesuit Conference, 1970.

Freire, Paulo. *Education for Critical Consciousness*. New York: Bloomsbury Academic, 1974/2013.

———. *Pedagogy of the Oppressed*. New York: Seabury Press, 1970.

Ganss, George E., translator. Ignatius Loyola, *Constitutions of the Society of Jesus*. St. Louis: The Institute of Jesuit Sources, 1970.

Groome, Thomas H. *Educating for Life: A Spiritual Vision for Every Teacher and Parent*. New York: Crossroad Publishing, 1998/2001.

———. *Sharing Faith: A Comprehensive Approach to Religious Education and Pastoral Ministry: The Way of Shared Praxis*. San Francisco, CA: HarperCollins, 1991.

———. *Will There Be Faith?: A New Vision for Educating and Growing Disciples*. San Francisco, CA: HarperOne, 2011.

Holland, Joe, and Peter Henriot, SJ. *Social Analysis: Linking Faith and Justice*. Revised edition. Maryknoll, NY: Orbis Books, 1983.

hooks, bell. *Teaching to Transgress: Education as the Practice of Freedom*. New York: Routledge, 1994.

Institoris, Henricus [Heinrich Kramer], and Jacobus Sprenger. *Malleus Maleficarum*. Translated into English by Christopher S. Mackay as *The Hammer of Witches: A Complete Translation of the* Malleus Maleficarum. Cambridge: Cambridge University Press, 2009.

Julian of Norwich. *Showings*. Classics of Western Spirituality. Mahwah, NJ: Paulist Press, 1977.

Littlehales, Margaret Mary. *Mary Ward: A Woman for All Seasons*. London: Catholic Truth Society, 1982.

Lonergan, Bernard. *Insight*. Volume 3 in *Collected Works of Bernard Lonergan*. 5th ed. Edited by Frederick Crowe SJ, et al. Toronto, Canada: University of Toronto Press, 1992.

Merici, Angela. *The Writings of St. Angela Merici*. Translated by Teresa Neylan. Ursulines of the Roman Union, 1969.

Noddings, Nel. *Caring: A Relational Approach to Ethics and Moral Education*. Berkeley, CA: University of California Press, 2013.

———. *Philosophy of Education*. 4th edition. New York: Routledge, 2018.

Pascal, Blaise. *Pensées*. Translated by A. J. Krailsheimer. New York: Penguin Classics, 1995.

Perkins, Pheme. *Jesus as Teacher*. New York: Cambridge University Press, 1990.

Rahner, Karl. "Christian Living Formerly and Today." *Theological Investigations*. Volume 7. Translated by David Bourke. New York: Herder and Herder, 1971.

Tertullian. *Prescription against Heretics*. Pickerington, OH: Beloved Publishing, 2014.

Tetlow, Joseph A. *The Spiritual Exercises of Ignatius Loyola*. New York: Crossroad Publishing, 2009.

Whitehead, Alfred North. *The Aims of Education and Other Essays*. New York: The Free Press, 1929/1967.

Note: All official church documents can be accessed on the Vatican website.

Index